IN PURSUIT OF EQUALITY IN HIGHER EDUCATION

IN PURSUIT OF EQUALITY
IN HIGHER EDUCATION

Edited by

Anne S. Pruitt
The Ohio State University

GENERAL HALL, INC.
Publishers
5 Talon Way
Dix Hills, New York 11360

IN PURSUIT OF EQUALITY IN HIGHER EDUCATION

GENERAL HALL, INC.
5 Talon Way
Dix Hills, New York 11746

Publisher: Ravi Mehra
Editor: Eileen Ostermann
Composition: *Graphics Division,* General Hall, Inc.

LIBRARY OF CONGRESS CATALOG CARD NUMBER: 86–080125

ISBN: 0–930390–68–7 [cloth]

Manufactured in the United States of America

Contents

Foreword: The Mission of the
Southern Education Foundation   **1**

Acknowledgments   **6**

Introduction: *Edgar G. Epps and Anne S. Pruitt*   **7**

Part 1: The *Adams* Case   **15**

1   **A Review of Early Decisions on *Adams* v.
*Richardson***
Gary D. Malaney   **17**

The Case 18, Dates 18, Decisions, 18, Other States 21, References, 21

**Part 2: Access and Progression:
Determinants of Success**   **23**

References 24

2   **Recent College and University Enrollment
Patterns of Black Students in States Affected
by *Adams* Litigation**
William F. Brazziel and Marian E. Brazziel   **25**

Findings 25, Suggestions for Further Study 28, Suggested Policy Initiatives 28

3   **Determining the College Destination of
Black Students**
Gail E. Thomas and Jomills H. Braddock II   **32**

Data 34, Findings 35, Summary and Policy Implications 36, References 38

4 Access, Retention, and Progression of Black Students Through the Two-Tier Florida Higher Education System the Individual
Charles M. Grigg **40**

The Florida System of Higher Education 42, Governance and Structure 43, Research Design 43, Results and Policy Implications 44, Needed Research 47, References 48

5 Racial Differences in College Student Achievement
Michael T. Nettles, A. Robert Thoeny, and Erica J. Gosman **49**

Model and Study Procedures 49, Summary of Findings 51, Cohort Attrition: Comparisons by Race and Predominant Race of University 51, Cohort Progression Rate: Comparisons by Race and Predominant Race of University 52, Individual-Level Progression Rates: Comparisons by Race and Type of University 53, College Grade Point Average: Comparisons by Race and Type of University 54, Student Antecedent Characteristics and College Attitudinal and Behavioral Characteristics: Comparisons by Race and Type of University 54, Faculty Attitudinal-Behavioral Characteristics: Comparisons by Race and Type of University 56, Causal Factors of Students' College Progression Rates 57, Causal Factors of Student College Grade Point Averages 58, Consequence of Progression and Performance to Employment 61, Conclusions 62

6 Institutional Effectiveness in the Production of Black Baccalaureates
Philip S. Hart **64**

Research Review 65, Findings 66, Solutions 69, Policy Initiative 71, References 73

7 Ending the White Monopoly on Graduate and Professional Education
James E. Blackwell **76**

Objectives of the Study 77, Method 77, Universe of Study 77, Data Collection 78, Data Analysis 78, Selected Findings 79, Recruitment 79, Financial

Aid 80, Applications 82, Admissions 83, Admission Criteria 83, Special Admission Programs 84, Enrollment 86, Medicine 87, Dentistry 88, Optometry 89, Pharmacy 90, Veterinary Medicine 90, Engineering 91, Law 92, Social Work 92, Degrees Conferred 93, Implications 93

Part 3: Aspirations and Career Choices of Black Students   95

8   The Educational Attainment Process Among Black Youth
Edgar G. Epps and Kenneth W. Jackson   **96**

Data 97, Findings 98, National Longitudinal Study (NLS) Males 98, National Longitudinal Study (NLS) Females 98, High School and Beyond Study (HSB) Males 98, High School and Beyond Study (HSB) Females 99, Additional Analyses 100, Summary 102, References 103

9   Black College Students and Their Major Field Choice
Gail E. Thomas   **105**

Data and Analyses 106, Findings 107, Summary and Conclusions 114, References 114

10   Factors Related to the Postbaccalaureate Careers of Black Graduates of Selected Four-Year Institutions in Alabama
Rhoda B. Johnson   **116**

Major Descriptive Findings 117, Major Inferential Findings 120, Policy Implications 121

Part 4: Social and Psychological Dimensions of the Learning Environment: Experiences of Blacks on College Campuses   122

11 Coping Strategies: Retaining Black
Students in College
Yvonne R. Abatso **123**

Purpose of the Study 124, Research Design 125, Results 126, A Coping-Retention Personality 126, Academic-Social Interaction on Campus 128, Experimental Study-Teaching of Coping Strategies 129, Summary and Discussion 130, References 131

12 College in Black and White:
Black Student Experiences on
Black and White Campuses
Walter R. Allen **132**

Overview of Research Findings: Undergraduate Students 134, Traditionally White Institutions (1981 Sample) 134, Traditionally Black Institutions (1983 Sample) 139, General Summary 144, References 145, Related Reports (available on request) 145

13 Mentoring and Networking
Among Blacks
James E. Blackwell **146**

Hypotheses 148, Method 149, Universe and Sampling Frame 149, Description of Instrument 149, Characteristics of Respondents 149, Nonrespondents 150, Variables 151, Findings 153, Role Models 153, Mentors 154, Networking 156, Discussion 157, References 160

**Part 5: The Significance of Financial Aid for
Black Students in Higher Education** **163**

14 Financial Access to Postsecondary
Education for Minority-Poverty Students:
A Look at the Recent Past and a View
of the Future
Jerry S. Davis and Kingston Johns, Jr. **164**

Changes in Access to Postsecondary Education 166, The Continuing Value and Need for Postsecondary Education 167, Past and Recent Trends in

Financial Aid 168, The Future of Financial Aid 170, Conclusion 173, References 173

15 A Study of Title III's Impact on Traditionally Black Institutions
Cameron Fincher
175

Survey Findings and Conclusions 176, Institutional Management 177, Program Improvement 178, Student Services 178, The Overall Value of Title III 179, General Implications 180

Part 6: The Employment of Blacks in Traditionally White Institutions
182

16 Black Employees in Traditionally White Institutions in the *Adams* States, 1975 to 1977
Anne S. Pruitt
183

Rationale 184, Design 186, Analysis of Black and White Employment in the Eight States 187, POA Analysis: 1975 187, POA Analysis: 1977 189, Analysis of Selected States 191, Arkansas 191, Florida 192, Georgia 192, Maryland 193, Discriminant Analysis 194, Conclusions 194, Postscript 196, Policy Implications 196, Suggestions for Further Study 198, References 199

Part 7: Summary and Conclusions
201

17 Highlights of the Studies and Some Policy Initiatives
Anne S. Pruitt
203

Access and Progression 204, Aspirations and Career Choices 205, Social and Psychological Dimensions of the Learning Environment 206, Financial Aid 206, Employment 207, Policy Initiatives 207, A Final Thought 209

The Authors
210

Yvonne R. Abatso 210, Walter R. Allen 210, James E. Blackwell 210, Jomills H. Braddock II 211, Marian E. Brazziel 211, William F. Brazziel 212, Jerry S. Davis 212, Edgar G. Epps 213, Cameron Fincher 213, Erica J. Gosman 213, Charles M. Grigg 214, Philip S. Hart 214, Kenneth W. Jackson 214, Kingston Johns, Jr. 215, Rhoda Barge Johnson 215, Gary D. Malaney 215, Michael T. Nettles 215, Anne S. Pruitt 216, A. Robert Thoney 216, Gail E. Thomas 217

Author Index
218

Subject Index
222

Tables

6.1   Effectiveness Quotient (EQ) Scores for B.A. and B.S. Degrees by Selected Race, Selected Years, and Total — All Institutions Combined   67

9.1   Regression Model of Black Students' College Major Choice — Total Sample (N = 915)   109

9.2   Regression Model of Black Males' (N = 2,555) and Black Females' (N = 659) College Major Choice   110

9.3   Regression Model of Black Students' College Major Choice — Blacks in Traditionally White Colleges (N = 125), Traditionally Black Private Colleges (N = 362), and Traditionally Black Public Colleges (N = 428)   111

Figures

4.1   Location of Control Points in the Flow of Undergraduate Students in a Two-Tier State University System (SUS)   45

9.1   Determinants of Black College Students' Major Field Choice   108

Foreword: The Mission of the Southern Education Foundation

The Southern Education Foundation, although incorporated in 1937 in New York City through the consolidation of three principal philanthropies, began its work in the area of race and education in 1867 with the founding of the Peabody Fund. The work of this fund continued and expanded in 1882 with the founding of the Slater Fund. In 1907 the Jeanes Fund was established, with another worthy mission that guided the Southern Education Foundation's work for many years after its incorporation.

For the most part, the mission of the funds was determined by the donors; however, the trustees were given wide discretion. In 1867, George Peabody, a merchant and banker, conveyed approximately $1 million to a group including Hamilton Fish and U.S. Grant. Peabody stipulated that the funds be used "for promotion and encouragement of intellectual, moral or industrial education among the young of the most destitute portions of the Southern and Southwestern states of our Union." This gift was supplemented with another $1 million in 1869. The Peabody Fund is credited with having influenced the establishment of public education in the South. It encouraged statewide systems of schools and helped create public opinion favorable to a tax program to support schools. In addition, the Fund stimulated the establishment of normal schools and teachers' associations, and it supported school consolidation.

In 1882, John F. Slater of Norwich, Connecticut, contacted Rutherford B. Hayes and others to inform them of his wish to place in their custody $1 million as a charitable fund devoted to "uplifting of the lately emancipated population of the Southern States and their posterity by conferring on them the blessing of Christian education." Slater wisely instructed the trustees that every expenditure should be determined solely by the convictions of the corporation itself as to the most useful disposition of its gifts. The Slater Fund is credited with helping develop private black colleges and stimulating vocational and industrial training, originating "country training schools," providing support for high schools for black students, stimulating increased training for black ministers, and upgrading the training of the faculties of black colleges.

1

In 1907, Anna T. Jeanes, a Philadelphia Quaker, conveyed $1 million to Booker T. Washington of Tuskegee Institute, Alabama, and to Hollis Burke Frissel of Hampton Institute, Virginia. Their instructions were to select a board to direct an endowment to be known as the Fund for Rudimentary Schools for Southern Negroes. Anna Jeanes specified that the income was not to be used for the benefit of large institutions but in the interest of community and country schools. This mission of improving education primarily for rural blacks in the South marked a first for a philanthropic agency.

The Jeanes Fund gave birth to the Jeanes Teachers, rural school teachers and supervisors who moved from one school to another. These teachers provided in-service education for local teachers and stimulated community organization. Their "homemakers' clubs" later became the federal government's home demonstration program. The teachers' work began in Virginia with the first teacher, Virginia Randolph. Support of this fund initially came solely from foundation income; however, state funds subsequently replaced private support. In 1936 and 1937 a memorial fund was established honoring Virginia Randolph, and in 1938 the monies were incorporated into the Southern Education Foundation, thus forming the fourth fund.

From its inception in 1937, the Southern Education Foundation continued many of the policies that the constituent funds had followed earlier. After a decade, some of these programs had been taken over by the states, and the Foundation moved into new areas of program interests in the field of race and education.

Until April 1, 1983, the Southern Education Foundation operated as a private foundation. On this date, the Internal Revenue Service officially recognized the Foundation as a public charity and granted an advance ruling to operate as one. The SEF request for status change was prompted by the Board's extensive review of the Foundation's program thrust and its determination of the need to enhance the Foundation's capacity for responding to issues of race, class, and education in the region. Although the Foundation continued to award small grants, an increasing share of SEF activities was devoted to the two operating programs — Public Policy and Higher Education. The new status provides the Foundation with greater flexibility in program design and in relations with agencies — public and private — from which it receives support. Accordingly, under public charity status, the Board has rededicated its resources to the realization of equality in education in the South.

The present SEF program consists of grant-making activity in the areas of early childhood education, equity in education, community involvement, networking, professional education, and higher education for minorities. In addition, the Foundation continues the work of its Public Policy and Higher Education operating programs. The latter program, which was designed in 1974 to address the specific issues of higher education desegregation relative to the *Adams* v. *Richardson* suit, has supported citizens' groups in an effort to enhance monitoring or *ad hoc* efforts; has commissioned 40 projects that resulted in the publication of numerous reports, monographs, and conference proceedings; has provided technical assistance by dispatching consultants or by making available small grants; and has convened conferences and consultants to address concerns identified by citizens.

In an effort to formalize the critical aspects of its program, in 1978 the Foundation established a Research Task Force. This body of six educators serves as the research arm of the Higher Education Program. It identifies problems of importance and seeks researchers to conduct projects. The Research Task Force has engineered the commissioning of 20 studies and the publishing of 14 monographs and is responsible for recommending the preparation of this volume.

This publication reflects the areas of research that were identified as critical by the Task Force members and several educational associations. For the most part, the research specifically focuses on issues relative to the *Adams* v. *Richardson* suit; however, broader higher education issues are investigated in instances where minorities are affected. SEF research has concentrated on access for minorities and the factors that prevent or aid the progression of students through a system; enrollment trends and patterns and career selection; the relationship between a community college system and the university system within a given state; the employment of blacks at all levels in public colleges and universities in the *Adams* states; successful efforts at producing black professionals; and barriers that prevent access, retention, progression, and graduation of blacks at the undergraduate, graduate, and professional levels.

SEF is encouraged that its research may have an impact, especially during a time when state systems across the South are exploring techniques of recruiting and retaining minority students; seeking ways to increase the pool of minority faculty and administrators; attempting to eliminate duplicate programs that are detrimental to traditionally black institutions; involving citizens' groups in the decision-making process; and ensuring that minorities are selected to serve on the governing boards of state higher education systems.

Many participants in the litigation of the *Adams* suit have described it as the largest and most comprehensive civil rights lawsuit in the history of American higher education. It certainly is becoming the longest. The Foundation hopes that the research contained in this volume can be used to resolve the issues pertinent to dismantling dual systems of higher education. SEF maintains that the findings have policy implications and should not be ignored. Thus, SEF is grateful that the work of the Foundation and of the principal investigators has been acknowledged to the extent of publishing this book and recognizing the significance of the studies.

The Southern Education Foundation also acknowledges with gratitude the Ford Foundation and its support of SEF's expanded Higher Education Program. Preparing this report was made possible by a Ford Foundation grant.

A list of other Foundation publications may be obtained by writing to the Southern Education Foundation.

Elridge W. McMillan, President

SOUTHERN EDUCATION FOUNDATION
340 West Peachtree Street, N.W.
Atlanta, Georgia 30308

Acknowledgments

The opinions expressed in this publication are those of the authors and are not necessarily those of the Southern Education Foundation. I have benefited from the advice of a number of persons who contributed their talents to the production of this volume. The Research Task Force, under the able leadership of James E. Blackwell, conceived the project. William Curlette, a Task Force member, critically read the entire manuscript, and James E. Blackwell provided enthusiastic support and advice as it took shape. I owe a special debt of gratitude to them. I express my appreciation to the staff of the Southern Education Foundation, especially Elridge McMillan, President; Karima Al-Amin, Higher Education Consultant; Jean Sinclair, Executive Associate; and Lauretta Travis, Secretary; and especially to the scholars who condensed into executive summaries the rich data contained in their monographs. William Unger's editorial work contributed greatly to the quality of this book. Karen Kreutzfeld typed the manuscript with patience and high competence, and my secretary, Jackie Hosley, served as an able conduit. I am deeply grateful to each of them. Finally, I wish to thank both Jules B. LaPidus, formerly Dean of the Graduate School at the Ohio State University, and Diether H. Haenicke, formerly Vice President for Academic Affairs and Provost, for their encouragement.

Anne S. Pruitt
Columbus, Ohio

January, 1987

Introduction

Edgar G. Epps and Anne S. Pruitt

This book results from the belief that research should provide the basis for intelligent change. It represents an important effort to maintain a source of data-based inquiry on desegregation in higher education. The prime consideration was to make the results of the Southern Education Foundation (SEF) studies of desegregation in public higher education available to a wide audience of individuals interested in equal educational opportunity, including school officials, counselors and teachers, legislators, other researchers, and graduate students. Studies reported herein were commissioned in the aftermath of the *Adams* v. *Richardson* court order, which required states with dual systems of segregated public higher education to dismantle them. A special interest was the expectation that the results would influence educational policy and practice.

The *Adams* court order, which is explored in greater detail by Gary Malaney in Chapter 1, arose out of the *Adams* v. *Richardson* lawsuit, initiated in 1970 by the National Association for the Advancement of Colored People (NAACP) Legal Defense and Educational Fund (LDF). In 1971, judges in the federal district court and the court of appeals instructed the U.S. Department of Health, Education, and Welfare (HEW) to secure plans from 10 states to take remedial actions to redress the wrongs of segregation and discrimination. These states, which became known as "*Adams* states," were Arkansas, Florida, Georgia, Louisiana, Maryland, Mississippi, North Carolina, Oklahoma, Pennsylvania, and Virginia. Currently, 19 states are encompassed by the *Adams* court order: the 10 listed above and Alabama, Delaware, Kentucky, Missouri, Ohio, South Carolina, Tennessee, Texas, and West Virginia.

Those remedial actions ordered by the courts concerned the admission, recruitment, and retention of students; the placement and duplication of program offerings among institutions; the role and enhancement of black institutions; and changes in the racial composition of the faculties involved. Set forth as criteria specifying the ingredients of acceptable desegregation plans, the remedial actions are often referred to as the *Adams* guidelines.

The Research Task Force of the Southern Education Foundation, formed in 1978, has taken as its mandate to assess carefully the progress being made toward eliminating inequality of blacks in higher education. It establishes priorities and funds small grants to scholars who are interested in researching topics and issues growing out of its priorities. Much talent resides in young scholars, who are often overlooked by funding agencies and publishers. The Task Force sought out such scholars in its effort to encourage their scholarship. Each author, whether emerging or more established, brought a background of scholarly experience and scholarly promise to the topics researched. Their vitae are summarized in the final section of this book. Their work is largely comparative in design, although experimental and longitudinal methods, as well as essays, are included.

The Task Force engaged in intensive discussion in the course of establishing a research agenda. We might wish that creating unitary systems of higher education would be as simple as opening the college gates. To the contrary, a multitude of questions emerge. For example, to what degree are black students entering and graduating from postsecondary educational institutions? What is the nature of their career aspirations and decisions? What kinds of encounters are they having with students and faculty in previously all-black or all-white institutions? What role do finances play in facilitating access to and graduation from higher educational institutions? To what extent are blacks being employed in traditionally white institutions?

Flowing from questions like these, among the earliest priorities established by the Research Task Force was the matter of access. It was believed that the first order of business was to find out what was happening to black students in states affected by the *Adams* case and in other states undergoing desegregation of higher education systems. Were black students entering traditionally white institutions in large numbers? If so, how did this trend affect student enrollment at traditionally black institutions? These questions are addressed in Chapter 2 by William and Marian Brazziel; it was one of the first studies commissioned by the Research Task Force. Also among the first group of studies commissioned was Charles Grigg's report, "Access, Retention, and Progression of Black Students through the Two-Tier Florida Higher Education System," which appears as Chapter 4 in this book.

The Task Force was also interested in how students choose colleges. What determines which students go to which colleges? Does attending desegregated secondary schools affect the college choice of black students? How much influence is exerted by family and friends? What role does family social status play in the choice process? These and similar questions are addressed in Chapter 3 by Gail Thomas and Jomills Braddock, who used survey data to examine the factors associated with college choice.

Beyond the issues of access and college choice, the Task Force wanted to know what was happening to students at different types of colleges. Are black colleges really more effective in retaining and graduating black students than are traditionally white institutions? What are the characteristics of institutions that are most effective in retaining and graduating black students? How important is the presence of black faculty? How important is financial aid in retaining students? These are a few of the questions addressed in the studies by Philip Hart (Chapter 6) and Michael Nettles *et al.* (Chapter 5). The results of this research should interest administrators and policymakers concerned about improving the effectiveness of institutions of higher education.

The issue of access to graduate and professional education was also among the first priorities of the Research Task Force. James E. Blackwell (Chapter 7) used institutional responses to a mailed questionnaire, supplemented by information from professional associations and interviews with administrators, to look at enrollment and graduation trends in graduate and professional schools over a 10-year period. He also examined factors that predicted differential rates of institutional success in recruiting and graduating black students. The results have important policy implications that should be seriously considered by educators and policymakers throughout the United States, as well as in the *Adams* states. The Blackwell work resulted in a major publication under the auspices of SEF, *Mainstreaming Outsiders: The Production of Black Professionals.*

In Part 3 the research focuses on black students' aspirations and career choices. Since blacks are underrepresented in higher education in the United States generally, as well as in the *Adams* states, the Task Force believed that information about the educational and occupational mobility process among black youth was needed. Among the pool of potential college students (high school seniors), what background, school, and personal factors predict high educational and occupational goals and attainment? Is it possible to identify ways of increasing the proportion of black high school graduates who are qualified to attend four-year colleges? The study by Edgar Epps and Kenneth Jackson (Chapter 8) addresses the general question of how the educational mobility process operates among black Americans. Using survey data from two national samples, they attempt to identify factors in secondary schools that might affect educational aspirations and attainment among black youths. They provide suggestions for improving secondary school curricula.

Black college students and graduates have tended to major in fields that lead to jobs in education and social service. Historically, this trend developed in response to limited career opportunities available to most blacks because of widespread segregation and discrimination in the labor market. Teaching, social service, and the professions offered job opportunities to blacks in sectors of the labor market that were relatively free of competition from whites. The legacy of this pattern of restricted opportunities is still reflected in the major field choices and career aspirations of black students. As Gail Thomas points out in Chapter 9, black college graduates in 1980 were underrepresented in the natural sciences and technological fields and overrepresented in education and the social sciences. Her study uses survey data to investigate the process of choosing a college major. The research has implications for both high school and college counselors.

Considerable speculation has occurred about the relative advantages or disadvantages of attending traditionally black institutions or traditionally white institutions. Since large numbers of black students are now enrolled in both types of institutions, information about the impact of institutional type on future careers of college graduates was deemed of great importance. Such information would be useful in helping address the question of the role of black colleges in a desegregated society. Other things being equal, do graduates of traditionally black institutions have career opportunities comparable to graduates of traditionally white institutions? Rhoda Johnson (Chapter 10) compared career outcomes for black graduates of traditionally black institutions and of traditionally white institutions in Alabama.

The studies in Part 4 address various aspects of the social and academic adjustment of black undergraduate, graduate, and professional school students on college campuses. In examining the coping strategies and support systems students use to help them survive in college and graduate school, Blackwell (Chapter 13) focused on networking and mentoring as two processes that could help explain graduate and professional school success, subsequent career development, and the occupational advancement of black professionals. His conclusions and recommendations provide clues that may help faculty and administrators improve the academic climate of graduate and professional schools for minority students.

Yvonne Abatso's study (Chapter 11) looked at the campus environment from a social–psychological point of view. She asked what personal traits of students are associated with successful coping on a college campus and if it is possible to teach students to use more effective coping strategies. She compared successful copers with less successful ones to determine characteristics that differentiate the two types of students. She also designed a program to improve the coping techniques of the less successful students. The results of this research provide useful suggestions for counselors and educators concerned with improving retention rates of black college students.

How do students feel about their college experiences on different types of college campuses? This is the general theme of Chapter 12 by Walter Allen, which uses survey data to assess student satisfaction with college and the institutional factors that encourage or discourage retention and academic progress. Student perceptions of how they are treated by faculty and peers, involvement in the institution's social life, and perceptions of discrimination are some of the variables examined in this research. The comparison of experiences on traditionally black and traditionally white campuses should be especially interesting to readers concerned about the role of black colleges in the 1980s and 1990s.

Part 5 includes two reports on the significance of financial aid for the higher education of black Americans. Chapter 14 reports on financial barriers to the higher education of black students; Chapter 15 discusses the results of a program to improve the effectiveness of small and developing institutions.

Several studies in this volume identify the availability of financial aid as an important factor in attracting, retaining, and graduating black students from both traditionally black and traditionally white institutions. Financial aid is even more important for graduate and professional school students. The American Council on Education Office of Minority Concerns reported that, in 1982, 35.6% of black families had incomes below the poverty level. Thus, it is not surprising that the majority of blacks enrolled in higher education require some financial assistance. The 1980s have seen a major change in the relationship of costs, income, and aid. In contrast to what could be said generally about the 1960s and 1970s, the 1980s represent depression years for higher education with regard to financial assistance. College has become more difficult for families to afford in the 1980s, and the impact on black students is especially harsh. A detailed discussion of financial barriers to higher education is presented in Chapter 14 by Jerry Davis and Kingston Johns.

The federal role in educational finance has a long and interesting history. One program with an important effect on traditionally black institutions was Title III of the Higher Education Act of 1965. In Chapter 15, Cameron Fincher uses survey data to assess the opinions of presidents of traditionally black institutions about the effectiveness of Title III and the impact of this type of financial assistance on their institutions.

Part 6 of this volume includes a study of black employees in traditionally white institutions. The importance of black faculty on white campuses for the academic adjustment and performance of black students is demonstrated by Blackwell and Allen in earlier chapters of this book. The Research Task Force identified employment as one of its major priorities for the first group of studies commissioned. Using data provided by the Office for Civil Rights of the Department of Health, Education, and Welfare for 1975 and 1977, Anne Pruitt performed a careful analysis of employment trends for these years (Chapter 16). Her conclusions provide many insightful recommendations for policymakers who want to improve on the less than spectacular track record of most institutions.

This book is by no means an exhaustive examination of the impact of the *Adams* guidelines. Those issues that seemed to be of most immediate and critical concern and that lent themselves to scientific scrutiny were funded first by SEF. Hence, a number of topics have yet to be addressed. Nor do the studies reported herein restrict their attention to the *Adams* states. Although *Adams* is the central focus, they target the overall progress, current status, and outlook for the future of black Americans in higher education.

In presenting this compilation of studies, we recognize that the desegregation of higher education is not static; since the Task Force began its work, changes have occurred in student and employee demographic data, college and university degree programs, state and federal funding, and student attitudes. We can take comfort in knowing that much of this change has been stimulated by the courts, the Office for Civil Rights, the Southern Education Foundation, state coalitions, and boards of regents. Desegregation is a dynamic phenomenon that requires constant monitoring and investigation. Thus, the research presented in this book provides benchmarks against which to observe the future and to influence changes.

It should be noted that nearly all the chapters summarize research that exists in much lengthier monograph form. Because we wanted this book to be useful to practitioners, authors were asked to write executive summaries in which they gave attention to solutions and policy initiatives. We wanted to assist practitioners in dealing with problems of effectively managing the desegregation process. Thus, more attention is given to solutions than to either research methodology or implications for further research. The executive summaries became chapters, which were then grouped by themes and linked together with appropriate introductory remarks. Readers who wish to examine for themselves the basic data from which these summaries and interpretations are drawn may secure the complete reports by writing directly to SEF.

The research reported in this volume addresses a broad range of issues pertinent to providing equality of educational opportunity for black Americans. The issues examined and the results reported should make interesting and informative reading for all persons concerned with the general problem of inequality of access to higher education in America. While the research is not directly generalizable to other minorities, the insights provided should be useful to administrators and policymakers whose interests focus on nonblack minorities.

PART 1

The *Adams* Case

Chapter	**1**	A REVIEW OF EARLY DECISIONS IN *ADAMS* V. *RICHARDSON*

A REVIEW OF EARLY DECISIONS IN *ADAMS* V. *RICHARDSON*

Gary D. Malaney

> No person in the United States shall, on the ground of race, color, or national origin, be excluded from participation in, or be denied the benefits of, or be subjected to discrimination under any program or activity receiving Federal financial assistance.
> — Title VI, Civil Rights Act of 1964

The above declaration has been this country's law since 1964, but there is yet to be total compliance. Although the statement refers to all programs and activities that receive federal assistance, this chapter concentrates on the activities associated with higher education.

Historically, the Office for Civil Rights (OCR) of the former Department of Health, Education, and Welfare (HEW) has been assigned the responsibility for enforcing Title VI regarding education. Some individuals have not been pleased with the way OCR and HEW have approached their responsibilities in this matter. Accordingly, in the fall of 1970, the NAACP Legal Defense and Educational Fund filed a class action suit in the federal district court in Washington, D.C., on behalf of 31 students, who were suing through their parents, and two citizens (Egerton 1982). The suit, known as *Adams* v. *Richardson,* was against HEW and OCR for defaulting on their obligations to enforce Title VI against the state of North Carolina.

The *Federal Supplement,* which provides the arguments and determinations of U.S. district courts, and the *Federal Reporter, Second Series,* which provides the arguments and determinations of U.S. courts of appeal, refer to the case as *Kenneth Adams, et al., Plaintiffs* v. *Elliot L. Richardson* (see 351, F.Supp. 636 [D.D.C. 1972] and 480 F.2d 1159 [D.C. Civ. 1973].) While the plaintiffs have remained the same, the case has undergone several name changes to reflect new HEW and Department of Education secretaries. These changes include *Adams* v. *Califano* and *Adams* v. *Bell.*

This case has become extremely important regarding the issue of equality of opportunity for access of students, faculty, and administrators.

In essence, the ruling affects all states that have been operating dual systems of higher education, which means the existence of historically separate institutions for whites and blacks. All such states were ordered to dismantle those systems, and this ruling has produced much debate and the usual wave of accompanying scholarly literature (see Blackwell 1981, 1982; Brazziel & Brazziel 1980; Egerton 1982; Fairfax 1978; Goddard 1980; Prestage 1982; Pruitt 1981).

The Case

Dates

The case has a long history of hearings, appeals, court orders and delays. The suit was first filed in late 1970, but the case was not heard until late 1972. On November 16, 1972, in the U.S. District Court, District of Columbia, Judge John H. Pratt delivered the first decision (351 F.Supp. 636 [D.D.C. 1972]; he amended the decision on February 16, 1973 (356 F.Supp. 92 [D.D.C. 1973]).

The original defendants appealed the decision, and the appeal was argued on April 16, 1973, with a decision reached on June 12, 1973 (480 F.2d 1159 [D.C. Cir. 1973]). The court of appeals affirmed all of Judge Pratt's order, with a modification of the injunction regarding higher education.

Almost four years later, the plaintiffs filed a Motion for Further Relief concerning the higher education phase of the litigation, and Judge Pratt handed down his Second Subsequent Order on April 1, 1977 (430 F.Supp. 118 [D.D.C. 1977]). Not satisfied with the action taken, the plaintiffs filed a Renewed Motion for Further Relief in 1983, and, on March 24, 1983, Judge Pratt delivered yet another order.

Decisions

The first decisions handed down in 1972 and 1973 found the defendants in violation of Title VI of the 1964 Civil Rights Act. In his Memorandum Opinion, Judge Pratt declared:

> On the basis of this record, it appears that, in certain of the areas about which plaintiffs complain, HEW has not properly fulfilled its obligation under Title VI . . . to eliminate the vestiges of past policies and practices of segregation in programs receiving federal financial assistance. (351 F.Supp. 637 [D.D.C. 1972])

In the Findings of Fact, regarding higher education, it was noted:

> Between January, 1969, and February, 1970, HEW concluded
> that the states of Louisiana, Mississippi, Oklahoma, North
> Carolina, Florida, Arkansas, Pennsylvania, Georgia, Mary-
> land, and Virginia were operating segregated systems of higher
> education in violation of Title VI.

It was also noted that HEW had requested that each of these states
submit a desegregation plan within 120 days. Five states totally ignored the
request, and five states submitted unacceptable plans. HEW failed to make
any formal comments, did not take any administrative enforcement action,
and did not refer the matter to the Justice Department for filing suits
against the states. HEW claimed that negotiations were still pending with
the states and that desegregating statewide higher education systems creates
special problems. HEW continued to provide federal funds to all 10 states.

In the Declaratory Judgment and Injunction Order, Judge Pratt said:

> Having once determined that a state system of higher education
> is in violation of Title VI, and having failed during a substantial
> period of time to achieve voluntary compliance, defendants
> have a duty to commence enforcement proceedings. (356 F.Supp.
> 92 [D.D.C. 1973])

He further required and enjoined the defendants to commence enforcement
proceedings within 120 days and to provide continuous data on the proceedings to the plaintiffs' counsel.

When the defendants appealed the district court's decision, the U.S.
court of appeals ruled in favor of the district court; however, there were
some slight modifications relating to the decisions affecting higher education. The court of appeals stated:

> We are also mindful that desegregation problems in colleges
> and universities differ widely from those in elementary and
> secondary schools, and that HEW admittedly lacks experience
> in dealing with them. (480 F. 2d 1159 [D.C. Cir. 1973])

The U.S. court of appeals felt that the defendants needed more time to
study the problems and to establish guidelines for desegregating statewide
systems of higher education. Because so much time had passed since the
first call for desegregation plans from the 10 states in question, the court

indicated that HEW should again ask for plans to be submitted within 120 days. The court further stated that HEW should be "in active communication with those states whose plans are not acceptable." The court felt that a state should have an additional 180 days after a plan had been declared unacceptable in order to revise the plan to acceptable standards. If an acceptable plan could not be formulated within 180 days, then HEW would have to initiate compliance procedures.

This decision was successful in bringing about action on the parts of HEW and all the states involved except Louisiana, which did not prepare a plan. HEW, in turn, referred the Louisiana case to the Department of Justice for commencement of enforcement proceedings. HEW also referred the Mississippi case when its plan was rejected. All the other state plans were accepted.

At this point, the plaintiffs filed a Motion for Further Relief, since they were not satisfied with HEW's actions. Judge Pratt, in issuing his Second Supplemental Order (430 F.Supp. 118 [D.D.C. 1977]), agreed with the plaintiffs and indicated that the higher education sections of all eight plans accepted by HEW "did not meet important desegregation requirements and have failed to achieve significant progress toward higher education desegregation." Judge Pratt indicated that none of the plans met the guidelines set forth by HEW.

Because the Louisiana and Mississippi cases had been transferred to the Justice Department, the Maryland case was before the court of appeals, and the Pennsylvania case was being negotiated between the defendants and plaintiffs, Judge Pratt issued no direct orders concerning these states. However, he did order and decree that the defendants

> shall promptly notify the states of Arkansas, Florida, Georgia, North Carolina, Oklahoma, and Virginia that the higher education desegregation plans submitted by them to HEW in 1974 are not adequate to comply with Title VI of the 1964 Civil Rights Act. (430 F.Supp. 118 [D.D.C. 1977])

He further ordered defendants to provide final guidelines or criteria for acceptable desegregation plans to the six states, the plaintiffs, and the court within 90 days of the order. He stated that the defendants should also require each state to submit a revised plan within 60 days of receiving the new guidelines and that the defendants should accept or reject the plans within 120 days after receipt.

In 1978 and 1979, the six states had plans accepted by HEW; since 1980, however, HEW has repeatedly informed the states that they have defaulted from their plans. Judge Pratt issued an order in early 1983 stating that the defendants, prior to the beginning of the 1983–1984 academic year, must receive from all states revised plans that were to be implemented by the fall of 1983 and were to be designed to ensure compliance to Title VI before the fall of 1985. In January 1983, Virginia had a revised plan accepted. Arkansas, Florida, Georgia, North Carolina, and Oklahoma had plans rejected, and a deadline of August 15, 1983, was set for revisions. Pennsylvania's deadline for submitting a plan was July 22, 1983. At this time, Maryland, Louisiana, and Mississippi faced lawsuits.*

Other States

The fact that the district court's decisions have shown that segregated public institutions of higher education are not going to be tolerated probably helped prompt OCR to initiate its own investigation of other states. In 1978 and 1979, OCR and the Department of Education "determined that vestiges of segregation remained" in eight additional states: Alabama, Delaware, Kentucky, Missouri, Ohio, South Carolina, Texas, and West Virginia. These states were ordered to submit plans to desegregate.

Plans have been accepted for Delaware, Kentucky, Missouri, South Carolina, Texas, and West Virginia.**

References

Adams v. *Califano,* 430 F.Supp. 118 (D.D.C. 1977).
Adams v. *Richardson,* 351 F.Supp. 636 (D.D.C. 1972).
Adams v. *Richardson,* 356 F.Supp. 92 (D.D.C. 1973).
Adams v. *Richardson,* 480 F.2d 1159 (D.C. Cir. 1973).
Blackwell, J. E.
    1981 *Mainstreaming Outsiders: The Production of Black Professionals.* Bayside, N.Y.: General Hall.
Blackwell, J.E.
    1982 Demographics of desegregation. In R. Wilson (Ed.), *Race and Equity in Higher Education.* Washington, D.C.: American Council on Education.

*As of spring 1985, Virginia, Arkansas, Florida, Georgia, Oklahoma, and the North Carolina Community College System operated under the acceptable plans. Louisiana operated under a court approved plan. Mississippi was in litigation and negotiations in Maryland were ongoing. — Ed.

**Alabama developed a plan that was unacceptable, and the matter has been referred to the Department of Justice to initiate litigation. Such action has taken place. — Ed.

Brazziel, W., & Brazziel, M.
    1980   *Recent College and University Enrollment Patterns of Black Students in States Affected by Adams-Califano Litigation.* Atlanta: Southern Education Foundation.
Egerton, J.
    1982   Race and equity in higher education. In R. Wilson (Ed.), *Race and Equity in Higher Education.* Washington, D.C.: American Council on Education.
Fairfax, J.
    1978   Current status of the Adams case: Implications for the education of blacks and other minorities. In College Entrance Examination Board, *Beyond Desegregation: Urgent Issues in the Education of Minorities.* New York: College Board.
Goddard, J. M.
    1980   *Educational Factors Related to Federal Criteria for the Desegregation of Public Postsecondary Education.* Atlanta: Southern Regional Education Board.
Prestage, J. L.
    1982   A political taxonomy of desegregation. In R. Wilson (Ed.), *Race and Equity in Higher Education.* Washington, D.C.: American Council on Education.
Pruitt, A. S.
    1981   *Black Employees in Traditionally White Institutions in the Adams States: 1975 to 1977.* Atlanta: Southern Education Foundation.

PART 2

Access and Progression: Determinants of Success

The number of black undergraduates enrolled full-time in American colleges and universities nearly doubled between 1970 and 1980. Blacks as a percentage of all full-time undergraduates increased from 6.8 in 1970 to 10.3 in 1976. This information, from a report of the National Center for Education Statistics (1983), reveals that this phenomenal increase coincided with activities at the federal and state levels to reduce barriers to equal educational opportunity.

Desegregation of student enrollment is a major ingredient in an acceptable state plan designed to dismantle the dual system of segregated higher education. Relevant sections of this criterion are drawn from the *Federal Register* and are quoted below (*Federal Register 1978*).

The states were ordered to "adopt the goal that for two year and four year undergraduate public higher education institutions . . . the proportion of black high school graduates throughout the state who enter such institutions shall be at least equal to the proportion of white high school graduates throughout the state who enter such institutions."

They are expected to "adopt the goal that there shall be an annual increase . . . in the proportion of black students in the traditionally white four year undergraduate public higher education institutions in the state system taken as a whole and in each such institution; and . . . adopt the objective of reducing the disparity between the proportion of black high school graduates and the proportion of white high school graduates entering traditionally white four year and upper division undergraduate public higher education institutions."

Moreover, they are expected to "adopt the goal that the proportion of black state residents who graduate from undergraduate institutions in the state system and enter graduate study or professional schools in the state system shall be at least equal to the proportion of white state residents who graduate from undergraduate institutions in the state system and enter such schools."

23

They are required to commit themselves "to take all reasonable steps to reduce any disparity between the proportion of black and white students completing and graduating from the two year, four year and graduate public institutions of higher education."

The states are required to commit themselves "to expand mobility between two year and four year institutions as a means of meeting" these goals. Finally, the states are required to commit themselves and all their "involved agencies and subdivisions to specific measures to achieve these goals."

Each study that follows targets a specific aspect of this very complex criterion. Chapter 2 by William and Marian Brazziel analyzes the participation of black students in all 19 states that now come under the *Adams* mandate. Given student opportunity to enroll in any college of their choice, are their participation rates increasing or decreasing? The Brazziels document trends and examine correlates of variability in state participation rates.

In Chapter 3, Gail Thomas and Jomills Braddock raise the question of the type of institutions attended. Charles Grigg focuses in Chapter 4 on the critical matter of community colleges as the so-called democratizer of higher education.

Problems of the quality of student programs in traditionally white versus traditionally black institutions are addressed by Michael Nettles and his colleagues in Chapter 5. Philip Hart proposes in Chapter 6 an effectiveness quotient to determine the institutional characteristics that enhance academic success for black students. In Chapter 7 on access and progression, James Blackwell describes participation rates of black students in graduate and professional schools. We know that this, the highest level of academic achievement, has been a stronghold of white students. Yet it is one that blacks headed for leadership in the academic and professional worlds must achieve access to and from which they must graduate.

References

Federal Register
>   1978   Revised criteria specifying the ingredients of acceptable plans to desegregate state systems of public higher education. Vol. 43, No. 32, Wednesday, February 15.

Hill, S. T.
>   1983   *Participation of Black Students in Higher Education: A Statistical Profile from 1970–71 to 1980–81.* Washington, D.C.: National Center for Education Statistics.

Chapter 2

RECENT COLLEGE AND UNIVERSITY ENROLLMENT PATTERNS OF BLACK STUDENTS IN STATES AFFECTED BY *ADAMS* LITIGATION

William F. Brazziel and Marian E. Brazziel

The study examined enrollment patterns of black undergraduate students in 19 states (Alabama, Arkansas, Delaware, Florida, Georgia, Kentucky, Louisiana, Maryland, Mississippi, Missouri, North Carolina, Ohio, Oklahoma, Pennsylvania, South Carolina, Tennessee, Texas, Virginia, and West Virginia) affected by *Adams* litigation and rulings. The research's general purpose was to ascertain the degree to which black students participated in the higher education enterprise and to identify trends signaling increases or decreases in this participation. One of the *Adams* criteria requires increases in the number of black students on white campuses, a subject the study also addressed, along with an assessment of state efforts to assure black student participation in the higher education enterprise.

The study documented increased black student participation in traditionally underrepresented fields of study, and a final section included regression equations developed to identify correlates for variability in state participation rates. Data from enrollment tapes of the Higher Education General Information Survey (HEGIS) for 1976 and 1978 formed the study's data core.

Findings

In 1976, 459,012 black undergraduates were enrolled in *Adams* states: 13.6% of the more than 3 million undergraduates enrolled in these states. Black population in these states was well over 16% of the total. When parity is expressed as a ratio of black enrollment to black population, the index for these states was .81.

This chapter is based on a previously published research monograph by William F. and Marian E. Brazziel: *Recent College and University Enrollment Patterns of Black Students in States Affected by Adams–Califano Litigation.* Atlanta: Southern Education Foundation, 1980.

Some 80% of the students were enrolled in public institutions in the states, and the number attending full-time was high compared to national averages. The ratio of public to private enrollment was also high. Black student enrollment in two-year colleges was higher in these states than in the nation as a whole.

When enrollment was examined according to definitions of parity, this condition was not reached for the states as a whole, but three states — West Virginia, Ohio, and Kentucky — reached or exceeded it. Oklahoma reached 99% of parity for 1976.

The data indicated that black enrollments increased in 1978 by approximately 3%. White enrollment in these states also increased, and the parity indexes remained about the same. Traditionally black four-year colleges lost enrollment, while black student enrollment at traditionally white four-year public colleges increased. Whether the latter's gains came at the former's expense is an unanswered question, and the possibility of a zero-sum game in these shifts does exist. Cross-racial enrollment is encouraged by *Adams* guidelines.

A significant percentage of black students attended traditionally white four-year colleges in the 19 states. Over 30% of the total number enrolled attended these schools, slightly over 33% attended traditionally black four-year colleges, and the rest attended two-year colleges, most of which were white. Wide variations are apparent in these patterns. Over 60% of West Virginia's black students, but only 11% of North Carolina's, were enrolled at traditionally white four-year institutions. Kentucky, Ohio, and Oklahoma were also high; Florida, Virginia, and Mississippi were also low.

One of the more heartening findings was black student increases in underrepresented fields of study. Students enrolled in business and management courses in 1978 had increased by 11,000 over the 70,000 enrolled in 1976. Over 12,000 engineering students were enrolled in 1978, up by nearly 2,000.

Black student enrollment in traditionally white public colleges was substantial and seemed to be increasing. Since *Adams* litigation involves public institutions, this finding should interest litigants. Indeed, in 1978, traditionally white public colleges enrolled half again as many black students (224,219) as did traditionally black public colleges (144,685).

The trend toward increased black student enrollment in traditionally white public colleges was pronounced. The figures are 111,322 for traditionally white campuses and 100,621 for traditionally black campuses. Enrollment on traditionally white public campuses increased by 4,000 students over a two-year period (1976–1978), while traditionally black public college enrollment decreased by 3,000 students. Again, these shifts involved public four-year colleges.

These shifts again raise the question of whether a zero-sum game was indeed occurring. Were white campus gains made at the expense of black campus losses? Only further research will tell. Data from this study indicated that such might be the case. Although the gains and losses of black and white campuses involved a head count of 7,000 students, total black enrollment for public four-year campuses increased by only 1,142 students, rising from 210,801 to 211,943. Further, states with black college losses matched those with white college gains.

The *Adams* guidelines indicated that increased overall black student enrollment and increased black student enrollment on white campuses were to go hand in hand. Parity would be reached, with black students enrolled on both black and white campuses. These data seem to indicate that such is not the case. Parity is *not* being reached. Black students on white campuses are matched by fewer black students on black campuses.

Adams criteria specifying goals for enhancing traditionally black colleges will be affected and perhaps jeopardized if enrollment on black public, four-year campuses is indeed markedly reduced. A certain enrollment level is necessary for program development and general institutional strength. Enrollment is thus a necessary ingredient of any enhancement program. Again, careful and immediate study is indicated here.

Several regression equations were developed to explore relationships between a set of predictor variables and the general participation rates of black students, black student enrollment on white four-year campuses, and state parity indexes for black enrollment. Generally, high participation rates and high parity indexes were closely related to type of state (northern, border, middle-south, deep south), black family income, the presence of black colleges, and the number of white regional public colleges and universities in a state. The latter have average admission standards, low tuition rates, and close proximity to population centers. Generally, northern and border states with higher black family incomes and a mix of black and white colleges had higher parity indexes for black enrollment. Black colleges and regional white state colleges were also important predictors of black enrollment on white four-year campuses. Black colleges were negatively correlated in this respect, however. The more black colleges in a state, the lower the black participation on white four-year campuses. Choice mechanisms seem to operate here. Given clear and open choices, many black students apparently choose black colleges.

In sum, the regression equations — and, indeed, the study's data — indicated the dynamics of diversity and choice in the participation process of black students in these states. States with high parity indexes for overall participation seem to offer choices and to promote diversity. A good mix of public and private, two- and four-year, and black and white colleges seems to be the key in these efforts, plus a genuine concern to involve black citizens in the higher education enterprise.

Suggestions for Further Study

Suggestions for further study include examining the operation of a zero-sum game in enrollment shifts between black and white four-year public institutions. Is such a game in progress? Are black student losses made up by white student gains? Is the rate of shift precipitant?

Enrollment analysis in all sectors might well be completed every other year to coincide with a biennial data collection on the NCES reports and tapes.

Widely publicized reports of black student enrollment drops in *Adams* states should be examined. The reports involve 1979 opening fall enrollment and attribute the rather sharp drop to foul-ups in student financial aid. These snarls stemmed, it seems, from a new management system installed by a U.S. Office of Education official who was hired to streamline the aid system and to eliminate abuses. The person has since departed, but whether the financial aid system recovers and whether black enrollment regains its former levels (if indeed there was a drop) remain to be seen.

Finally, an analysis of possible drops in baccalaureate degree production seems necessary at this juncture. Some 60,000 black students earn baccalaureates each year, with traditionally black colleges accounting for nearly half the total. Dropout rates of black students in traditionally white colleges are high. A psychic toll is exacted on many students, and many experience more than a little hostility. These factors drive down graduation rates. If a rapid flow of black students onto white campuses occurs, baccalaureate degree production will probably be affected. How much or how seriously remains to be seen. Again, serious study is indicated.

Suggested Policy Initiatives

This study has revealed implications for policy initiatives that might be mounted by the U.S. Department of Education and by state boards and commissions of higher education. Four such initiatives come to mind.

First, the *Adams* criteria of enrollment parity *and* graduation of black students should be placed at the top of the policy priority list. As this study showed, enrollment parity is shamefully low in many states, and baccalaureate graduation is barely half what it should be. Other Southern Education Foundation studies will show that black graduate and first professional degree production is a national disgrace. The most valuable contribution the Department of Education can make to implement *Adams* mandates is to encourage the bending of every oar to accomplish parity in black enrollment *and* graduation.

Second, the *Adams* criteria that specify enhancing traditionally black colleges and universities should also be placed at the top of the priority list. Discrimination in funding, program allocation, and mission has prevailed for a hundred years on these campuses, and it still prevails. If further legislation is needed to strengthen relevant civil rights laws, the Department of Education should seek it. Funding and program allocation parity is a must.

Third, the concept of racial balance in *Adams* colleges, which has occupied the energies of many of those working toward desegregation in colleges and universities, might well be replaced by a concept of cross-racial enrollment. Racial balance is a concept that is used in desegregating public schools. The concept has worked well, but it cannot be applied successfully in desegregating colleges and universities in the *Adams* states. It would work to the detriment of black colleges. Indeed, it would mean the end of many black colleges.

States most successful in producing black baccalaureates are states such as Ohio, which has many black students enrolled at traditionally white colleges and a sizable number of black students enrolled at traditionally black colleges. Cross-racial enrollment of this nature in every *Adams* state would seem to be the ideal concept to be employed in this work. On the other hand, rhetoric about racial balance has already sparked a March on Washington by concerned black Americans to protest all *Adams* initiatives. More protests are planned. The good that *Adams* initiatives can achieve can be greatly damaged by pursuing improper goals.

Fourth, a variety of policies should be developed to encourage integration. However, the policies of urging large-scale program transfer and of urging large-scale remedial programs on four-year campuses should be changed.

Program transfer at Savannah State and at Armstrong State in Georgia was a total failure. Black students did not enroll in the teacher education programs that were transferred to Armstrong. White students did not enroll in the business programs that were transferred to Savannah. Black baccalaureate production was cut in half at the two schools.

Extensive remedial programs should be confined to community colleges. Rightly or wrongly, many professors on four-year campuses do not like remedial programs and are contemptuous of students who need such programs to correct deficiencies. Further, when large numbers of black students are enrolled as special students, this contempt is generalized to *all* black students on campus. The September 1980 issue of *Ebony* contains a piece by Alvin Poussaint that explicates this dynamic. High visibility seems to be the problem. White colleges can offer remedial education to white students (and black colleges to black students), and the students suffer little from professorial contempt and hostility. After the freshman year, upper-division professors cannot identify who did or did not come to campus with deficiencies. Black students on white campuses are visible, however, and are often tagged with a deficiency stereotype regardless of their preparation.

Extensive use of transitional study programs in community colleges, coupled with the practice of publicizing the unusual strengths of many black enrollees, will enable many *Adams* states to avoid the errors of other states that tried the special-program approach. Further, this study's data indicated that a rapid, natural build-up of black students on white campuses is occurring without special programs.

Policies that encourage cross registration, consortia programs, and other cooperative efforts will bring about a significant amount of integration. Funds are available from the Department of Education to promote consortia for operational efficiency. Adding funds to encourage consortia for integration would help greatly.

Some multi-campus colleges and their feeder high schools engage in a policy of racial steering. Black students are encouraged to enroll at traditionally black campuses, while white students are encouraged to enroll at traditionally white campuses. Guidance counselors, teachers, admission officers, recruiters and others are involved in this policy. Reversing it will be difficult, but reversal will promote integration.

Policies facilitating easy transfer within a college system will promote integration. Many students would spend a year or two on a campus on which they were members of a minority group if transfer to another college were simple. Transfer in many systems, however, is not simple. Students lose financial aid entitlements, their credits are not accepted, and they experience other problems. Most are rightfully wary of experimentation in such a context.

Coupling easy transfer with well-funded black colleges replete with new, attractive programs should result in more white students on black campuses. As noted above, the build-up of black students on white campuses seems to be occurring rapidly and needs little stimulation. Admissions officers on black campuses should maintain contact with black students on white campuses, however, to offer the disaffected the opportunity to transfer to a black college and graduate. Too often, disaffection has meant complete withdrawal, loss of entitlements, and loss of credits. Easy transfer and maintaining contact could save many of these students.

Chapter 3

DETERMINING THE
COLLEGE DESTINATION OF
BLACK STUDENTS
Gail E. Thomas and Jomills H. Braddock II

Within the past decade, a substantial number of black students have gained access to college. In fact, between 1973 and 1979, black enrollment in U.S. colleges and universities increased more rapidly than white enrollment (Astin & Cross 1977; Bayer 1973). By 1980, however, black student enrollment in U.S. undergraduate institutions had leveled off. In 1982, blacks constituted only 8% of the four-year college population and 10% of the two-year college population.

Most public reports on the status of black students in higher education have not considered the types of colleges that these students attend. Nevertheless, where black students pursue their education is consequential for several reasons. First, investing in higher education remains the major alternative for upward mobility for most blacks. Second, black students' ability to obtain access to graduate and professional education largely depends on the type and quality of their undergraduate education. For example, the fact that a larger proportion of black undergraduates attends two-year rather than four-year colleges has major implications for their subsequent educational attainment. Black students must make the transition from two-year to four-year colleges to qualify for advanced higher education. Third, the problems of prompt graduation (Thomas 1981) and retention (Braddock 1981) for blacks in traditionally white colleges and universities also affect their access to graduate and professional schools.

Until recently, most major investigations of students' access to college and educational attainment were based on white samples (Hauser 1971; Sewell, Haller, & Ohlendorf 1970; Sewell, Haller, & Portes 1969; Sewell & Shah 1967). Recent investigations involving black samples generally fall into

This chapter is based on a previously published research monograph by Gail E. Thomas and Jomills H. Braddock II: *Determining the College Destination of Black Students.* Atlanta: Southern Education Foundation, 1981.

three broad categories. First, several large-scale descriptive studies have examined black student enrollments and degree attainment at various levels of higher education and their representation within major fields throughout higher education (Blackwell 1981; Brown & Stent 1977; Grigg 1980; Mingle 1979; Thomas 1980). These investigations show that black students are underrepresented in access and degree attainment at the graduate and professional school levels. In addition, they reveal that black students are underrepresented in the hard and technical sciences (i.e., the natural sciences, mathematics, and engineering) and in advanced professional fields (law, medicine, and dentistry).

Second, descriptive studies about the experiences of black students in traditionally white colleges have been conducted (Allen 1981; Boyd 1977; Smith 1980; Willie & McCord 1972). This research shows that the academic and social experiences of black students on traditionally white campuses vary depending on their family and academic background and their previous experience in predominantly white environments. Most of these studies have also reported that many black students encounter some adjustment problems (e.g., alienation, academic difficulties, teacher bias) in traditionally white colleges.

The third group of studies on black college students has investigated race and sex interactions affecting the educational attainment process (Portes & Wilson 1976; Thomas 1981; Thomas, Alexander, & Eckland 1979). The major concerns of these studies have been with (1) the number of years of schooling that students attain; (2) the transition of students from high school to college; and (3) the prompt graduation of students in four-year colleges. These investigations have shown significant race and sex interactions, suggesting that factors influencing the college entry and educational attainment process vary for blacks and whites and for males and females.

The issues of who goes where to college and what factors determine the college destination of students have not been systematically addressed for black students. For whites, Astin (1965) found that American colleges and universities differ substantially in the types of students they enroll. Astin employed colleges as the unit of analysis and examined student characteristics within various institutions to determine why students were enrolled in their respective colleges. He found a high correlation between the characteristics of entering freshmen and the colleges and universities they attended. Astin concluded that where students attend college is a function of two decisions: one made by the student and the other made by college admission officers. First, students choose a college or university that meets their personal aspirations and goals and that satisfies the expectations of their peers, family, teachers, and counselors. Then college admission officers accept or reject applicants based on criteria that include academic credentials, student goals and aspirations, the needs and goals of the college or university, and the quality and quantity of the available applicant pool.

In this study, the student, rather than the institution, was the unit of analysis. Focusing on the student, we examined a number of factors that affect the type of college that black students attend. These factors included the personal characteristics of students (family background, standardized test performance, educational aspirations, perceptions about colleges and universities); their academic and precollege program experiences within high school (their curriculum placement, high school rank, course preparation in mathematics and science, and their participation in Upward Bound or Talent Search); the influence of "significant others"; and the characteristics of the high schools (region, racial composition) that black students attend. We were specifically interested in determining what factors influenced the enrollment of black students in two-year versus four-year colleges and in traditionally black versus traditionally white colleges.

Data

The National Longitudinal Survey (NLS) of the High School Senior Class of 1972 was the data set used in this study. The survey, which is under the auspices of the National Center for Education Statistics (NCES), was conducted to determine what happened to students after they left high school, as indicated by their educational and vocational plans and experiences. A representative sample was drawn of twelfth graders who were enrolled in some 1,200 U.S. public, private, and church-affiliated secondary schools.

The project employed a two-stage probability sample, with schools as first-stage sampling units and students as second-stage units. Schools located in low-income areas or with a high proportion of minority students were oversampled in order to obtain an adequate representation of black students and other racial minorities (Mexican, Native American, and Asian). Approximately 21,600 high school seniors participated in the Base Year (1972) survey and completed a questionnaire that dealt with their post-high-school plans, family background, and previous educational experiences.

Base-Year (1972), First- (1973), Second- (1974), and Third-Year (1976) follow-up data were used in this study. Between the Base-Year and Third-Year follow-up surveys, approximately 51% of the blacks ($N = 1,608$) made the transition to some type of college. This subsample of blacks was employed in this study.

Findings

Cross-tabulations and multiple regression analyses were employed to evaluate factors that determine the college destination of black students. The latter procedure permitted an assessment of the simultaneous and separate contribution of the independent variables to the variation in the dependent variable(s). In addition, it provided a basis for determining the predictive power of the independent variables by interpreting the Coefficient of Determination (R^2).

Findings from the descriptive data revealed interesting distinctions among blacks who attended various types of colleges. For example, among black females, students who attended highly selective colleges and private colleges were from higher socioeconomic status backgrounds than were their counterparts who attended less selective colleges or public colleges.[1] These differences were less pronounced among black males. The racial composition of the high school that black students attended also affected the type of college that they attended. Black males and females who attended predominantly white colleges and black males who attended highly selective colleges were much more likely to be graduates of traditionally white high schools than were black students who attended traditionally black colleges. Also, black males and females who were enrolled in a high academic, as opposed to a general or vocational, curriculum were disproportionately more likely to attend a four-year college, a private college, or a college of high selectivity than were their counterparts who were enrolled in a nonacademic high school curriculum.

The findings from multiple regression analyses showed that the independent variables were not very powerful in predicting access to two-year versus four-year colleges. Eleven (for southern males) to 16% (for nonsouthern females) of the variance in this dependent variable was explained by these variables. Past models of college access employing similar variables have been more predictive for whites (Portes & Wilson 1976; Thomas, Alexander, & Eckland 1979).

---

[1]College selectivity is defined as the mean SAT score of the student body for each institution. —Ed.

Second, the findings indicated that the variable that had the greatest influence on four-year college access differed for students depending on their sex and region. For southern males, the status of the college (as measured by admission standards, academic reputation, and curriculum offerings) was the most important factor affecting their access to a four-year college. For nonsouthern males, their college options (i.e., the number of colleges to which they were accepted) most influenced their access to four-year colleges. For southern females, educational expectation was the most important determinant of four-year college access, whereas high school academic preparation was the most important determinant for nonsouthern females. However, both of these variables had a negative rather than a positive effect on four-year college attendance for southern and nonsouthern females. This means that southern black females with high educational expectations and nonsouthern black females with high academic performance in high school are more likely to attend two-year than four-year colleges.

The results from the regression analyses also showed that the independent variables were not highly predictive of attending a traditionally white versus a traditionally black college. The percentage of variance explained for subgroups ranged from .098 to .165. However, the results showed that, for southern and nonsouthern black males and black females, high school racial composition (i.e., attending a predominantly white high school) was the most important determinant of attending a traditionally white college. Educational expectation was also a significant factor affecting the access of southern males to traditionally white colleges. However, this variable did not have a significant influence on attending a traditionally white college for the other subgroups. Finally, the results suggested that, among black males and black females, students with the greatest number of college options (i.e., acceptance offers) were more likely to attend a traditionally white college than were black students with fewer college options.

Summary and Policy Implications

Our objective in this chapter was to examine factors that determine the college access of black students to two-year versus four-year colleges and to traditionally black versus traditionally white colleges. Regional and sex differences were evaluated when examining this issue. The sex, regional, and personal background differences that were found suggested that educational administrators and policymakers may need to devote more effort to learning about the diverse characteristics and educational backgrounds of black students so that they can more effectively match potential black undergraduates with various colleges and universities. Findings from this study also indicated that the college destination of black students is, to a great extent, contingent upon the family resources that these students have, the type of high school and high school curriculum that they were enrolled in, and the academic and motivational skills that they bring to the college environment. Also, the admission process and the characteristics and mission(s) of colleges and universities themselves assume a very important role in the college access and destination of black students. Therefore, college recruiters and high school counselors may need to provide more detailed and effective counseling to inform students and their parents of the requirements and tradeoffs associated with gaining access to and matriculating in various types of colleges and universities.

A second and more subtle implication from our findings concerned the role of black colleges in recruiting black high school students. It has been consistently argued that America's traditionally black colleges must be better supported morally and financially to compete effectively with traditionally white colleges for black students (Institute for the Study of Educational Policy 1976); Thomas, McPartland, & Gottfredson 1981). Our findings suggested that the ability of black colleges to compete with traditionally white colleges also depends on their success in recruiting black students from predominantly white high schools. Our findings showed that attending a predominantly white high school was positively related to attending a traditionally white college. Thus, recruiters from traditionally black colleges must find more effective strategies to increase their pool of applicants from predominantly white high schools. This will obviously depend on the future level of state and federal support for black colleges. It will also depend on the ability of black colleges to convey their strengths and unique attributes to black students who are likely to be attracted to, and are likely to be recruited by, white colleges.

Finally, our study confirmed Astin's (1978) observation that where students go to college is a critical issue that requires detailed and systematic investigation. In addition, the consequences of black students' undergraduate college destination for their subsequent higher education achievement and occupational attainment need to be examined. This is very important because educational attainment (especially at the graduate and professional school levels) remains the primary mechanism for the occupational and upward mobility of black students and for black Americans in general.

References

Allen, W. R.
  1981 Correlates of black student adjustment, achievement, and aspirations of a predominantly white Southern university. In Gail E. Thomas (Ed.), *Black Students in Higher Education: Conditions and Experiences in the 1970s*, pp. 126–141, Westport, Conn.: Greenwood Press.

Astin, A. W.
  1965 *Who Goes Where to College?* Chicago: Science Research Associates.

Astin, A. W.
  1978 *Four Critical Years.* San Francisco: Jossey-Bass.

Astin, H. S., & Cross, P. H.
  1977 *Characteristics of Entering Black Freshmen in Predominantly Black and Predominantly White Institutions: A Normative Report.* Washington, D.C.: Higher Education Research Institution.

Bayer, A. E.
  1973 The new student in black colleges. *School Review, 81,* 415–426.

Blackwell, J. E.
  1981 *Mainstreaming Outsiders: The Production of Black Professionals.* Bayside, N.Y.: General Hall.

Boyd, W. M.
  1977 Black undergraduates succeed in white colleges. *Education Record, 58,* 309–315.

Braddock, J. H.
  1981 Desegregation and black student attrition. *Urban Education, 14,* 403–418.

Brown, F., & Stent, M. D.
  1977 *Minorities in U.S. Institutions of Higher Education.* New York: Praeger.

Grigg, C. M.
  1980 *Access, Retention and Progression of Black Students through the Two-Tier Florida Higher Education System.* Atlanta: Southern Education Foundation.

Hauser, R. M.
  1971 *Socioeconomic Background and Educational Performance.* Rose Monograph Series, Washington, D.C.: American Sociological Association.

Institute for the Study of Educational Policy
  1976 *Equal Educational Opportunity for Blacks in U.S. Higher Education: An Assessment.* Washington, D.C.: Howard University.

Mingle, J. R.
  1979 *Degrees Awarded in the Nation and the South: 1976–1977.* Atlanta: Southern Regional Education Board.

Portes, A., & Wilson, K. L.
  1976 Black-white differences in educational attainment. *American Sociological Review, 41,* 414–431.
Sewell, W. H., Haller, A. O., & Ohlendorf, G. W.
  1970 The educational and early occupational attainment process: Replications and revisions. *American Sociological Review, 35,* 1014–1027.
Sewell, W. H., Haller, A. O., & Portes, A.
  1969 The educational and early occupational attainment process. *American Sociological Review, 34,* 89–92.
Sewell, W. H., & Shah, V. P.
  1967 Socioeconomic status, intelligence and the attainment of higher education. *Sociology of Education, 40,* 559–572.
Smith, D. H.
  1980 *Admission and Retention Problems of Black Students at Seven Predominantly White Universities.* Washington, D.C.: National Advisory Committee on Black Higher Education and Black Colleges and Universities.
Thomas, G. E.
  1980 Race and sex group equity in higher education: Institution and major field enrollment statuses. *American Educational Research Journal, 17,* 171–181.
Thomas, G. E.
  1981 College characteristics and black students' four-year college graduation. *Journal of Negro Education, 50,* 328–345.
Thomas, G. E., Alexander, K. L., & Eckland, B. K.
  1979 Access to higher education: The importance of race, sex, social class, and academic credentials. *Social Review, 87,* 133–156.
Thomas, G. E., McPartland, J. M., & Gottfredson, D. C.
  1981 Desegregation and black student higher education access. In G. E. Thomas (Ed.), *Black Students in Higher Education: Conditions and Experiences in the 1970s,* pp. 336–356. Westport, Conn.: Greenwood Press.
Willie, C. V., & McCord, A. S.
  1972 *Black Students at White Colleges.* New York: Praeger.

Chapter **4**   ACCESS, RETENTION, AND
PROGRESSION OF BLACK
STUDENTS THROUGH THE
TWO-TIER FLORIDA HIGHER
EDUCATION SYSTEM
Charles M. Grigg

This study addresses the question of whether a state system of higher education based on different levels or tiers provides equal access and equal opportunity for minority students to achieve their academic and professional goals. Specifically, it investigates access distribution, retention, and progression of minority students using Florida community colleges as the initial entry point to get a baccalaureate, graduate, or professional degree.

When the California Master Plan for Higher Education was published in 1960, it became the best-known planning document in the country. One of the key concepts developed in this Master Plan was access to higher education. However, the document defined accessibility in two different ways. First, it set specific admission standards that made the universities and the state colleges selective and the community colleges completely open door. Second, it called for locating community colleges within commuting distance of most, if not all, prospective students. Willingham (1970) reported that "free access higher institutions in California are almost exclusively the public community colleges because only those in the top third of their high school class are admitted to the state colleges" (p. 55). Eulau and Quinley (1970) reported that "the popularity of junior colleges was clearly reflected in the responses of state legislators and executive officials. They were more positive in their evaluation of these colleges than of any other aspect of higher education covered in the survey" (p. 113). The authors also indicated that an important factor in the favorable evaluation of junior colleges was the multiple functions they could perform. For instance, there are

This chapter is based on a previously published research monograph by Charles M. Grigg: *Access, Retention and Progression of Black Students through the Two-Tier Florida Higher Education System.* Atlanta: Southern Education Foundation, 1980.

liberal-arts-oriented institutions from which sophomores could transfer to four-year institutions, and there are vocational training centers that provided a place for late bloomers to serve the community. But in their concluding remarks the authors state that "many state officials gave high priority to expanding junior colleges. They saw many advantages to these schools — economy, accessibility, and curricula oriented to the basic vocational needs of individuals" (pp. 177–178).

From the beginning of the junior college movement, the question raised by many was whether these colleges were just extensions of high school and, as such, terminal program institutions. This argument was particularly relevant for those state systems that followed the California Master Plan. As early as 1970, Willingham pointed out that the poor, whether scoring high on tests or not, would, by economic necessity, gravitate to the community colleges; without economic support, they would gravitate to the senior institutions within commuting distance.

Bowles and Gintis (1976) see the two-year college phenomenon as a way to resolve the conflict between the university's elite-training functions and the greatly expanded number of students enrolled. An expanded number of students in higher education has thus been facilitated without undermining the elite status and function of the established institutions. Karabel (1972) cites a national study by the American Council on Education that points up the sharp differences between students' social origins and their attendance at various types of institutions. The survey revealed that 62% of students enrolled at public two-year colleges came from families with an income under $12,500. This compares to students at public universities, where only 44% of the students enrolled came from families with an income under $12,500.

In many respects, the community college represents a big holding operation for students who cannot afford to attend a senior institution. Bowles and Gintis (1976) label community colleges places where the majority of students are "programmed for failure." In contrast, Clark (1960) identifies this process as a "cooling out" process, bringing students' hopes into line with the realities of the job market. Bowles and Gintis summarize this situation by indicating that at least three times as many entering community college students want to complete four or more years of college as actually succeed. Less than half receive even the two-year Associate of Arts degree. Clark provides some insight into this process and partially explains how the community colleges control the number enrolled in college preparatory programs:

In the junior college, the student does not so clearly fail, unless he himself wishes to define it that way, but rather transfers to terminal work . . . . The terminal student can be made to appear not so radically different, e.g., an "engineering aide" instead of an "engineer" and hence he goes to something with a status of his own. (p. 570)

Most previous educational research involving race and sex comparisons has not focused on the type of higher education institutions that students attend. Instead, the concern has been primarily with investigating who goes to college and the factors that determine college entry and subsequent educational attainment. Although this research addresses an important part of the issue of educational access, it does not address the type of higher education institutions that students attend and their educational activities and experiences in such institutions.

It is safe to say that all those who view the role of community colleges in higher education would agree that they do well in providing middle-level training in nursing, computer work, office skills, and the health fields. The question remains, however, how effective the community colleges have been in providing college preparatory programs for those who wish to continue their college education at a senior institution. Both Blackwell (1977) and Fairfax (1977) point out the critical need to have more black students entering graduate and professional training. In those states that rely on community colleges to be the equal-access point in higher education, the question is posed whether equal opportunity to progress to the next level of education is a reality or a myth.

The Florida System of Higher Education

The reason for conducting research in Florida is that, among the *Adams* states, Florida has progressed furthest in establishing and using community colleges to implement the equal-access, equal-opportunity provision.

In Florida's commitment to equal access and equal opportunity in public higher education, as adopted by the State Board of Education on September 6, 1977, the state reaffirmed the goal of assuring equal educational opportunities in the Public Community College System and the State University System. Further, the state committed to ensuring that the system as a whole and each institution would be open and accessible to all students and would operate on an equal-opportunity basis, without regard to race.

Governance and Structure

The Florida State Board of Education is composed of seven elected state officials; it has general supervision for all public education in Florida, including the Division of Community Colleges and the State University System. Each of Florida's 28 community colleges is governed by a district Board of Trustees, which is appointed by the governor, approved by the State Board, and confirmed by the Senate. These 28 community colleges, 14 of which also serve as area vocational–technical centers, are the major component of the first tier. They provide opportunity for post-high-school education at the freshman–sophomore level.

The State University System is governed by a statewide Board of Regents, which is appointed by the governor, approved by the State Board, and confirmed by the Senate. Florida's state universities operate on a "two-tiered" system. Five universities accept first-time-in-college students and upper-division and graduate students, while the other four universities enroll students at the upper-division and graduate levels only. Florida A. and M. University, Tallahassee; The University of Florida, Gainesville; The University of Central Florida, Orlando; The University of South Florida, Tampa; and Florida State University, Tallahassee, are the four-year institutions. The University of North Florida, Jacksonville; Florida Atlantic University, Boca Raton; Florida International University, Miami; and The University of West Florida, Pensacola, are upper-division institutions. All are traditionally white institutions except Florida A. and M., which is the only state traditionally black institution. The State University System has a policy that limits lower-level enrollment to ensure that most high school graduates begin their college education in a community college.

In 1971, an articulation agreement between the Division of Community Colleges and the State University System assured access to upper-division levels in any one of the nine universities for all those with an Associate of Arts degree.

Research Design

This study addressed the general question of whether a state system of higher education based on dual responsibility and different levels or tiers is effectively providing equal access and equal opportunity for minority students. Specifically, the study evaluated the system's effectiveness in providing minority students with access, distribution, retention, and progression.

The process was conceptualized as evaluating the flow of students through the system by identifying critical points at which minority students suffer differentially as compared to white students. Figure 4.1 diagrams the two-tiered system and indicates the three potential routes by which a high school graduate might pursue a bachelor's degree. Student flow into the system begins with the recruitment of high school graduates. Approximately two-thirds of first-time college students enter the community college system. The other one-third enters the two-tier State University System.

Differentiation begins at this point. Students entering four-year universities are "mainliners," with the prospect of a continuous four years of uninterrupted undergraduate education in a comprehensive university with graduate and professional programs. Route *B* in the diagram represents the mainliners. Route *A* — entrance through community colleges — represents the transfer flow of students. After receiving their Associate of Arts degrees, this group must transfer to either upper-divisional — Route *C* — or to the mainline — Route *D*. Each route has critical control points (Figure 4.1) where minority students suffer relative to white students.

The study concentrated on student flow through the system, using published and unpublished data for the three years 1976–1979. Published data for community colleges were drawn from *Equal Access–Equal Opportunity* for Florida community colleges, fall 1976 through fall 1978. Data on the State University System were drawn from the Board of Regents publication *Desegregation Status Report*, 1977–1978 and 1978–1979. Information on the number and distribution of Associate of Arts graduates transferring to the State University System was drawn directly from the tapes of the 1977–1978 and 1978–1979 Feedback Studies. Retention data were drawn from the 1976–1977 Longitudinal Study. Both studies, which were conducted by the Division of Community Colleges, involved special tabulation to meet the purposes of this study.

Results and Policy Implications

The enrollment pattern in the two-tier system from 1970 to 1978 speaks to the success of the first objective. The proportion of all undergraduates in the state who enrolled in community colleges increased from 55% in 1970 to 61.2% in 1978. The proportion of black undergraduates in community colleges increased more rapidly than that of whites. In 1970, 54.2% of all blacks enrolled were in community colleges; by 1978, the percentage had

FIGURE 4.1.

Location of control points in the flow of undergraduate students in a two-tier state university system (SUS).

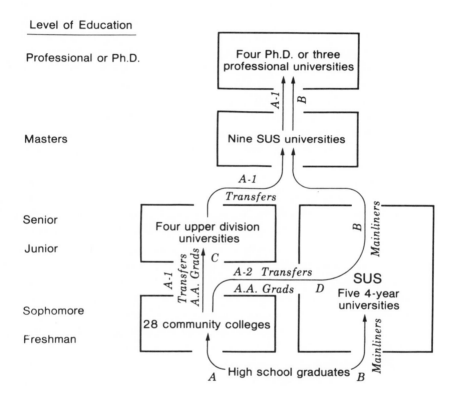

Student Flow Control Points

A & B   First-time entrance of high school graduates

C & D   Break in institutional affiliation entrance of transfer students into two-tiered SUS

increased to 65. White community college undergraduate enrollment increased from 55.2% in 1970 to 61% in 1978.

Even more impressive than the concentration of total undergraduate enrollment in community colleges is the concentration of first-time entrance of high school graduates. In 1977, 75% of all white high school graduates entered community colleges; in 1978, the percentage had increased to 77. These figures can be compared to 78.2% of all black high school graduates in 1977 and to 79.4% in 1978.

Community colleges have assumed the burden of undergraduate enrollment, but a higher proportion of blacks than of whites is enrolling. The figures also point up the fact that a smaller proportion of blacks than of whites is taking the mainline route. As a result, a higher proportion of blacks faces the discontinuity of transferring to the State University System as juniors. At this point, a higher proportion of these transfer students continues in an upper-division university—Route C—than transfers to the mainline—Route D (Figure 4.1).

To best evaluate how well the two-tier system fulfills its commitment of equal access, retention, and progression of black students, specific control points were identified in the student flow. At each point, a differential loss by blacks occurred that reduced black representation in the flow of students moving through the system. At each control point, the structural reasons for these differential losses by blacks have been identified.

The student flow into the system begins with the recruitment of high school graduates. Parity analysis indicated a black deficit for both 1977–1978 and 1978–1979 for both the Community College System and the State University System. The absolute loss in black students from the system was 1,712 for 1977–1978 and 2,915 for 1978–1979.

The second control point occurs at the disjunction of the two systems, where Associate of Arts recipients transfer to the State University System. There are two estimates of the progression rate from one system to the other. A first study indicated a differential in progression rate of 9 to 14%, while a second study indicated from 14 to 31%. Using these two studies as high and low estimates of differential loss will result in an absolute black student loss of from 151 to 343 in 1977–1978 and from 244 to 554 in 1978–1979.

The final control point is the retention of community college transfers in the State University System. Persistence rates for transfer students are as much as 10 points lower than for mainliners for both blacks and whites. The data indicated that black and white transfer students fare less well than mainliner students and that white transfer students fare better than black transfer students.

Special mention should be made of the role of Florida A. and M. University, the only traditionally black institution in the State University System. In accordance with the *Adams* guidelines, there must be a commitment to increasing the total proportion of white students attending this institution. A less than 2% white enrollment in 1979 had increased to 8.4% in 1978 — an increase from 58 to 381 white students. In 1970, Florida A. and M. University enrolled 27% of all blacks in public higher education. By 1978, it enrolled only 15.4% of all blacks. Black representation in the student body decreased only 6.7% between 1970 and 1978.

Our studies indicated that very few blacks choosing the two-plus-two route applied for admission to the two professional programs — law and medicine — and that the few who did were not admitted to law school. White applicants taking the two-plus-two route had a better chance. White applicants admitted from the two-plus-two route account for the acceptance group's proportion of the applicant pool.

The Florida system of higher education is one approach to redirecting the flow of students seeking a college education into community colleges. However, Florida has not solved several common problems inherent in this approach. First is the problem of increased black underrepresentation at the system's upper levels. Black concentration in the system's lowest stratum does not guarantee that the entire system has accorded access to blacks. This problem is particularly severe in the traditionally white four-year universities. Second, black student losses at the point of transfer to senior institutions are substantial. This is true for Florida and for other states with large black concentrations in community colleges.

Needed Research

This study identified points in the two-plus-two system where black student loss was significant. Further research is needed to study the retention on community college campuses of black students seeking the Associate of Arts degree.

Black student loss at the point of transfer from community colleges to the State University System is severe. Little is known about why this loss ocurs. Do students find jobs in their own communities? Do they postpone their goals to a later date?

Finally, retention studies of black community college graduates should be conducted within the State University System for both four-year and upper-division institutions. More answers are needed about the differential loss of black students.

References

Blackwell, J. E.
   1977   *The Participation of Blacks in Graduate and Professional Schools: An Assessment.* Atlanta: Southern Education Foundation.
Bowles, S., & Gintis, H.
   1976   *Schooling in Capitalist America.* New York: Basic Books.
Clark, B. R.
   1960   The cooling out function in higher education. *American Journal of Sociology, 65*(6), 569–576.
Eulau, E., & Quinley, H.
   1970   *State Officials and Higher Education.* New York: McGraw–Hill.
Fairfax, J.
   1978   Current status of the Adams case: Implication for the education of blacks and other minorities. In College Entrance Examination Board, *Beyond Desegregation: Urgent Issues in the Education of Minorities.* New York: College Board.
Karabel, J.
   1972   Community colleges and social stratification. *Harvard Educational Review, 42*(4), 521–562.
Willingham, W. W.
   1970   *Free-access to Higher Education.* New York: College Entrance Examination Board.

Chapter 5

RACIAL DIFFERENCES IN
COLLEGE STUDENT
ACHIEVEMENT
Michael T. Nettles, A. Robert Thoeny,
and Erica J. Gosman

For many years now, efforts made to desegregate and integrate higher education institutions in the United States have focused largely on attracting larger numbers of underrepresented or minority-race students to traditionally single-race campuses. While many university officials have simultaneously concerned themselves with the impact of integration on quality of learning and performance, the social and legal interests have been biased toward quantitative changes, such as the numerical increase of black students on traditionally white university campuses and of white students on traditionally black campuses. While quantitative concerns are important and are deserving of social and legal attention — and the attention of educators — the qualitative matters of equality of student performance and the usefulness of a college education must receive equal attention.

This chapter is an empirically based effort to ascertain the effects of desegregation on black and white college student performance. Specifically, the study focuses on determining the differences between black and white college student performance as measured by attrition rates, progression rates, and grade point averages at different types of colleges and universities, when students are in the racial minority or majority on their campus, and the effect of progression rates and grade point averages on students obtaining employment after completing college.

Method and Study Procedures

The study involves 30 universities of 5 different types located in 10 southern and southern border states in the United States. Six universities of

This chapter is based on research supported by The Ford Foundation, The Tennessee Higher Education Commission, and the Southern Education Foundation.

each of the following types participated in the research: (1) traditionally white large public research universities; (2) traditionally black public universities; (3) traditionally white public regional universities; (4) traditionally white private comprehensive universities; and (5) traditionally black private universities.

The study was conducted in four phases; in each phase, a different survey instrument was used to collect data. In the first phase, the Institutional Data Questionnaire (IDQ) was administered to each of the 30 universities to collect cohort attrition and progression rates and cohort average SAT scores, average family income, financial aid sources and amounts, major fields of study, and the size and racial composition of each university's student body and faculty.

In the second phase, the Student Opinion Survey (SOS) was administered to 7,428 students at the 30 participating universities. Randomly selected were 150 white students and 150 black students from each university's combined sophomore, junior, and senior classes. When minority representation on a campus was less than 150 students, the entire population of minority students was surveyed. The SOS obtained data regarding each student's academic, demographic, behavioral, and attitudinal characteristics, as well as students' perceptions of their university and college experiences.

The Faculty Opinion Survey (FOS) was administered to 894 randomly selected faculty members, approximately 30 from each participating university. At each institution, approximately two-thirds of the sample were of the majority racial group. The FOS gathered information regarding faculty members' backgrounds and teaching styles and their opinions about student attrition, progression, and performance. The survey also included questions about faculty attitudes, behaviors, and perceptions of the racial situation on their campus and their level of satisfaction with their university.

Finally, the Employer Opinion Survey (EOS) was administered to 524 employers who regularly recruit and actually employ graduates from the 30 participating universities. These employers were asked to rank the criteria they considered most important in their screening process and to express their opinions about college students' progression rates and grade point averages as hiring criteria when compared with other criteria.

The IDQ was administered to all 30 colleges–universities. The SOS was mailed to 7,428 students, and 4,094 (65%) usable responses were received. The FOS was mailed to 894 faculty members, of whom 706 (79%) responded. The EOS was mailed to 524 employers, producing 354 (67.5%) usable responses.

Summary of Findings

Cohort Attrition: Comparisons by Race and Predominant Race of University

Cohort attrition is the percentage of entering freshmen who drop out of college at any time during the first five years of enrollment. Data for these analyses were obtained from the IDQ.

Overall, black college students have a much higher annual and long-term attrition rate than do white college students. Over a five-year period, 55.7% of black cohorts drop out of college compared to 38.4% of white cohorts. Racial differences in attrition rates vary, however, depending on the predominant race of the university. At traditionally white universities, in general, black students have higher attrition rates over five years than do white students, and at predominantly black universities, white students experience higher attrition rates over five years than do black students. Also, attrition rates at traditionally black universities for black students and white students combined over five years are higher than the attrition rates of black and white students combined at traditionally white universities. An interesting fact is that both black and white students at traditionally black public universities have higher attrition rates than do black students at traditionally white universities.

These data indicate the severe need for colleges and universities to address the high attrition problems of black students at both black and white institutions. The data also indicate the great need for colleges and universities to improve the retention rates of both black and white students when they are in the racial minority group on their campus.

This study did not follow up college dropouts to determine why they dropped out, whether they had plans to reenter their college, or whether they transferred to another university. Such a follow-up would inform us whether attrition rates are attributed to academic problems or dissatisfaction with the college or university attended or to other reasons. In the case of attrition, because there was no follow-up of dropouts, this study is confined to recommending that colleges and universities give closer attention to their students' attrition to determine the reasons why they are dropping out of college and to design programmatic solutions to these attrition problems. What this study does contribute in terms of attrition is an indication of the magnitude of the attrition problem and of the types of students affected at various types of universities.

Cohort Progression Rate: Comparisons by Race
and Predominant Race of University

Cohort progression is the percentage of entering college freshmen who become sophomores after one year of enrollment, juniors after two years, and seniors after three years, and the percentage who graduate after four and five years of enrollment. This is a measure of efficiency of the college experience and is a more qualitative indicator of student performance than are attrition rates. Progression rates indicate not only that students stay in school but also tell whether they progressed from one grade level to the next higher level. Data for these analyses were obtained through the IDQ.

White students, overall, have faster progression rates annually and long term than do black college students. After five years of enrollment, 92% of white students who persist in college graduate, compared to 78% of black students. When the total entering cohort is considered, including dropouts, 56% of white cohorts graduate after five years, compared to 35% of the black cohorts.

As with cohort attrition rates, cohort progression rates vary by predominant race of the university. At traditionally white universities, progression rates of black and white persisters are nearly equal—91.7% of the white persisters graduate after five years, compared to 88.9% of the black persisters. When considering the total entering cohort, however, a higher percentage of white students progresses annually and actually graduates, obviously reflecting the higher attrition rates of black students at white universities. At white universities, 56.5% of the white total entering cohort graduates after five years, compared to 48.6% of the black entering cohort.

At traditionally black public universities, white persisters have a faster progression rate than do black persisters, but, considering the overall entering cohort, a larger percentage of black students progresses annually and actually graduates than is the case with white students at black universities. At black public universities, 77.1% of the white persisters graduate after five years, compared to 72.7% of the black persisters. From the total entering cohort, however, only 14.2% of the white students graduate within five years of being admitted, compared to 28.6% of the black entering cohort. This again reflects the higher attrition rate of white students at black public universities.

Black student persisters at traditionally white universities have faster progression rates than both black and white persisters at traditionally black universities. Recall that 88.9% of black student persisters at white universities graduate within five years of initial enrollment, compared to 72.7% of black persisters at black universities and 77.1% of white persisters at black universities. Additionally, a greater percentage of black entering cohorts at white universities graduates after five years than of black cohorts at black universities and white cohorts at black universities.

These progression-rate data indicate a need for colleges and universities to distinguish between progression rates of total cohorts and persisters, because aggregate cohort progression rates over a period of years may also reflect some attrition rates. However, the data presented on cohort progression rates indicate that, in addition to improving black students' retention rates at white universities, some attention should be given to eliminating the modest difference between black and white persisters' progression rates. Of even greater concern is the need for black public colleges and universities to improve the progression rates of both black and white student persisters. A greater understanding of the progression challenges is provided by the analyses below.

Individual-Level Progression Rates: Comparisons by Race and Type of University

Progression rates are also measured by the average number of credit hours students successfully complete per term of enrollment. These progression-rate data were obtained through the SOS. Additional data were obtained through the SOS and the Faculty Opinion Survey (FOS) to assist in identifying the causal factors for student college progression rates.

Consistent with the performance patterns found in cohort attrition and cohort progression, white students have faster progression rates in terms of actual number of credit hours successfully completed each term. Overall, white students average 15.3 credit hours per term, compared to 14.4 per term for black students. These rates also vary by type of university and by the student's race. For white students, the fastest progression rates in credit hours per term are found at the white large public universities, followed in descending order by white private universities, white regional public universities, and predominantly black public universities. For black students, the fastest progression rates are found at traditionally black private universities, followed in descending order by white large public universities, white regional universities, white private universities, and black public universities.

These progression rates measured by average credit hours support the cohort progression-rate findings. The data indicate a need for overall improvement of black student progression, particularly at white private and black public universities, as well as improvement in white student progression rates at black public colleges and universities.

College Grade Point Average:
Comparisons by Race and Type of University

Individual student cumulative grade point averages were also collected through the Student Opinion Survey. White students were found to have higher grade point averages than black students—a letter grade equivalent to B compared to a letter grade equivalent bordering $B-$ and $C+$. For both black and white students, grade point averages differ significantly at every type of university where comparisons can be made. For white students, the highest grade point averages are earned at white private universities, followed in descending order by black public universities, white regional universities, and white large public universities. For black students, the highest grade-point averages are earned at black private universities, followed in descending order by black public universities, white private universities, white regional public universities, and white large public universities.

A few important and interesting implications can be drawn from the racial and institutional comparisons of student college grade point averages. First, it is important that the highest college grade point average for black students, earned at traditionally black private universities, is lower than the lowest grade point average earned by white students, earned at traditionally white public universities. This is the first indication that race may be a significant factor in student college grade point averages. Second, it is important to note that, unlike with progression rates, black students achieve their highest grade point averages at the two types of black universities. Recall that, although black students progress fastest at black private universities, they progress slowest at black public universities. The rank ordering for college grade point averages by university differs from the rank ordering of progression rates.

Student Antecedent Characteristics and College Attitudinal and
Behavioral Characteristics: Comparisons by Race and Type of University

Even though academic performance may be the most important qualitative measure of the college experience, student personal and academic characteristics and attitudes are also important reflections of quality. Therefore, these factors, too, are important in the racial desegregation or integration of colleges and universities.

Racial and minority–majority status comparisons of four antecedent (precollege) characteristics and seven attitudinal characteristics reveal that, for the overall college population, black and white students are dissimilar. Black and white students do not significantly differ from each other on only one antecedent characteristic — age — and on only one attitudinal characteristic — academic motivation. On the three remaining antecedent characteristics measured in this study, white students had significantly higher SAT scores, higher high school grade point averages, and higher socioeconomic status. These differences in antecedent characteristics exist at all types of universities except black public universities, where white students are significantly older than black students.

The lower SAT scores and high school grade point averages clearly indicate that black students are receiving less adequate preparation for college than are white students. It is an important obligation of public policy-makers and lawmakers to assure that black elementary and high school students receive better preparation at both levels than they currently receive so that they will be better prepared for college.

Antecedent characteristics obviously cannot be changed by university educators and administrators after students are admitted into the university. Nevertheless, they are important racial group differences that universities must recognize in their effort to assure that quality educational experiences are provided to the full range of students admitted. Further, these findings argue for establishing stronger partnerships between universities and high schools where black students are enrolled. University educators should work closely with elementary and secondary educators to assure that black students receive better academic preparation at the elementary and secondary school levels than they currently receive.

On the seven attitudinal factors, black students and white students overall are equally academically motivated but are significantly different on the remaining six factors. White students are significantly more academically integrated and are more committed to their universities than are black students. Black students have greater feelings of racial discrimination, greater social integration, more interfering problems, and greater financial need than do white students. Students are not the sole determinants of their college experience; factors of academic integration, commitment to the university, interfering problems, and feelings of racial discrimination represent student interaction with faculty and with other university components. University faculty and administrators must assume their share of responsibility for these relationships in an effort to enhance the quality of the college experience for black students. Similarly, black students must assume increased responsibility for assuring a better college experience by improving their own interaction with faculty, administrators, and other components of their campuses.

At the three types of white universities, the only difference from the overall findings is that white and black students are equally socially integrated. At white regional universities, black students are less academically motivated than are white students. At black public universities, the differences from the overall findings are that black students have greater commitment to their university than do white students, but white students have greater feelings of racial discrimination. The two races are equally academically integrated and show no differences in terms of interfering problems at black public universities.

In general, these student characteristics indicate that black students and minority students on the various types of campuses are not as satisfied with their college experience as are white students and majority students. As a major part of the desegregation process, universities would benefit from efforts to facilitate greater academic integration and commitment for black students and to reduce the racial discrimination felt by black and white students when they are in the minority group on campus. Also, the greater interfering problems and financial needs of black students require the continued attention of both educators and policymakers.

Faculty Attitudinal–Behavioral Characteristics: Comparisons by Race and Type of University

Because students are not the sole determinants of their college performance, faculty attitudes and behaviors are also a major subject of analysis. Faculty attitudes and behaviors are primarily used in this study to determine their effects on student performance. Although total faculty attitudes–behaviors at the different universities are the important measures, comparisons between black and white faculty are made to assure that they are not significantly different and therefore do not differently affect student performance and because such comparisons are central issues in the desegregation process. Specifically, two arguments are often advanced. First, black students need a sufficient number of black faculty on campus to (1) serve as role models; and (2) allow black students to have strong relationships with campus faculty. Second, black faculty are able to establish relationships with black students that serve to improve the black students' college performance.

There are overall differences between black and white faculty and between majority and minority faculty when all five types of universities are combined, but black faculty and white faculty on each type of campus are very much alike when compared to each other. For all five university types combined, black faculty have more contact with students outside the classroom, are more likely to have nontraditional teaching styles, and show greater concern for student development than do white faculty. There is no difference in their feelings of discrimination or their satisfaction with their university. In contrast, at each of the three types of white institutions, black faculty are significantly more likely to exhibit nontraditional teaching styles and to have significantly greater feelings of racial discrimination than are white faculty, but otherwise their attitudes are not significantly different. At black universities, white faculty have greater feelings of racial discrimination than do black faculty members, but otherwise they are not different, except that black faculty have greater contact with students at black private universities than do white faculty members.

In general, at all five types of universities, black faculty and white faculty are more alike in attitudes and behaviors than they are different. Minority-race faculty feel more racial discrimination, regardless of whether it is on a black or a white campus. Black faculty on white campuses generally have more nontraditional teaching styles. Since neither faculty feelings of discrimination nor teaching styles are consistent and stable predictors of student performance, however, one should not expect an increase in minority faculty to lead to increased academic performance of minority students.

The need for more black faculty is evident throughout higher education and is central to the desegregation process, even though it does not appear to affect student performance. The purpose of role modeling and the importance of racially diverse faculties may be justified on other grounds, such as the improvement of minority student attitudes and behaviors and satisfaction with their university.

Causal Factors of Students' College Progression Rates

Nineteen academic, attitudinal, and behavioral characteristics are significant predictors of student college progression rates. The characteristics of students with faster progression rates are, in order of decreasing importance, (1) to be enrolled at a large university; (2) to be in a younger college-age group; (3) to have faculty with a high degree of concern for student development; (4) to attend college a long distance from home; (5) to have low commitment to their university; (6) to have high high school grade point averages; (7) to have relatively low satisfaction for their university; (8) to have low financial need; (9) to be highly socially integrated; (10) to have a high SAT score; (11) to be highly academically motivated; (12) to work relatively few hours on a job while in college; (13) to have faculty with low satisfaction with their university; (14) to live in on-campus housing; (15) to have degree aspirations beyond a bachelor's degree; (16) to have few interfering problems; (17) to attend a college with a racial composition similar to that of their high school; (18) to have a faculty with little contact with students outside the classroom; and (19) to be married.

While many of the variables that are significantly related to progression rates are academically oriented, some are not. For example, faculty concern for student development, student high school grades, faculty satisfaction with their university, faculty contact with students, student commitment to the university, student SAT scores and academic motivation, and living in on-campus residence halls are all educational factors that understandably relate to student performance. Conversely, size of university, student age, distance a student attends college away from home, financial need, job hours, and marital status do not appear on the surface to have any educational significance, yet they significantly influence student college progression rates.

This suggests further that, while progression rate is a performance indicator, it may not be as strong a performance indicator as other measures of outcomes. Progression rates serve best, perhaps, as a measure of efficiency of the college experience and are important to state legislators. Legislators are often faced with the basic issue of how long they should supplement a college student's education with state tax funds. Normal progress is also a requirement by the federal government in approving renewal of financial aid awards. These governmental requirements make progression rates an important issue for minority students.

Causal Factors of Student College Grade Point Averages

The significant predictors of overall college grade point averages include 21 student, faculty, and institutional characteristics. In decreasing order of importance for students with relatively high grade point averages are (1) high academic motivation; (2) high grade point average in high school; (3) high academic integration; (4) high SAT scores; (5) a low level of satisfaction with the university; (6) high faculty–student contact outside of class; (7) few interfering problems; (8) high feelings of racial discrimination; (9) faculty with nontraditional teaching styles; (10) being in the racial majority; (11) being white students; (12) low social integration; (13) living in on-campus housing while in college; (14) higher degree aspirations; (15) low financial need; (16) attending a smaller university; (17) attended a private high school; (18) being male; (19) attending college a long distance from home; (20) having taken courses at another university; and (21) being married.

In contrast to progression rates, the strongest predictors of college grade point average represent student cognitive abilities. Nonacademic variables related to student college grade point averages are fewer than those related to progression rates. This is further evidence that college grade point averages and progression rates are two different types of performance measures that require different characteristics, attitudes, and behaviors. The predictors of high college grade point averages that are not predictors of fast progression rates are low social integration, high faculty–student contact, and attendance at a small university. Characteristics that predict fast progression rates but exert no influence on college grade point averages are young age, low number of hours working a job, attending a high school and college with similar racial compositions, high faculty dissatisfaction with the university, and high faculty concern for student development. Thus, institutions that attempt to address their students' slower progression rates should adopt different strategies than they used for addressing the problem of lower college grade point averages.

It is particularly important that race is found to be a significant predictor of student college grade point averages. The fact that race is a significant predictor of grade point averages indicates that, unlike with progression rates, universities should target special efforts toward producing higher grade point averages among black students. Efforts made by universities aimed at students with relatively low academic integration, low high school grade point averages, low SAT scores, many interfering problems, and high financial need will not pertain to all black students, but they are likely to raise the grade point averages of many who were discovered in this study to possess these characteristics.

Several significant predictors at the overall level are also significant predictors at each of the five types of universities included in the study. Specifically, students with high grade point averages at all five types of universities have relatively high academic motivation, high high school grade point averages, high academic integration, and low commitment to their universities. Low financial need and high SAT scores are significant predictors of high college grade point averages at all types of universities except the traditionally black public universities. Additionally, race is significant at the three traditionally white universities, with white students predicted to have a higher grade point average than black students, but race is not a predictor of grade point average at black public and black private universities. Recall, too, that at those two types of universities, black students have higher grade point averages than do black students at traditionally white institutions. The remaining variables are significant at some types of universities, but not at others, with no explainable patterns.

The two college student performance measures of progression rate and college grade point average have 10 significant predictors in common, although they exhibit varying degrees of strength. Student characteristics that contribute to both fast progression rates and high grade point averages are high SAT scores, high high school grade point averages, living in on-campus housing, being married, attending college a great distance from their permanent homes, degree aspirations beyond a baccalaureate, low financial need, low commitment to their universities, high academic motivation, and few interfering problems.

The two performance measures also have some unique predictors. Student characteristics that produce high college grade point averages but do not produce rapid progression are being white, being female, having attended a private rather than a public high school, being in the racial majority on campus, being a transfer student, having high academic integration, having high feelings that the institution is racially discriminatory, having high contact with faculty outside the classroom, and having faculty with a nontraditional teaching style. Three of the four variables that predict faster progression rates but not college grade point average are working a low number of hours on a job while in college, attending a college with a similar racial composition as one's high school, and having a faculty with a high concern for student development. The fourth variable—social integration—is positively related to progression rate but negatively related to grade point average. High social integration is related to rapid progression but to lower grade point averages. These differences in the predictors for progression rate and grade point average indicate that these are two distinctly different measures of student performance.

Some predictors of both progression rates and college grade point averages are conditions that institutions are not inclined to change even though they appear significantly to affect student performance negatively. In the case of progression rates, these are high faculty contact with students outside the classroom and high student commitment to the institution. In the case of grade point average, the predictors are high student commitment to the institution, high faculty satisfaction, and high faculty contact with students outside the classroom.

Conversely, there are conditions that indicate something negative about an institution that positively affect student performance. Faculty dissatisfaction, high feelings of racial discrimination, and low social integration are significant predictors of high student grade point averages; low student commitment to the university, faculty dissatisfaction, and low faculty contact outside the classroom are significant predictors of faster progression rates. While the interpretation of each variable may serve to justify or explain its relationship to high performance, these are not characteristics that universities should promote. As has been noted in this analysis and elsewhere, there is more to value in the college experience than academic performance, however measured.

It is important to call special attention to factors that are discovered to be nonsignificant predictors when these discoveries are contrary to initial speculation. The most noteworthy of such factors in this study is that socioeconomic status is not among the significant predictors of student college performance—either in terms of progression rates or grade point averages. In this study, as is typical, socioeconomic status consists of three elements: (1) parents' occupation; (2) parents' educational attainment; and (3) parents' income. The fact that socioeconomic status is not significant implies that, while student performance in college may somewhat depend on the by-products of the parents' socioeconomic status (e.g., high school preparation and low financial need), students from families with low socioeconomic status are not in an academically disadvantageous position in college provided they receive adequate precollege educational preparation and their in-college financial and other needs are met.

Consequence of Progression and Performance to Employment

The consequence of progression and performance was measured by requesting employers to indicate the relative importance of the two performance measures among other criteria they use in their decisions to hire college graduates. This information was obtained through the Employer Opinion Survey.

Employer rankings of the seven most important criteria used in deciding to employ college students are, in order of most important to least important, (1) major field of study; (2) prior work experience; (3) college grade point average; (4) type of college attended; (5) relevance of specific college courses taken; (6) personal characteristics; and (7) progression rate. While grade point average is among the top criteria, progression rate is the least important, relatively. Nonetheless, progression rate is not thought to be totally unimportant by employers. Responding to an open-ended question on the survey, employers agreed that progression rate is viewed as an indicator of a student's expected performance on the job. The high ranking of college grade point average further indicates that colleges and universities need to give greater attention to increasing the grade performance of black students. If this is not done, black students will continue to be in a relatively disadvantageous position in the labor market.

Conclusions

The fact that black college students overall have lower performance levels than white students signals a need for new efforts at addressing the qualitative aspects of college and university desegregation and integration. Universities need to take specific, long-term measures to assist black students to improve their retention rates, progression rates, and college grade point averages. This study suggests that university officials should not confine themselves to one approach in addressing this observed difference in the performance of their white and black students; rather, they should employ several approaches, ranging from addressing differences in student precollegiate performance and personal characteristics up to differences in student attitudes about college and student behaviors in college, as well as faculty attitudes, teaching styles, and teacher behavior toward students. Universities must also focus their attention on different factors in attempting to resolve the differences in college attrition when comparing college progression rates with college grade point averages. Finally, because racial differences in attrition, progression, and college grade point averages and the student characteristics related to each vary by type of university, different universities must attempt different strategies to address their own unique problems.

These factors of attrition, progression, and college grade point average have important implications for the qualitative improvement of racial integration in universities. With the anticipated stabilization of enrollment patterns during the 1980s, dramatic improvement in the qualitative aspects of integration–desegregation is not likely to be achieved through admission and recruitment efforts that have proven successful over the past decade. Universities must shift a part of their attention in the short and long term to producing equality in the qualitative aspects of the college experience.

Chapter 6

INSTITUTIONAL EFFECTIVENESS
IN THE PRODUCTION OF
BLACK BACCALAUREATES
Philip S. Hart

Historically, black colleges and universities have played a critical role
in the undergraduate education of black Americans. The majority of these
institutions, founded after the Civil War, were for nearly a century the only
choice of black students interested in a college education. The civil rights
movement of the 1960s and the subsequent federal legislation served to
open the doors of traditionally white instititions (TWIs) to blacks — in many
cases for the first time — and many of them were recruited eagerly.

Access to TWIs opened up for black students in the late 1960s. At the
same time, traditionally black institutions (TBIs) also experienced surges in
enrollment that began in 1969 and lasted for nearly a decade. Taken
together, this surge of interest in black undergraduates created widening
opportunities and access for this group to earn a baccalaureate degree.

But now, officials of many private black colleges say that enrollments
are slipping, and there is serious concern about the future. To an extent,
this enrollment slippage is a problem for public black colleges also. Black
undergraduate enrollment at TWIs has also peaked and fallen off.
However, even though the number of black students attending colleges has
more than tripled in the last 20 years, to about 1.3 million, the percentage at
black colleges has declined from 82% in 1965 to around 28% in 1981.

There is evidence (Astin 1975, 1977, 1982; Brazziel & Brazziel 1980;
Claffey 1981; Hart 1984) that TBIs have been more effective than their white
counterparts in moving black students through to the bachelor's degree.
This ambition and determination to succeed among black students is evident at the undergraduate level — nearly two-thirds of the men and more
than two-thirds of the women who entered black colleges in 1972 planned to

This chapter is based on a previously published research monograph by Philip S. Hart: *Institutional Effectiveness in the Production of Black Baccalaureates.* Atlanta: Southern Education
Foundation, 1984.

continue beyond the bachelor's degree. In all colleges, somewhat over half the men and only 43% of the women planned graduate work.

The overall trends suggest a difficult time for all undergraduate institutions, however, and TBIs will be particularly affected. Today's black undergraduate student faces a situation that includes declining enrollments, a reduction in financial aid programs, a reduction in student support services, a decrease in faculty size, a decrease in library volumes, and a concern about educational quality.

This chapter summarizes a study of factors identified as most important to institutional effectiveness in the production of black baccalaureates. An "effectiveness quotient" has been developed by the author as an overall measure of institutional effectiveness. This effectiveness quotient, or EQ, is a function of total black enrollment and total earned degrees by black undergraduates in all institutions or by individual institutions. The EQ serves as a dependent variable in examining a set of independent variables. Comparisons are made by institution type (public, private, TBI, TWI), institution size, and other variables in an effort to identify, describe, and measure those salient factors that serve to enhance institutional effectiveness in producing black baccalaureates.

Measures of input–output are also used in the analysis model, thus suggesting a concern for institutional efficiency. Researchers interested in studying organizations and institutions are usually concerned with measures of effectiveness and efficiency (Hart 1974; Parsons 1956; Sower 1976; Sower & Miller 1964). For our purpose, effectiveness refers to an institution's ability to produce black baccalaureates in an efficient manner, where efficiency reflects using the most effective means to secure a given goal.

Retrenchment, due to the loss of resources, is hitting colleges and universities hard and is having detrimental effects on the values, structure, and norms in these institutions. Institutional systems that input resources into colleges and universities are reducing their support. Those of us still in the academy were forewarned in the 1970s to be prepared for institutional contraction (*Daedalus* 1974, 1975; Sower 1976).

Research Review

The research problem of concern in this study is measuring institutional effectiveness in undergraduate colleges and universities. In addition, the most salient factors contributing to institutional effectiveness in producing black baccalaureates are identified and described. A further concern is how these salient factors can be translated into policies and practices for undergraduate institutions that have not traditionally served black students.

The research method consists of a three-stage design. Stage 1 encompasses an analysis of undergraduate enrollment and earned degree data for all four-year colleges and universities for the academic years 1972–1973, 1974–1975, 1976–1977, 1978–1979, and 1980–1981. A national norm of effectiveness (EQ) is derived for each year, by race. In Stage 2, a 4% sample of TWIs and a 17% sample of TBIs is drawn, yielding an institutional sample of 84 TWIs and 18 TBIs. A spread sheet was then created for each available study year, with figures for each institution in the sample.

From the spread sheets for each available study year, a top 10 was determined for all institutions with the highest EQ scores. Next, a top five for TBIs was determined using the same method. Then, the number and percentage of TWIs and TBIs above and below the national norm EQ were determined. Comparisons were then made between the institutional sample in Stage 2 and the universe of undergraduate institutions in Stage 1.

Next, a research review was conducted that identified 31 studies that examine persistence among black undergraduates and/or institutional effectiveness among undergraduate colleges and universities. Meta-analysis, or research synthesis (Glass 1976, 1977; Hedges & Olkin 1983; Hunter, Schmidt, & Jackson 1982; Light 1982; Light & Pillemer 1984), is the technique used to evaluate the quantitative findings of these studies in order to identify the most salient factors in persistence to the degree.

Using factor-analysis techniques, correlations, multiple regression analysis, and meta-analysis, the strongest factors in persistence are identified. These factors serve as the cause, or independent variable. Institutions in the Stage 2 sample are organized according to the EQ score, and percentiles are created that serve to group high-, medium-, and low-index institutions. The persistence factors are grouped into three categories: institutional factors, individual factors, or contextual factors.

This phase of the research concludes with the testing of 10 null hypotheses that relate to institutional effectiveness and persistence.

Findings

As seen in Table 6.1, there has been a trend of declining institutional effectiveness in relation to blacks, whites, and Asians over the 1972–1973 to

1980-1981 period. The data in Table 6.1 also reveal a decline in the ability of black, white, and Asian undergraduates to persist in obtaining a baccalaureate degree.

TABLE 6.1.

Effectiveness Quotient (EQ) scores for B.A. and B.S. degrees by selected race, selected years, and total—all institutions combined

Year	Black	White	Asian	Total
1972–1973	.10	.11	.12	.13
1974–1975	.08	.13	.12	.12
1976–1977	.07	.12	.09	.11
1978–1979	.10	.13	.11	.13
1980–1981	.07	.11	.09	.08

Source: U. S. Department of Education, Office for Civil Rights. *Racial, Ethnic and Sex Enrollment Data from Institutions of Higher Education,* Fall 1972, 1974, 1976, 1978, 1980. U. S. Department of Education, Office for Civil Rights. *Bachelor's Degrees Conferred by Institutions of Higher Education by Race, Ethnicity, and Sex: Institution, State and Nation, 1976–1977, 1978–1979, 1980–1981.*

The aggregate data also suggest that black students were less likely to persist to baccalaureate completion than either white or Asian students. The overall declining trend signals a problem in retention for all three racial groups. Examining enrollment and earned degree figures for black students in engineering developed by Blackwell (1982) and reanalyzed by Hart (1984) indicates a decline in EQ scores for engineering and all other fields. This trend suggests something akin to a revolving-door policy by colleges and universities in relation to black students.

In this regard, Astin's (1982) educational pipeline suggests that whites are 1.2 times more likely to graduate from high school than are blacks, are 1.3 times more likely to enter college than are blacks, yet are 1.9 times more likely to complete college than are blacks. This disparity in persistence suggests the importance of structural factors in inhibiting the access and progression of black undergraduates.

Among these structural factors are the fact that the median black family income has remained approximately 60% of the median white family income and that the unemployment rate among blacks remains about twice as high as the white unemployment rate. During a period of institutional retrenchment in higher education, both these structural factors conspire to put financial pressures on the average black undergraduate such as to make it close to twice as likely that white undergraduates will complete college.

In 1972–1973, 69% of TBIs were above the national norm for institutional effectiveness, while 53% of TWIs were above the national norm. In 1980–1981, fully 100% of TBIs were above the national norm, compared to 84% of the TWIs. Over the decade of study, TBIs consistently outperformed TWIs in graduating black students.

The top 10 institutions for the 1972–1973 to 1980–1981 period consist of 7 private colleges, 2 Massachusetts institutions, 2 in Connecticut, and 1 in New Hampshire. There is one TBI in the aggregate top 10. Private, prestigious, and selective institutions dominate the rankings.

In regard to the top five TBIs for the 1972–1973 to 1980–1981 period, Fisk and South Carolina State are the most consistent in that four of five academic years they were in the top five. However, Southern University had the highest mean rank and the most appearances in the overall top five ranking.

As rankings for each study year and the aggregate indicate, the 90th percentile is dominated by TWIs that are private, prestigious, and selective. The TBIs are clustered in the 75th to 90th percentile, while the bulk of TWIs are below the 75th percentile.

The most powerful institutional predictors of institutional effectiveness for all years combined are attending a four-year college, followed by attending a TBI, access of black students to the institution, whether the student was supported by scholarships or grants, and the percentage of black faculty. The most powerful individual predictors are involvement in campus life, good high school grades, parental aid for those attending TWIs, living in a dormitory, and high socioeconomic status. The most powerful contextual factors for all years combined are attending college in the Northeast and litigation status. These findings suggest that baccalaureate completion is more probable by attending a college in the Northeast or a TBI in an *Adams* state.

For all institutions that are most effective over the 1972–1973 to 1980–1981 period, half are in the Northeast, 7 out of 10 are private, the majority charge above-average tuition and fees, all are residential rather than commuter institutions, 4 are in *Adams* states, only 2 are weak in terms of access, the majority have student populations of more than 500 and less than 10,000, and most are prestigious and selective, with generous per-student expenditures.

Among the top five TBIs over the study period, as expected, all are in *Adams* states, three are private, two are considered prestigious and selective, all have student populations above 500 but less than 10,000, all have equal access for black students, and each has a majority of black faculty.

The type of student most likely to persist to the degree is a female who is receiving parental aid (particularly those attending a TWI), who is of high socioeconomic status, who has good high school grades, who does well on aptitude tests, who possesses good study habits, who lives in a dormitory (especially during the first year), and who maintains a high level of involvement with campus life. The ongoing value of the TBIs is their ability to admit, retain, and graduate students who do not necessarily meet the ideal criteria.

Among the null hypotheses tested, the author determined that TBIs are more effective than TWIs, private institutions are more effective than public ones, private TBIs are more effective than public TBIs, a larger percentage of black faculty implies a higher EQ score, more effective institutions are more likely to have special admissions and retention programs, more effective institutions are more likely to have a higher quality of financial aid, SAT scores do not relate to effectiveness, there is no relation between the student–faculty ratio and effectiveness, and higher per-student expenditures imply higher institutional effectiveness.

Solutions

Potential solutions for improving institutional effectiveness in producing black baccalaureates need to address questions of access, retention, and graduation. During the halcyon period of black undergraduate enrollment, colleges and universities were rewarded for their efforts in enrolling black students. There was limited incentive built in for colleges and universities to retain and graduate black students. Thus, a revolving-door policy seems to have become the norm, particularly for TWIs.

As seen earlier, black undergraduates are below the national norm in terms of institutional effectiveness in graduating them. One possible solution may be to develop a reward system for institutions based on their ability to graduate black students. If a college or university exceeds the national norm in any academic year, then some form of financial incentive should be forthcoming from the state or federal level.

It is also important to encourage black students to do well in high school and to continue to try and improve the quality of elementary and secondary education. Further, in that nearly two of five black under-graduates begin their college careers in community colleges, it is crucial to improve the articulation between two-year colleges and four-year colleges and universities.

Structural factors, such as the relatively higher rates of black unemployment and lower median family incomes, also demand solutions. The chronic black youth unemployment problem makes it difficult for college-bound black youngsters to work and save for their education, as do many of their white counterparts.

The inability of the broader society and of the black community effectively to reduce the impact of these structural factors poses a long-term problem. Possible solutions include job-creation strategies, the willingness of employers to hire and promote black workers, the growth and expansion of black businesses, an end to wage discrimination, and employer willingness to hire black youth. Access to higher education will continue to be problematic if solutions to these structural factors are not found.

TWIs need to examine TBIs more closely in terms of what makes the latter more effective in producing black baccalaureates. Perhaps a consortium of TWIs could be organized to operate as a study group to examine TBIs, with the goal of determining what TBIs are doing that better enables them to retain and graduate black students. This consortium could then recommend steps that TWIs could take to improve their ability to admit, retain, and graduate black students.

Other ways in which administrators and practitioners can move to solve the problems attendant to producing black baccalaureates include improving the access of black students to a college education. It is also important to try and finance a black student's college education with scholarships and grants, not loans. Loans sharply inhibit the production of black baccalaureates. For TWIs, it is particularly important to recruit, hire, and promote black faculty aggressively. The value of black faculty role models is well established in the TBIs.

Black students on TBI and TWI campuses should be encouraged to become actively involved in the life of the campus community. High involvement usually means a greater likelihood of persistence to the degree. Oftentimes, on TWI campuses, black students become socially isolated from the broader campus society. TWIs, as well as black and white students, must meet the challenge of opening up involvement in campus life.

The production of black baccalaureates seems to be facilitated when colleges and universities have special admission and retention programs. A high-quality financial aid program and high per-student expenditures also go a long way in promoting the production of black baccalaureates.

Unfortunately, there is a growing sentiment in U.S. society and on many of our campuses that blacks in general and black undergraduates specifically do not warrant special attention. This sentiment, in combination with a scarcity of resources on many of the nation's campuses, makes the search for solutions to the production of black baccalaureates a particularly problematic one.

However, there are instances where problems have been addressed without large expenditures. On the campus where I teach, the university chancellor has arranged for James E. Blackwell and me to meet with key staff in admissions, financial aid, and support services in order to explore ways to improve the university's ability to produce black baccalaureates. At the University of Colorado–Boulder, upon the urging of a black member of the Board of Regents, a comprehensive study and program for action has been developed. It is aimed at improving the University's ability to admit, retain, and graduate black and minority students.

In both these instances, a special sensitivity to the plight of black students on white campuses is exhibited by key black faculty and board members. Earlier, the critical role of black faculty in both TBIs and TWIs was touched upon. It is equally important to have active black members of boards of trustees, particularly on TWIs. In addition, a critical mass of black administrators is crucial.

The search for solutions to the problem of increasing the production of black baccalaureates needs to be couched within a nonexpansionist agenda for U.S. higher education. The solutions will need to be creative and reasonable in their costs. TBIs have been successful in producing black baccalaureates for over a century within an environment that expects them to be creative and cost-efficient. It is not too much to ask that TWIs accomplish the same objective within similar constraints.

Policy Initiative

From a policy viewpoint, institutional effectiveness can be enhanced through actions that increase the access of black students to higher education, supported adequately by scholarships and grants, in institutions with a reasonable percentage of black faculty and adequate per-student expenditures. Knowledge, commitments, decision-making strategies, and the power of those interested in increasing institutional effectiveness could well continue to focus the policy discussion around these particular institutional factors. It will remain a difficult debate as long as Reagan administration policy has the effect of controlling malleable factors (Blackwell & Hart 1982).

At the level of boards of trustees, particularly at TWIs, policies should be adopted that encourage the institution to enroll black undergraduates at a level equal to the proportion of blacks in the state. TWIs should also initiate a policy that targets scholarship aid to black and minority students in a proportion beyond their numbers. TWIs should also formulate a policy for hiring black faculty according to the proportion of blacks in the state.

At the state level, legislation is needed that provides incentives for public institutions to recruit black students, faculty, and staff aggressively. Progress in meeting specified recruitment and hiring goals should be tied to funding levels. It also seems appropriate to create a pool of scholarship funds that can be made available to those institutions that meet their recruitment and hiring goals. Policy initiatives are also needed at this level that can assist TBIs in upgrading their programs and facilities. In order to be effective, blacks will need to form coalitions with other minorities and sympathetic whites. A key is to be able to indicate that improving the ability of colleges and universities to produce black baccalaureates will benefit all undergraduates.

At the federal level, the sizable deficit poses a particular problem for higher education. The Reagan administration's budget-cutting proposals aim to reduce the student-aid entitlement program. Government aid to college students provides grants and low-interest tuition loans. The budget for fiscal year 1986 would restrict outright stipends to students from families earning $30,000 or less. This proposal would profoundly affect the ability of black undergraduates to earn college degrees.

In addition, it would be more difficult for students to claim that they are independent of their families, as increasing numbers have done to qualify for nonrepayable grants. The total estimated saving over three years is $2.1 billion, but with significant negative effect on the college completion chances of black students.

The National Education Association (NEA) figures that the likely targets of budget cuts would restrict student-aid eligibility, consolidate grant programs, reduce the size of loans and awards, and raise loan fees.

However, the NEA feels that pro-education forces appear strong enough to deflect most of these cutback efforts.

Most federal higher education programs were up for renewal by Congress in 1985. For example, the Higher Education Act expired September 30, 1985. According to the NEA, that act will have wide support in Congress. Another key issue is the direction William Bennett charts for higher education as the Secretary for the U.S. Department of Education.

The issues at the federal level suggest a policy agenda that is organized around deflecting the impact of higher education cutbacks and lobbying support for the various higher education programs that will be up for renewal. For example, black educators should consider organizing a lobby based in Washington, D.C. Also, the organization of a political action committee (PAC) should be considered. It is highly doubtful that any costly higher education initiative will find widespread congressional support. However, a well-organized lobby and well-funded PAC could help consolidate support around blacks and higher education.

TBIs remain important in terms of providing access to higher education in an effective manner to tens of thousands of black students. Aside from private four-year colleges located in the Northeast, TBIs remain, as a group, the most effective institutional type in producing black baccalaureates. Compared to the private four-year northeastern colleges, however, the TBIs graduate a significantly larger number of black students per year.

The task of improving access to and the performance level of higher education will continue to be a difficult agenda item. This chapter is an attempt to identify, describe, and measure the most salient and malleable factors in persistence among black students and to prescribe broad approaches for improving institutional effectiveness.

References

Astin, A.W.
   1975 *Preventing Students from Dropping Out.* San Francisco: Jossey-Bass.
Astin, A.W.
   1977 *Four Critical Years.* San Francisco: Jossey-Bass.
Astin, A.W.
   1982 *Minorities in American Higher Education.* San Francisco: Jossey-Bass.

Blackwell, J.E.
  1982 Demographics of desegregation. In R. Wilson (Ed.), *Race and Equity in Higher Education,* pp. 28–70. Washington, D.C.: American Council on Education.
Blackwell, J. E., & Hart, P.S.
  1982 *Cities, Suburbs and Blacks.* Bayside, N.Y.: General Hall.
Brazziel, W., & Brazziel, M.
  1980 *Recent College and University Enrollment Patterns of Black Students in States Affected by Adams–Califano Litigation.* Atlanta: Southern Education Foundation.
Claffey, C.E.
  1981 Black private colleges an "endangered species." *Boston Globe,* November 27, pp. 1–17.
Daedalus.
     American higher education: Toward an uncertain future. Vol. 1, Fall 1974; Vol. 2, Winter 1975.
Glass, C.V.
  1976 Primary, secondary and meta-analysis of research. *Educational Researcher, 5,* 3–8.
Glass, C.V.
  1977 Integrated findings: The meta-analysis of research. *Review of Research in Education, 5,* 351–379.
Hart, P.S.
  1974 *Problems in Organizational Renewal.* Ph.D. dissertation, Michigan State University.
Hart, P.S.
  1984 *Institutional Effectiveness in the Production of Black Baccalaureates.* Atlanta: Southern Education Foundation.
Hedges, L.V., & Olkin, I.
  1983 Regression models in research synthesis. *American Statistician, 37,* 137–140.
Hunter, J.E., Schmidt, F.L., & Jackson, G.B.
  1982 *Meta-analysis: Cumulating Research Findings across Studies.* Beverly Hills: Sage.
Light, R.J.
  1982 *Synthesizing outcomes from several research studies — supplementary material.* Paper presented to the Boston Chapter of the American Statistical Association.
Light, R.J., & Pillemer, D.B.
  1984 *Summing up: The Science of Reviewing Research.* Cambridge, Mass.: Harvard University Press.
Parsons, T.
  1956 Suggestions for a sociological approach to the theory of organizations. *Administrative Science Quarterly, i,* 63–65, 225–239.

Sower, C.A.
  1976 An experimental sociology of institutional renewal. *Rural Sociology, 41,* 7–24.
Sower, C., & Miller, D.A.
  1964 The changing power structure in agriculture: An analysis of negative versus positive organization power. Reprint from James H. Copp (Ed.), *Our Changing Rural Society: Perspectives and Trends.* Ames: Iowa University Press, 127–158.
U.S. Department of Education, Office for Civil Rights
      Racial, Ethnic and Sex Enrollment Data from Institutions of Higher Education, Fall 1972, 1974, 1976, 1978, 1980. Washington, D.C.: GPO.
U.S. Department of Education, Office for Civil Rights
      Bachelor's Degrees Conferred by Institutions of Higher Education by Race, Ethnicity, and Sex: Institution, State and Nation, 1976–1977, 1978–1979, 1980–1981. Washington, D.C.: GPO.

Chapter 7   ENDING THE WHITE MONOPOLY ON GRADUATE AND PROFESSIONAL EDUCATION

James E. Blackwell

For approximately three decades between the mid-1930s and the mid-1960s, the National Association for the Advancement of Colored People (NAACP) and the Legal Defense and Educational Fund (LDF) waged a relentless legal struggle against racial discrimination in higher education. The legal assault against discrimination and segregation in publicly supported institutions was initially directed against those graduate and professional schools in southern and border states that barred blacks from admission. The success achieved by these organizations in persuading the U.S. Supreme Court to declare unconstitutional state-imposed barriers, such as make-shift or newly constructed separate professional schools or the use of mandatory out-of-state tuition grants as a substitute for admission to the graduate or professional school in the applicant's state of residence, paved the way for a few blacks to matriculate at, and graduate from, the traditionally white institutions (TWIs) that previously excluded them. Only token numbers of blacks were affected, however.

This situation began to change in the 1960s, and in most significant ways, as increasing numbers of blacks enrolled in graduate and professional schools all across the country. This change was facilitated by the civil rights movement and by a process of consciousness raising among a broad array of Americans about the degree to which discriminatory, segregative policies and practices, and a nationwide monopoly on higher education, had prevented a significant portion of Americans from participating in the educational opportunity structure. Not only was the legal mandate to desegregate institutions recognized, but a moral commitment was made by individuals and groups at federal and local levels and in the public and

This chapter summarizes some of the more important findings reported in James E. Blackwell, *Mainstreaming Outsiders: The Production of Black Professionals.* Bayside, N.Y.: General Hall, 1981.

private sectors to accelerate the desegregation process. By the end of the 1960s, however, it remained apparent that many southern states continued to operate essentially dual, segregated systems of higher education, despite their unconstitutionality. Efforts to dismantle such systems achieved a new momentum in the *Adams* case. In 1978, this writer began a major analysis of recruitment, enrollment, and graduation trends of black students in graduate and professional schools.

Objectives of the Study

The central objectives of this study were to (1) make some determination of how successful institutions were in their recruitment, enrollment, and graduation of black graduate–professional school students during the 1970s; (2) ascertain what factors best predict success in the enrollment and graduation of black graduate–professional school students; (3) demonstrate the degree to which quantitative and qualitative criteria are used as the bases for admission decisions across racial lines; (4) assess the degree to which black enrollment and graduation trends from graduate–professional schools are influenced by *Adams* case litigation status; (5) ascertain whether or not black student chances of achieving greater equality of access and of graduating are related to institutional control (i.e., public or private); and (6) make at least a preliminary assessment of the *Bakke* case's impact on existing affirmative efforts to include more blacks in graduate–professional schools and on their subsequent graduation from these institutions.

Method

Universe of Study

The specific focus of attention was the professions of medicine, law, dentistry, optometry, veterinary medicine, engineering, pharmacy, and social work and black enrollment in and graduation from doctoral degree programs. Because of the constraints of manageability and feasibility and of the probability of institutional cooperation, the original goal of including as "cases" the 1,162 professional schools identified with these fields of study was modified. This decision led to a two-pronged approach for data collection and analyses. One approach consisted of survey research techniques. The second approach used content analysis of data filed by all professional schools in these fields with their professional associations.

Ultimately, this approach also led to the development of 743 institutional cases and a trend analysis based on information about all professional institutions.

Data Collection

Two sets of data were obtained. The first set was obtained from responses to a mailed institutional inventory, supplemented with information provided by professional associations. This inventory or survey resulted in 743 cases that could be scrutinized carefully through a variety of statistical procedures and analyses. The second data set consisted of the results of interviews with administrators and of an analysis of institutional data, such as annual surveys, collected by the various professional associations from professional schools and graduate institutions. This source provided information about graduates of the more than 2,000 U.S. graduate and professional schools.

The institutional inventory was divided into 22 parts, with a total of 62 items. It was designed to obtain specific institutional data about race, institutional control, type of professional school, and *Adams* litigation status with respect to black student recruitment, applications, enrollment and graduation; number of black faculty on the staff, full- or part-time; and special admission, recruitment, and minority-retention programs for every year between 1970 and 1979. Open-ended questions addressed special problems experienced by institutions with respect to enrolling and retaining black students, academic support programs, and the roles performed by minority affairs officers, student organizations, and other informal associations in the recruitment, enrollment, and retention through graduation of black students.

Data obtained through interviews also focused on problem areas. The content analysis of institutional data reported to associations helped to construct 10-year trends by profession in the enrollment and graduation of black professional school students.

Data Analysis

The study's research component identified three dependent variables: (1) first- year enrollment; (2) total enrollment; and (3) graduation from professional school. The 12 predictor variables were (1) presence and number of black faculty in the professional school; (2) presence of a special recruitment program; (3) presence of a special admission program; (4) presence of a retention program; (5) presence of a minority affairs officer; (6) *Adams* case litigation status; (7) location of the institution; (8) type of institutional control; (9) quality of financial aid program; (10) quality of scholarship program; (11) presence or absence of a black college in the state; and (12) number of professional schools in the state.

In this analysis, the Statistical Package for the Social Sciences was utilized. Simple coefficients of correlation were obtained, and multiple regression techniques were employed to ascertain the effects, if any, of the predictor variables on the dependent variable. A stepwise regression technique was used to identify the most powerful predictors of each of the three dependent variables at three points during the 10-year period studied.

Trends were constructed in tables and graphs that depicted the absolute numbers and percentages of black students enrolled and their total enrollment and graduation for each year of the 10-year period from 1970 to 1979. These trends were determined for each of eight professions studied and by the annual production of doctoral degrees by race and subject areas. Enrollment and graduation fluctuations were explained in terms of structural, institutional, and societal conditions that impacted on the predictor or dependent variables.

Selected Findings

Recruitment

The recruitment of black students for professional schools was uneven and inconsistent during the 1970s. Enormous differences were found in the quality of commitment and support from institutions, from public and private sectors, and from professional associations to facilitate recruitment efforts designed to increase black student participation in professional school education. Not unexpectedly, the overall quality of recruitment programs varied by professions as well as by institutions. About 75% of the institutions among the 743 survey cases reported the presence of recruitment programs for black students at varying times during the decade. Although a substantial proportion of these programs were genuine efforts, many were actually cosmetic programs — impressive in structure but never supported by a serious institutional commitment to implement them. However, some institutions that made serious efforts toward implementation were unsuccessful. Their lack of success may be attributed to such factors as a reputation for an unfavorable institutional climate, characterized by general hostility to black students or by faculty and student lack of enthusiasm for the presence of black students; admission requirements heavily weighted toward traditional, cognitive criteria; inadequate financial aid packages; lack of black faculty; lack of a critical mass of black students; and an unfavorable geographic location.

Nevertheless, several institutions were quite successful in recruiting black students for their professional school (s). The most successful institutions were those whose recruitment programs were supported by external funds, such as federal grants and support from private foundations. The primary beneficiaries of these efforts were schools or colleges of medicine, law, dentistry, pharmacy, and engineering. Colleges of optometry and veterinary medicine, with the notable exception of the School of Veterinary Medicine at traditionally black Tuskegee Institute in Alabama, were generally unsuccessful in recruiting black students during the 1970s.

Successful recruitment programs relied on a variety of strategies to persuade members of the targeted group to apply for admission. Among the more widely used techniques were developing a wide array of promotional materials (e.g., brochures, circulars, slides, and films about the institution and its student life and educational programs); using a special recruitment staff for visits to high schools, traditionally black colleges, and TWIs in which a sizable number of black students were enrolled; involving faculty and students in the recruitment process, especially as hosts during the campus visits of targeted students; special programs for high school and college advisers; and establishing linkages between the professional school, faculty advisers, alumni associations, and state, regional, and national associations for assistance regarding financial support, information dissemination, and general recruiting.

Special recruitment programs began to fade as federal funds decreased, as institutional commitment to these efforts waned, and as the *Bakke* case made its way toward the U.S. Supreme Court for final resolution in 1978.

Financial Aid

During the 1970s, approximately 50% of all black students enrolled in a professional school came from families whose annual income was less than $10,000. In some fields, such as dentistry, at some institutions, four years of training cost as much as $40,000. Though the high cost of professional education places it out of reach for all but the affluent, irrespective of race, it is virtually impossible for an overwhelming majority of black students to advance through a professional school without some form of financial aid. For instance, in 1976–1977, 90% of first-year dental students at Loma Linda University, 80% at Georgetown, 75% at the University of Southern California, 85% at Harvard, and 90% at Temple had to rely on loans to finance even the first year of dental education. This situation was repeated at several institutions and in most professional fields of study throughout the 1970s. A disproportionate number of black students were compelled to rely heavily on loans to finance their education.

Nevertheless, thousands of black students benefited from scholarships that helped defray the costs of both graduate and professional school education. Examples of major scholarship programs that aided black students included the federally funded Health Professions Scholarship and Health Professions Loan Program, the G-POP Program, the Minority Fellowship Program of the National Institute of Mental Health (NIMH), and private-sector funding from the Robert Wood Johnson Foundation, the Ford Foundation, the Alfred P. Sloan Foundation, the Carnegie Foundation, the Josiah T. Macy Foundation, and the Rockefeller Foundation. In addition, fellowship programs for blacks and other minorities were established specifically in such fields as medicine, dentistry, engineering, law, and social work and in some doctoral-degree disciplines, such as the social and behavioral sciences.

Despite the existence of a substantial number of financial assistance programs at varying points during the 1970s, these programs were inadequate to meet the diverse needs of increasing numbers of black students for financial assistance. Neither were they able to keep pace with the escalating costs of graduate and professional education. Near the middle of the decade, funds to assist minority students began to shrink, while others became inaccessible with the implementation of more restrictive eligibility requirements. Further, many of the minority scholarship programs mounted by the federal government and by several professional associations came under a well-orchestrated, vigorous attack from persons who regarded special financial assistance programs as a form of so-called reverse discrimination. Shifting priorities also contributed to the loss of scholarships and other funds once available to minority students. Near the end of the decade, significant improvements were made in the availability of money for graduate and professional education. Some institutions had also done a better job of disseminating information about the existence of financial aid programs by which blacks and other minorities could benefit. Fluctuations in the enrollment patterns of black students in the various fields of study mirrored changes in the availability of financial aid programs during the 1970s.

Applications

As early as the 1950s, following the upsurge in college enrollment and graduation after World War II, graduate and professional schools experienced an unprecedented demand for admission. The initial pressure came from white students who saw graduate and professional degrees as a major instrument for their social mobility and as a means to acquire lucrative financial rewards. Yet options then available to black students were quite restrictive; consequently, the numerical impact of black student enrollment on the TWIs had been negligible even in institutions outside the South.

Applicant pressure from larger and larger numbers of well-qualified students not only led to an increase in the number of graduate and professional schools but, inevitably, to a significant rise in admission standards. Almost simultaneously, major civil rights organizations and black students also began to exert enormous pressure on institutions for admission of black and other minority students. One response was the development of recruitment programs designed to increase the applicant pool of students previously excluded from full participation in graduate and professional education programs.

Applicant activity varied tremendously during the 1960s and 1970s; however, after the initial upsurge in the number of blacks who applied to professional schools during the early 1970s, there was relatively little change in the percentage that black applicants actually made of the total number of applications filed. This point may be illustrated in the field of medicine. In 1960, some 14,397 applicants filed 54,662 applications to the 86 medical schools then in existence. In 1970, some 24,987 persons filed an average of 6 applications—a total of 148,797 applications. Only 1,250, or 0.8% of all applications, were from black students. The number of applications from black students rose to 2,186 in 1972 and climbed only to 2,592 in 1979–1980, when the number of medical colleges had increased to 126. By 1979–1980, however, the total number of applications filed had spiraled upward to 335,982, or 9.2 per person. In 1980, the 40,000 applicants to U.S. medical schools were competing for 16,930 first-year seats in 126 institutions.

Importantly, whereas applicant activity increased significantly among students as a group interested in the profession of medicine, it remained virtually stalled at about 2,500 for black students from 1972 through the remainder of the decade.

Similar patterns occurred in dentistry and law. Interest in engineering continued to expand at a much faster rate than in any other profession during the 1970s. Notable and somewhat dramatic declines in black student applications to schools of social work and colleges of optometry, pharmacy, and veterinary medicine occurred after peaking near the mid-1970s.

Admissions

Admission Criteria

As increasing numbers of black and other minority students applied for admission to professional schools particularly, even with the construction of expanded numbers of professional schools, allegations were widespread that blacks were being given preferential treatment over "better-qualified" white applicants. Most frequently, these charges rested on presumed racial differences in performance on quantitative measures for admission and/or on erroneous assumptions that institutions relied exclusively on quantifiable criteria in making admission decisions. No institution determines admission eligibility solely on the basis of such traditional measures as test scores and grade point averages. Both traditional (the more quantitative) and nontraditional (the more qualitative) measures are employed by most institutions in determining eligibility for admission to graduate and professional schools. The most commonly used quantitative measures during the 1970s were test scores (e.g., GRE, LSAT, MCAT, VMAT, OCAT, and the DAT), grade point average (GPA), and the quality of the undergraduate college. The most often cited qualitative measures were motivation, relevant work experience, communication skills, personality characteristics, and promise as a professional. Letters of recommendation were of special importance as admission committees assessed qualitative factors used in admission decisions. Just as a rank on objective measures could determine either inclusion or exclusion, qualitative assessments made of the applicant contributed heavily in these considerations. Qualitative factors could also be the source of bias either in favor of or against an applicant because of their subjective nature.

Admission standards increased dramatically in most professional schools during the 1970s. There seemed to be a direct correlation between raised standards and increased pressure for admission. In effect, in most professions studied, the greater the enrollment pressure, as evidenced by the absolute applicant volume, the higher the standards. Similarly, decisions to raise admission qualifications were also affected by space limitations. Consequently, a number of persons who appeared qualified, if admission officers and committees had adhered strictly to the more traditional measures, were denied admission. Many of these persons found it difficult to accept the fact that institutions employed a mix of qualitative and quantitative factors that resulted in the admission of minority students who scored lower on test scores. They failed to understand that, at these institutions, test scores were not the sole criterion employed in this process.

This situation triggered a national debate over the relative weights to be assigned to such factors as test scores and to nonquantitative measures. Those persons who advocated a so-called meritocracy insisted on test scores, grade point averages, and other quantitative measures as the exclusive basis for rendering admission decisions. Those persons who were more concerned about the abuses of test scores and about heavy reliance on them as a restrictive barrier to the more often excluded groups and those persons who insisted on the value of qualitative measures as instruments for assessing motivation to succeed, perseverance, determination, and promise as a professional argued for greater reliance on evaluative criteria. The national debate intensified as adversaries prepared to defend their positions in the cases of *DeFunis* v. *Odegaard* and *Alan Bakke* v. *The Board of Regents of the University of California/Davis.*

As the *Bakke* case made its way through the various levels of the judiciary, several professional schools began to reformulate their admission policies and to redirect them in ways that demonstrated heavier reliance on such factors as test scores. By 1978, shortly after the U.S. Supreme Court rendered its decision in the *Bakke* case, it seemed evident that the downturn in black enrollment in many professional schools reflected the implementation of more restrictive admission policies.

Special Admission Programs

The primary function of special admission programs was to increase the enrollment chances of those students, especially underrepresented minorities, who possessed special talents, skills, and qualitative characteristics not particularly evidenced in test scores and grade point averages. Although a significant number of black students entered through regular admission procedures, a large number used the special admission route to a professional school. Medical, dental, and law schools were more likely to establish special admission programs during the 1970s than were other professional schools. In fact, approximately 75% of the medical and dental schools and more than half of all law schools operated such programs at some time during the 1970s. Schools and colleges of optometry and pharmacy also operated them, but not to the same degree as other professional schools. Optometry was such an underchosen field that its applicant-to-admittee ratio was exceptionally high for most students. The primary problem was the inability of most optometry schools to mount a recruitment program attractive enough to woo black students. Very few of the 24 colleges of veterinary medicine ever operated special admission programs. Neither did they aggressively recruit black students. Consequently, the TWI schools of veterinary medicine have never moved beyond token representation of blacks in their student bodies.

The number of special admission programs declined during the latter half of the 1970s. One of the primary causes of this decline was the virulent attack levied against these programs by right-wing, conservative, neoconservative, and formerly liberal persons and groups. Opponents of these programs considered them unconstitutional, discriminatory, and demeaning or stigmatizing to minorities. They were not willing to accept the argument that these programs were morally justified and educationally sound because they made allowances for the persistence of racism against minorities, for test biases, and for discriminatory grading practices that helped to lower the performance of some minority students on these measures. They also objected to rigid set-aside programs that allocated a specific number of places or seats for minority students for which other students could not compete. That argument was supported by the U.S. Supreme Court as it rendered its *Bakke* decision in 1978. Significantly, in the same decision, the Court found constitutionally defensible the use of the race variable in admission decisions when it served a compelling state need. Further, the Court granted considerable latitude to institutions to use special admission programs, as long as they were not specifically race-based and were expanded, for instance, to include economically disadvantaged students from all races. In general, those institutions that were seriously committed to diversity in the student body composition and to expanded educational opportunity made the modifications necessary to retain their programs and sometimes to expand them into even more viable programs. Uncommitted institutions found a publicly acceptable rationalization to abolish their programs. Hence, a decline was quite apparent at the end of the 1970s.

Enrollment

In terms of absolute numbers and percentages of black students enrolled in graduate and professional schools during the 1970s, the findings in this study reveal that progress was uneven. In many ways, enrollment trends showed significant gains followed by declines and stagnation. Statistical analyses of the 743 cases studied revealed that the most powerful and persistent predictor of first-year and total enrollment was the presence and number of black faculty in the professional school. In every instance, this variable was significant beyond the .05 level of confidence. Clearly, the most successful institutions regarding black student enrollment during the 1970s were those institutions with black faculty in the professional school. Conversely, the least successful were those that had none or had black faculty in either token or inconspicuous roles. It appeared, therefore, that the larger the number of black faculty, as in schools of social work, for instance, the greater the number of black students.

With respect to first-year enrollment in a professional school, other powerful predictors of black student enrollment were (1) the quality of financial aid; (2) the number of professional schools within a state; (3) not being under *Adams* litigation to desegregate; and (4) type of institution. In addition to the black faculty variable, the most powerful predictors of total black student enrollment in professional schools were (1) presence of a special admission program; (2) quality of financial aid; (3) proportion of blacks in the state's population; and (4) number of professional schools within the state.

These predictors suggest that black students are more likely to be enrolled in those institutions with a favorable financial assistance program for them; in those states where two or more professional schools in a given field reduced barriers attributed to a restricted number of available seats for applicants as a whole; and in those states that were not under the mandate to dismantle a dual system of higher education. The latter situation reflects the more positive steps taken by several northern and midwestern states to recruit and enroll significant numbers of black students aggressively . Only near the end of the 1970s did the *Adams* litigation appear to have a major impact on the enrollment of black students in professional schools. Even then, some *Adams* states and some professional schools within institutions were more determined to expand educational opportunity than were others.

During the first part of the 1970s, private institutions were considerably more successful in enrolling black professional school students than were public institutions. However, from about 1974 to the end of the decade, public institutions began to outdistance private ones regarding black student matriculation. This change may be evidence of the fact that the number of blacks in a state is also significantly correlated with high enrollment. A larger potential pool of students exists with large numbers of resident blacks; further, as enrollment demands increased, public institutions were more likely to be the recipients of legal and public pressure for admission.

With respect to total black student enrollment, the presence of special admission programs was also a major predictor of enrollment. In effect, these programs did assist a sizable number of black students to gain access to various professional fields of study during the 1970s. This finding also suggests that black students were more likely to enroll in professional schools if they operated a special admission program than if they did not.

Medicine

In 1968–1969, approximately 60% of the 266 first-year black medical school students were matriculated at the medical college of Howard University and Meharry Medical School. Forty percent were dispersed among 54 of the 97 medical schools operating in the United States at that time. Forty-three schools of medicine enrolled not a single black student. The 266 black first-year students represented 2.7% of all first-year medical students. By 1970, the number of blacks in first-year classes had almost tripled to 697, which in turn represented 6.1% of all first-year medical students. In 1975, the 1,027 black first-year students constituted 7.5% of total first-year students. Significantly, 1975, the same year the *Bakke* suit began to work its way through the various courts, was the peak year for the proportion of black students enrolled in first-year medical school classes. Thereafter, their percentages declined and stabilized at about 6.4% in 1979–1980. The absolute number of blacks in first-year classes climbed only to 1,108 by the end of the decade.

Only 23 of the more than 100 medical colleges that operated throughout the 1970s were relatively successful in enrolling black students in first-year classes. Seven of these were in the *Adams* states. Of that number, four are located in Pennsylvania, one in North Carolina, one in Maryland, and one in Florida. Forty-four medical colleges enrolled fewer than 50 black students during the 1970s.

In 1970, the total enrollment of 1,509 black students in all medical colleges represented 3.8% of the 40,238 students enrolled in all classes. By 1975, total U.S. enrollment had increased to 55,848; of that number, 3,456, or 6.2%, were black students. The black proportion of total enrollment peaked in 1975 at 6.3% and began a steady decline in 1975 that was never halted during the remainder of the decade. Hence, in 1979–1980, when total black student enrollment rose to 3,627 of a national total of 63,800, blacks actually constituted only 5.6% of total enrollment. It seems that the *Bakke* suit had a chilling effect on the admission of black students to medical schools and colleges. At the same time, it is also highly probable that some of the black students who may have gone into medicine were probably attracted to less time-consuming fields, such as engineering, which did not require them to defer gratifications for four or more years after college graduation before they could begin to earn a decent living. Nevertheless, an important fact remains: The presence of an additional 40 medical colleges in 1980 over the number in existence in 1968–1969 did not result in the kind of upsurge in the total number of black medical students that the additional space might have suggested. That space went primarily to white students, especially white females, who constituted in excess of 20% of medical school students by 1980. In effect, the white monopoly on professional education was only moderately affected by wider inclusion of black and other minority students.

In 1980, Howard and Meharry medical colleges, traditionally black institutions, enrolled only 20% of all blacks in medical colleges. Nevertheless, their 20% constituted as many black students as the combined black student enrollment of 74 medical colleges in the United States. As the decade ended, the addition of two new medical colleges would also improve the opportunities for medical education for black Americans. They were the Medical College of Morehouse College and the undergraduate medical education program at the Charles Drew Medical Center in Los Angeles.

Dentistry

In 1970, one-third of the 52 colleges of dentistry in the United States did not enroll a single black student in their first-year classes. Thirty percent of them enrolled only 1 black first-year student, and 25% enrolled between

2 and 5 black students in their first-year dental classes. The dental schools of Meharry and Howard University enrolled 86 (41%) of the 185 black first-year dental students in 1970. Only 19 black students, less than 10%, were enrolled in the first-year classes of the 13 schools of dentistry located in the *Adams* states.

The number of blacks matriculated in first-year classes in the dental schools in the *Adams* states increased to 35 by 1974 and to 46 in 1979–1980. The most successful institutions in the *Adams* states with respect to the enrollment of black first-year dental students were the University of Maryland, the University of Georgia, and the University of Pittsburgh.

In 1970, black students represented 4% of all first-year matriculants. The peak year for blacks in first-year classes was 1975, when the 298 students in first-year classes constituted 5.1% of all dental students in that class. By 1979–1980, a downturn in the number and proportion of blacks in first-year dental classes was apparent, since the 274 black students constituted only 4.4% of the 35,702 students in first-year classes. Yet the total number of dental schools had expanded to 60.

With respect to total enrollment in U.S. schools of dentistry in 1970, the dental schools at Meharry and Howard University accounted for 62% of the 451 black students enrolled. Only 4 TWIs enrolled 10 or more black students, and 8 of the 51 U.S. mainland dental schools did not enroll a single black student. The 451 blacks in dental schools in 1970 represented 2.7% of the total dental school enrollment of 16, 553. By the end of the decade, 1979–1980, the absolute number of black dental students had climbed to 1,009, or 4.4% of a total dental school enrollment of 22,482. However, the 977 blacks in dental school in 1975–1976 actually reached a higher proportion, 4.7% than was represented by a larger absolute number of black dental students in 1979–1980. Clearly, the slight increases in the number of black dental students were not keeping pace with the proportion of nonblack students matriculated in these institutions.

Optometry

At no point during the 1970s did blacks represent a major proportion of students matriculated at the 13 schools and colleges of optometry in the United States. For instance, in 1970, the 15 black optometry students represented 0.5% of the 2,826 students enrolled in all optometry colleges. The peak year for total black student enrollment was 1976, when the 89 black students made up 1.89% of the nation's 4,177 optometry students. By

1979–1980, however, there was a sharp decline to only 48 black students, or 1% of a total enrollment of 4,500 optometry students. The most successful institution for enrolling black students in this field was Indiana University. This success was due largely to the aggressive and sustained efforts of a single black faculty member in that college of optometry who was able to mobilize varied resources to recruit and enroll a significant number of black students. The sex ratio of blacks in optometry schools also shifted during the 1970s. For instance, in 1970, 87% of all black optometry students were males. By 1979–1980, however, black women, with 54%, constituted a majority of blacks in this field of study.

Pharmacy

In 1970 and 1971, black students constituted a mere 1% of all students matriculated in the 50 traditionally white pharmacy schools in the United States. Specifically, in 1971, for instance, although the 618 black pharmacy students represented 3.7% of the total pharmacy enrollment, 353 of the 618 black students were enrolled in 1 of the 4 pharmacy colleges located at traditionally black institutions, or TBIs: Florida A. & M. University, Howard University, Texas Southern University, and Xavier University of New Orleans. The total percentage of black pharmacy students actually peaked early in the decade — 1972–1973 — at 6.6%. The absolute number of blacks in pharmacy continued to rise, but the proportion that blacks represented of total enrollment declined. For instance, in 1979–1980, the 958 black B.S. pharmacy students constituted only 4.2% of total baccalaureate pharmacy students, and 54.3% of those students were enrolled at the four TBIs. Only the University of Maryland among white pharmacy schools in the *Adams* states enrolled a significant number of black students in pharmacy. In 1979, that institution matriculated a total of 31 black pharmacy students and was among the top six institutions in the nation with respect to the number of blacks studying for a baccalaureate degree in pharmacy.

Veterinary Medicine

Schools of veterinary medicine have been the most resistant to the kinds of recruitment practices necessary to attract significant numbers of black students. The major exception, for obvious reasons, is the College of Veterinary Medicine at Tuskegee Institute, a TBI located in Alabama. It is estimated that, between 1970 and 1974, this institution accounted for more than 90% of all blacks studying in this field. In the *Adams* states, the record of black student enrollment was then and continues to be dismal. For instance, between 1973 and 1980, the School of Veterinary Medicine at Louisiana State University enrolled 2 of the 9 blacks who applied; the University of Mississippi, which opened its school in 1977, matriculated 3 of the 16 black applicants; the University of Tennessee, whose school also opened in 1977, enrolled 1 of its 2 black applicants. Between 1969 and 1979, only four black students enrolled in the DVM program at the University of Georgia. By 1980, with 24 schools of veterinary medicine in the United States, 80% of all blacks in pursuit of DVM degrees were still matriculated at Tuskegee Institute.

Engineering

In terms of absolute numbers of black students enrolled in first professional degree programs, engineering was singularly the most successful field during the 1970s. For instance, in 1970, the 1,289 black students enrolled in baccalaureate degree programs constituted 1.7% of the 71,661 students studying for the B.S. in engineering degree. By 1979–1980, the 6,339 black first-year engineering students represented 6.1% of the 103,724 first-year engineering class in the United States. Similarly, with respect to total enrollment, there was an upward spiral in black student enrollment. Specifically, in 1970, the total black student enrollment of 4,136 constituted 2% of a total U.S. enrollment of 194,727. By 1979–1980, the total black baccalaureate engineering enrollment of 14,786 was 4.3% of the 340,488 students studying for a B.S. degree in engineering at 282 institutions. Six of those institutions were TBIs: Howard University, North Carolina A. & T. University, Prairie View A. & M. University, Southern University, Tennessee State University, and Tuskegee Institute.

The major stimulus for this sharp upturn in the number of blacks studying engineering was the combination of a concerted effort by the federal government and aggressive action taken by private foundations and the corporate structure to support recruitment efforts to increase the representation of blacks and other minorities in this profession. Programs such as Minorities in Engineering, the Minority Education Engineering Effort (ME³), and the Committee on Minorities in Engineering combined with the efforts of private foundations and corporations such as the Alfred P. Sloan Foundation and General Electric to pioneer in expanding enrollment opportunities for blacks and other minorities.

Although black student enrollment also expanded at the graduate level, black M.S. degree students rose only from 0.7% in 1971 to 1.3% (only 357 students) of total 1980 enrollment. At the Ph.D. level in 1980, only 109 black students, or 0.8% of 13,461, were enrolled. The *Adams* states had no significant black student enrollment at the graduate level in engineering.

Law

First-year black student enrollment in schools of law almost doubled between 1969 and 1979. The absolute number rose from 1,115, or 3.8% of 29,128 first-year law students, to 2,002, or 5.7% of the 34,632 first-year law students in the 164 ABA-approved schools of law in 1979. With respect to total enrollment in U.S. ABA-approved law schools, black students never exceeded the 4.6% of total enrollment they registered in 1976–1977. In 1979–1980, the 5,257 black students in law represented only 4.2% of the 122,860 students studying law in the United States. Hence, not only are blacks still underrepresented in this field but their proportion in the total law school enrollment is declining. The law schools at the TBIs of Howard University, Texas Southern University, Southern University, and North Carolina Central University account for a significant proportion of the total number of blacks in law schools. Further, these four institutions are considerably more desegregated than are the majority of schools of law at TWIs.

Social Work

Only in social work was parity ever attained, as measured by the ratio of black student enrollment to the proportion of blacks in the total population. Throughout the 1970s, the total black U.S. population was slightly less than 12%. In 1970, however, the 975 blacks enrolled in the first year of MSW degree programs represented 14.5% of the 6,699 first-year students. That percentage peaked at 15.7% in 1972–1973, when there were 1,226 black first-year students out of a total first-year enrollment of 7,788. By 1979–1980, however, it had fallen to 9.3%, or 799 of 8,056 first-year MSW students. In the *Adams* states, at the MSW level, the most successful institutions for enrolling black students were the University of Maryland and Virginia Commonwealth University, which maintained a black student enrollment of at least 10% through most of the 1970s. The least successful institution in the *Adams* states was the University of Oklahoma.

Degrees Conferred

The findings in this study showed that the most powerful predictors of graduation of black students from professional schools were the presence and size of the black faculty and the presence of a retention program. The salience of the black faculty variable has already been discussed. However, retention here includes a broad range of factors, including varying degrees of academic support systems, viable black student organizations, the ability to participate in buzz sessions or study groups, and community support systems, as well as an institutional climate regarded as somewhat favorable. In other words, the presence of a mechanism that facilitated learning under less than perpetually stressful situations, accompanied by a sense of mutual support in a positive social network, helped to retain black students through graduation.

During the 1970s, graduate and professional schools produced 5,286 blacks with the M.D., 1,436 with the D.D.S., 200 with the O.D. degree, 6,967 with a first professional degree in engineering, and 6,694 with a doctoral degree. The peak year for producing black doctorates was 1977, when 1,109 blacks received doctoral degrees. In general, blacks received less than 4% of the doctorates conferred during the decade.

One of the major problems in producing blacks with doctoral degrees is the maldistribution of blacks in fields of study. They were overrepresented in education, in which more than 50% of all blacks with doctoral degrees are concentrated, and seriously underrepresented in all other fields, especially the physical, mathematical, and biological sciences. Even so, the average of 1,000 blacks who earn a doctoral degree each year remains a dismal number that is inadequate to meet the societal need for more blacks with this degree.

Implications

The problem of underproduction of blacks with professional degrees and the current monopoly the white population holds on graduate–professional education can be ameliorated only if concrete steps continue to be taken by graduate institutions, the public and private sectors, and the federal government. Specifically, there is a critical need for (1) a strong institutional, governmental, and corporate commitment to provide resources for recruiting, enrolling, and retaining much larger numbers of black students in the nation's graduate and professional schools; (2) the creation of a positive learning environment at the institutional level; (3) the recruitment, hiring, and tenuring of much larger numbers of blacks in faculty roles and the hiring of blacks in positions of power, influence, and trust in academic administration; (4) the development of strong networks between black students and influential mentors among black faculty and administrators; (5) the establishment of viable linkages between professional schools, colleges, and school systems in order to foster interest in graduate and professional education and to share information about curriculum requirements and the expectations for academic performance in graduate and professional schools; and (6) expanded financial aid packages provided by the federal government through substantial scholarships, by the private sector, and by institutions to assist needy and deserving black students who wish to pursue graduate and/or professional education. Without such provisions, it is unlikely that the overall problem of inequality of access evidenced by the underrepresentation that still persists will disappear in the foreseeable future.

PART 3

Aspirations and Career Choices of Black Students

Coupled with the goal of making access to higher education a reality is the realization that the opportunity structure figures heavily in the determination of aspirations. It is no news that college-educated blacks are heavily represented in the social sciences and education. Neither is it news that the colleges open to them in generations past — traditionally black colleges — offered courses of study primarily in these fields. Moreover, it is a tendency of an oppressed people to gravitate to those disciplines that will enable them to understand their condition and to work to alleviate it. Also, a racially and sexually biased labor market sends unmistakable signals about where employment is available and how sexually stereotyped the world of work is.

As a consequence, the availability of previously closed institutions as well as previously limited job opportunities can have a profound impact upon aspirations. At a time when opportunities for women are expanding, both race and gender are fertile areas for analysis. Edgar Epps and Kenneth Jackson in Chapter 9 explore the applicability of the traditional status-attainment model for black youth. Next, Gail Thomas addresses the factors that motivate black students' choice of a college major. Rhoda Johnson follows by explaining the impact on job placement of attending traditionally black versus traditionally white institutions.

Chapter 8

THE EDUCATIONAL
ATTAINMENT PROCESS
AMONG BLACK YOUTH
Edgar G. Epps and Kenneth W. Jackson

Despite the gains of the past two decades, the overall rate of college attendance by blacks in the United States is still considerably below that of
whites. In 1982, blacks accounted for 8.0% of enrollment in four-year institutions and 10.3% of enrollment in two-year institutions (National
Center for Education Statistics 1984). In the *Adams* states, black
undergraduates constituted 13.6% of total enrollment, while the black college-age population in these states is almost 20% of the total (American
Association of University Professors 1983; Brazziel & Brazziel 1980). These
figures suggest that there is still considerable room for improvement in
educational attainment among blacks.

The research reported here seeks to assess the process by which educational attainment is generated in the black population. Specifically, our efforts are an attempt to determine the mechanism that generates educational
mobility among black Americans. The basic theoretical orientation for our
analysis is the Wisconsin model of status attainment (Sewell, Haller, &
Portes 1969). This model and its variants, in their traditional form, have
not worked very well to explain the black educational attainment process
(Hout & Morgan 1975; Kerckoff & Campbell 1977). We contend that this
problem is due primarily to an inadequate specification of a critical dimension within the status-attainment model. That is, the Wisconsin model and
its variants are basically social–psychological models emphasizing the
primary role played by social–psychological influences. These factors,
usually measured in terms of influential others and aspirations, serve as key
mediators of the effects of earlier social circumstances, such as one's school
career or family history.

This chapter is based on a previously published research monograph by Edgar G. Epps and
Kenneth W. Jackson: *Educational and Occupational Aspirations and Early Attainment of
Black Males and Females.* Atlanta: Southern Education Foundation, 1985.

We contend that social–psychological factors are not as central to generating educational attainment for blacks as they are for whites. We hypothesize that the school dimension is of considerably more importance than the social–psychological dimension for blacks.

In this research, we attempt to modify the traditional status-attainment model. This modification consists primarily of respecifying the school dimension, with the other dimensions (background and social-psychological) remaining basically unchanged. The rationale for respecifying the school dimension is that we believe that this component represents a very critical aspect of the status attainment process for blacks. If our hypothesis concerning the importance of the school dimension is correct, respecifying this dimension should increase the model's explanatory power for blacks. The results could also provide a basis for making recommendations about schooling that could help to increase black participation in higher education.

Data

Data for this analysis were taken from the 1972 National Longitudinal Study (NLS) and its 1980 follow-up and from the 1980 High School and Beyond (HSB) study and its 1982 follow-up. Both are national samples selected to be representative of high school seniors in the United States at the time the data were collected. The analyses reported in this research are based on the following sample sizes: HSB males, 259; NLS males, 167; HSB females, 324; NLS females, 319.

The estimation techniques used in the analyses are those usually found in status-attainment research. These strategies, commonly referred to as path analytic techniques, have proven to be quite informative with respect to understanding the dynamics of educational attainment.

The model's basic dynamics are assumed to be as follows. Background factors (socioeconomic status, ability) are those crucial elements that the individual brings to the attainment process. These factors are then assumed to have a direct impact on those school factors (track, semesters of course work taken, grades) that are relevant for subsequent attainment. The effects of these school factors are then mediated by the social–psychological factors (influential others, aspirations) that, in turn, have a direct impact on status. As we view the process for blacks, the social–psychological component should have a relatively weak mediating effect on school factors.

Findings

National Longitudinal Study (NLS) Males

The model accounts for about 31% of the variance in educational attainment in this cohort of black males. The significant direct influences were ability, track, influential others, and aspirations. Except for track, the school component, contrary to our expectations, did not exert much influence on educational attainment. Ability was by far the most important determinant of educational attainment ($b = .353$), while the aspirations variable was second in importance ($b = .196$). The pattern observed here is similar to that usually found for white males. That is, ability is the most important background factor, and social–psychological factors tend to mediate the effects of other background and school factors.

National Longitudinal Study (NLS) Females

The model was slightly more successful for females than for males, accounting for just over 34% of the variance in educational attainment. We also find that the school component tends to be more significant for females. Both track ($b = .195$) and grades ($b = .105$) have substantial direct effects on educational attainment. As was the case for males, however, ability ($b = .275$) and aspirations ($b = .331$) stand out as the most important determinants of educational attainment.

Since aspirations are the most crucial determinant of educational attainment, we asked which factors are most important in generating aspirations. We find that the only important determinants of aspirations are the school factors (grades, semesters of course work taken, and track). It is interesting to note that the only school variable that significantly affected male aspirations was grades, with most of the important determinants being related to the student's background. In contrast, for females, the school factors mediate both background and ability and directly influence educational attainment. Thus, our hypothesis is at least partially supported for NLS females.

High School and Beyond Study (HSB) Males

We find that the model explains approximately the same amount of variance in educational attainment for HSB males (29%) as for NLS males

(30%). However, there are differences in the effects of certain variables. Unlike for NLS males, HSB male educational attainment is influenced considerably more by school factors. For NLS males, background and social-psychological factors were more important. For HSB males, however, the background factors had no direct impact on educational attainment; only aspirations, among the social-psychological variables, had any significant effect. Nevertheless, although aspirations had the strongest effect (b = .448) both track (b = .123) and semesters of course work (b = .166) also had significant direct effects on attainment. It should be noted that the pattern for HSB males is similar to that for NLS females. Grades, semesters of course work taken, and track were all significant determinants of aspirations. The differences observed for the two male cohorts suggest the possibility that a very fundamental shift in the generation of educational status may have occurred between 1972 and 1980. If this is indeed the case, it would appear that attaining high levels of education has become less dependent on individual ascriptive and/or motivational factors and more dependent on institutional–school factors.

High School and Beyond Study (HSB) Females

With respect to educational attainment for females, we do less well with the HSB cohort (25% of variance explained) than with the NLS cohort (34% of variance explained). As was the case for the NLS females, two school factors (track and grades) have rather substantial direct influences on educational attainment. Only semesters of course work taken was unimportant among this group of school factors. However, course work does affect educational attainment indirectly through its effect on aspirations. Aspirations, as was the case for NLS females, had the strongest direct influence on educational attainment (b = .334).

The factors responsible for generating educational aspirations are substantially different for HSB and NLS females. For NLS females, the principal influences were all school factors. In the HSB cohort, not only were school factors important but background (both socioeconomic status and ability) also exerted a significant direct effect on this variable. This finding implies a slight shift away from the more institutional factors observed in the NLS cohort to an emphasis on the more ascriptive and/or motivational individual components in the HSB group. This is not to imply that school factors are unimportant; they still have a significant impact on aspirations. But they are not sole determinants of aspirations for the HSB females, as they are for the NLS females.

We find then, that for the HSB females, the process by which educational attainment is generated has also shifted. Although it is not as substantial as the shift for males, our findings indicate a general tendency in recent years for background factors to increase their influence. The fact that we account for no more than 34% of the variance in educational attainment for NLS females and only 25% for HSB females suggests that other factors (presumably unmeasured) are also contributing to the variance in educational attainment. That is, we suspect that the variables typically included in this kind of research are becoming less influential and that perhaps some previously unidentified variables are becoming more important.

Additional Analyses

In an effort to see if early-attainment processes differ from the pattern observed for HSB seniors, we applied our model to HSB sophomores. We can look only at the generation of aspirations for this cohort (rather than educational attainment). For sophomore *males*, school factors tend to dominate in terms of their influence on aspirations. In fact, all three school variables entered into the model (track, courses taken, and grades) directly influence aspirations. Socioeconomic status and influence of significant others also had strong direct effects on aspirations. What is different about the sophomore male results is the decreased importance of ability. For senior males, ability had a significant direct influence on all relevant dependent variables except educational attainment. For the sophomores, ability directly influenced only grades and track, and in neither case was it the most important influence.

For sophomore *females,* socioeconomic status, track, courses taken, grades, and influential others all have significant direct effects on aspirations. For senior females, the only difference was that ability also had a significant direct effect, and grades did not. Socioeconomic status had a stronger impact on subsequent variables for sophomore females than for any other cohort. This tends to provide additional support for our contention that there seems to be a general trend, especially among females, away from the more structurally oriented dimensions, such as school factors, and toward the more individually oriented background characteristics. This does not indicate that school factors have diminished in importance. Rather, our results seem to indicate that socioeconomic status is becoming a more salient factor in generating educational attainment among black American females.

In an attempt to improve the specification of the school component, we conducted an analysis in which additional school variables were added to the model, and occupational and educational aspirations were entered as separate variables rather than as a composite. This analysis involved the HSB senior cohort. Three additional variables were added to the model: type of school the student attended (public or private), whether or not the student had taken remedial or advanced courses, and achievement as measured by standardized tests. A different measure of ability was also used (the combined scores of a picture–number test, a mosaic comparison test, and a visualization test instead of the math, reading, and vocabulary tests).

Including the additional variables does not greatly alter our results. While differences are observed, the basic findings remain unaltered. For *males*, we find that courses taken and educational aspirations are the only two variables that have any significant direct effect on educational attainment. This differs from the original specification only in that track also had a significant direct effect that does not show up now. The amount of variance in educational attainment explained by the model only increased from 29 to 31%. It is interesting to note that, in this specification, we are able to account for over 55% of the variance in achievement for black males. This is quite substantial, given other attempts at explaining achievement.

Note that in the original model we combined educational and occupational aspirations to form a composite measure of "aspirations." In the alternate model, where occupational and educational aspirations were entered separately, we find that almost all the influential determinants of aspirations in the original model are attributable to educational aspirations. The major difference between the two models is with respect to the influence of background factors. In the original model, ability had a strong direct effect on aspirations; in the alternate model, socioeconomic status influences aspirations along with the school factors (track, courses, grades, achievement test scores).

For *females,* the results are similar to those for males. There is only a slight improvement in accounting for the variance in educational attainment (27% as compared to 25%). Unlike the male results, however, ability has a significant direct effect on educational attainment along with grades and educational aspirations. Educational aspirations are predicted by socioeconomic status, ability, track, courses taken, grades, and influential others. We also do a good job of predicting achievement among females, accounting for 42% of the variance. It is interesting to note that, for both sexes, achievement test scores do not influence educational attainment. Our basic conclusion for the results of the alternate specification is that the overall pattern observed in the original specification is not substantially changed.

Summary

Our analysis has revealed that the relative importance of school factors tends to vary depending on which cohort one is observing. We found that, for NLS males, school factors were relatively unimportant, with social–psychological factors being more important. Although doing a respectable job of accounting for educational attainment, our assumptions were not correct for NLS males. School factors, even after being specified in a more representative manner, did not dramatically increase our understanding of the generation of educational attainment for NLS males.

We also found that this pattern did not generalize to the HSB sample. Using the HSB data to estimate a similar model, we found that school factors contributed significantly more to explaining educational attainment than did any of the other dimensions considered. This finding indicated that a major shift away from the individual background factors had taken place. In other words, what goes on in schools seems to matter considerably more for black males in the 1980s than it did in the early 1970s.

Our analysis indicated that, for females, the generation of educational attainment was already based on the more institutionally related school factors in the early 1970s. School-related factors were by far the most critical elements in this process for females. Thus, the process found for the 1980 cohort of males was similar to that found for females in the early 1970s.

This process, however, has not remained stable. Our analysis revealed a slight shift for females over time. That is, for females, background factors tended to be more important in the 1980s than they were in the 1970s. This is not to say that school factors decreased in importance. The analysis revealed that school factors continued to be important but that background factors increased in importance for the 1980 HSB females.

Thus, given the relative stability of the school factors for the two female cohorts, as well as the shift toward an emphasis on school factors among males, it is likely that the pattern observed for females tends to be the pattern that males will follow at a later point in time. If this assessment is correct, we can expect that background factors will also become more relevant for black males in the future.

It is interesting to note that, in the alternate model using HSB data, we do a good job of predicting achievement as measured by tests. The variables that had a positive effect on achievement for males were socioeconomic status, ability, type of school (public or private), track, grades, and educational aspirations. For females, ability, track, courses taken, grades, and educational aspirations were positive influences. What is somewhat puzzling in this analysis is the fact that achievement (measured by standardized test scores) appears to be unrelated to educational attainment. This is contrary to expectations and provides clear support for the notion that aspirations may be more important for educational attainment among blacks than is measured achievement. One possible explanation for this seeming anomaly is the well-known fact that achievement tests do not measure blacks' accomplishments very well. Thus, the students' personal ambitions tend to be somewhat more important than achievement test scores in predicting actual attainment.

However, this interpretation must be viewed with caution because of one major limitation of the HSB data. That is, these students have been out of high school only two years. This means that our measure of educational attainment is constrained by the fact that students have not had sufficient time to complete their education. Future follow-up surveys may find that, with additional variance in educational attainment, better prediction is possible. This limitation does not apply to the NLS data to the same extent because students in that cohort had been out of high school for eight years.

What we can say is that the model we have used permits us to identify, to a certain degree, the basic pattern associated with generating educational attainment. Also, we can point out that there is support for our contention that, as things now stand, the more institutionally relevant school variables are among the critical elements in the educational attainment process for both black males and black females. These factors profoundly influence educational attainment in terms of both direct and indirect effects. Aspirations are very important, but they serve primarily as mediators of school factors, since they are almost wholly generated by these institutional influences.

References

American Association of University Professors
   1983   *Footnotes, 1,* 4.
Brazziel, W., & Brazziel, M.
   1980   *Recent College and University Enrollment Patterns of Black Students in States Affected by Adams–Califano Litigation.* Atlanta: Southern Education Foundation.

Hout, M., & Morgan, W. R.
    1975 Race, sex and educational attainment. *American Journal of Sociology, 81,* 364–394.
Kerckhoff, A., & Campbell, R. .
    1977 Black–white differences in the educational attainment process. *Sociology of Education, 50,* 15–27.
National Center for Education Statistics
    1984 *The Condition of Education, 1984 edition.* Washington, D.C.: GPO.
Portes, A., & Wilson, K. L.
    1976 Black–white differences in educational attainment. *American Sociological Review, 41,* 414–431.
Sewell, W. H., Haller, A. O., & Portes, A.
    1969 The educational and early occupational attainment process. *American Sociological Review, 34,* 551–569.

Chapter 9

BLACK COLLEGE STUDENTS AND
THEIR MAJOR FIELD CHOICE
Gail E. Thomas

The persistent gap in race and sex differences in income favoring whites and males has been partly attributed to differences in the major field choice and career aspirations and decisions of men and women, and blacks and whites. Recent data for 1980 by the Office for Civil Rights indicate that black and female baccalaureate degree recipients continue to be over-represented in education and the social sciences and underrepresented in the natural and technical sciences. This trend has persisted for at least four decades. Investing in education and the social sciences yields lower earnings for undergraduates than does investing in the natural and technical sciences.

Given the importance of college major choice for career achievement and the persistent race and sex gap in occupational attainment, this inquiry sought to understand what factors motivate black students' choice of a college major. Several theories have been formulated regarding the career aspirations and vocational choices of college students. Many of these theories have not been empirically tested, however, especially with reference to black students. This study was therefore designed to assess the relevancy of these theories to understanding the college major choice of black students.

Past studies about the major field choice and career aspirations of race and sex groups have been primarily descriptive. These inquiries have focused on the career intentions and actual major field choices of males and females and blacks and whites during various time periods (Admissions Testing Program 1983; Brown & Stent 1977; Lederer 1983; Thomas 1980; Trent 1983). A few previous studies have assessed the major field choice and career aspirations of college students more extensively.

This chapter is based on a previously published research monograph by Gail E. Thomas: *Black College Students and Factors Influencing Their Major Field Choice.* Atlanta: Southern Education Foundation, 1984.

Koch (1972) employed economic theory to test the hypothesis that students select undergraduate majors that offer them the highest economic returns from their educational investments. Koch compared cross-sectional data on income by major field with the enrollment of students in various major fields in 1970 and in 1971 and found that students' major field choice was significantly related to the labor market value associated with various majors. Accounting, mathematics, and economics had higher economic rates of return and higher student enrollments than did education, sociology, history, the fine arts, and the social sciences.

Cebula and Lopez (1982) retested Koch's (1972) economic incentive theory and extended Koch's hypothesis by noting that, apart from the monetary value of various majors, students' major field choice was also influenced by the change in earning differentials over time associated with the major field, the job prospects of the major, and students' GRE scores. This study indicated that earning differentials among fields and differences in the rate of change in earnings among fields were the two most important factors affecting students' major field choice.

Studies by Davis (1966) and Thomas (1981) applied sociological rather than economic theory to examine additional nonmonetary factors associated with students' major field choices and career aspirations. Davis (1966) argued that, by the time of college entry, because of previous family, school, and community socialization, students' career aspirations and orientations are fairly crystallized and are unlikely to change substantially. His results showed that early career expectations and aspirations and sex (i.e., being male or female) were the two most important determinants of students' career aspirations. Thomas' 1981 findings confirmed Davis' 1966 hypothesis regarding the importance of students' early career aspirations. Thomas' results showed that, for blacks and whites, the ascriptive attribute of sex and early expectations of pursuing a specific major were the two most important determinants of major field choice.

Data and Analyses

The data for this analysis were based on a subsample of 927 black college juniors and seniors who participated in a 1982 survey involving 2,100 black and white students that was conducted at Johns Hopkins University. Student participants were enrolled in eight four-year colleges and universities in the South Atlantic states. Five of these institutions were traditionally black, and three were traditionally white.

Students who participated in the study were officially majoring in one of 13 selected major fields: (1) mathematics; (2) chemistry; (3) physics; (4) biology; (5) accounting; (6) economics; (7) engineering; (8) social work; (9) psychology; (10) sociology; (11) nursing; (12) education; and (13) business management. Approximately 900 black students participated in the study. Students were asked to complete a 78-item questionnaire designed to assess various theories about their major field choice and career orientation.

Findings

Multivariate analysis was used to address the question of what factors determine the major field choice of black students. Differences in the educational and occupational attainment process have been found in previous research for males and females and for students in different types of colleges. Therefore, separate regression analyses were constructed for black males and black females and for blacks in traditionally white institutions (TWIs) and in public and private traditionally black institutions (TBIs).

Figure 9.1 presents the regression model and variables included in the analysis. Although a causal sequence is implied by the ordering of the independent variables in the first six panels in Figure 9.1, interest was primarily in the influence of the independent variables on the major dependent variable—college major. Therefore, relationships between independent variables were not examined. The major dependent variable, college major, is a dichotomous variable that can be viewed as majors of low versus high competitiveness or as nontraditional versus traditional majors. The biological, natural, and technical sciences and entrepreneurial fields (i.e., business and economics) are considered highly competitive majors. Recent data on earnings by major field were used to determine the relative demand or competitiveness of college majors. Nontraditional or highly competitive majors were coded 1, while more traditional and less competitive majors (i.e., education, the social sciences, and other fields) were coded 0.

Tables 9.1 to 9.3 present the results from regression analyses for the total sample of blacks, for black males and black females, and for blacks in TWIs and in private and public TBIs. Columns 1–5 of Table 9.1 show the influence of various independent variables when other independent variables are included or not included in the regression equations. Column 5 represents the "full" or complete equation, with all variables included. Collectively, these variables explain 31% of the variance in black students' college major choice. This improves on previous efforts (Thomas 1981) to explain

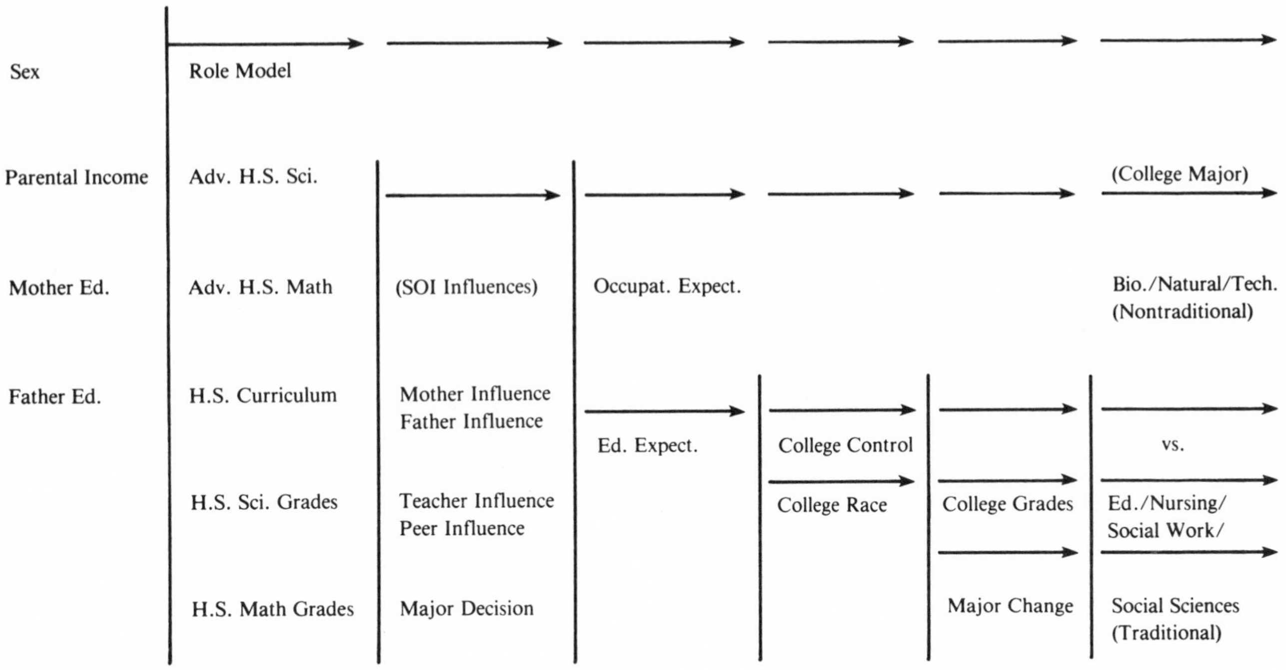

FIGURE 9.1.

Determinants of black college students' major field choice. The causal relationships among independent variables within panels are not examined because the primary interest is the impact of the independent variables on the major dependent variable—college major.

TABLE 9.1

Regression model of black students' college major choice — total sample ($N = 915$)[a]

Independent Variables	(1) College Major	(2) College Major	(3) College Major	(4) College Major	(5) College Major
Sex	.290[b]	.268	.224	.222	.213
Father's Education	.126	.095	.063	.066	.069
Mother's Education	.003*	−.018*	−.031*	−.033*	−.036*
Advanced Science		.050	.045*	.054	.056
Advanced Math		.119	.112	.126	.125
High School Math Grades		.157	.127	.119	.135
High School Science Grades		.016	.099	.111	.124
Educational Expectations			−.151	−.152	−.143
Occupational Expectations			.321	.328	.341
College Control				−.047*	−.058*
College Race				−.112	−.122
College Grades					.097
R^2	.106	.203	.289	.300	.308

[a]Analysis is based on SPSS subprogram regression option Pairwise Deletion. The number of cases ($N = 915$) is based on the N for the major dependent variable — major field choice.

[b]Coefficients are standardized regression coefficients.

*Coefficients are less than twice their standard error.

TABLE 9.2

**Regression model of black males' (N = 2,555) and
black females' (N = 659) college major choice[a]**

	Black Males	Black Females
Father's Education	.006[b]	.021
	.030*	.083
Mother's Education	−.025	−.002
	−.121*	−.009*
Advanced Science	.118	.062
	.111*	.048*
Advanced Math	.133	.202
	.094*	.129
High School Math	.021	.105
Grades	.042*	.178
High School Science	.068	.094
Grades	.115*	.143
Occupational Expectations	.007	.014
	.196	.390
Educational Expectations	−.097	−.091
	−.175	−.137
College	−.074	−.044
Control	−.085*	−.044*
College	−.137	−.181
Race	−.112*	−.124
College	.015	−.056
Grades	−.037	−.105
R^2	.112	.309

[a] Analysis is based on SPSS subprogram regression option Pairwise Deletion. The number of cases for black males ranged from 217 to 258 and for black females from 526 to 668.

[b] The top coefficients are the unstandardized values, and the bottom coefficients are the standardized (beta) coefficients.

* Coefficients are less than 1.5 times their standard error.

TABLE 9.3.

Regression model of black students' college major choice — Blacks in traditionally white colleges (N = 125), traditionally black private colleges (N = 362), and traditionally black public colleges (N = 428)[a]

	Blacks in White Colleges	Blacks in Priv. Black Colleges	Blacks in Pub. Black Colleges
Sex	.323[b]	.144	.309
	.299	.133	.274
Father's Education	−.016	.020	.036
	−.065*	.083*	.126
Mother's Education	.028	−.032	.005
	.017*	−.137	.017*
Advanced Science	.003	.110	.041
	.002*	.084	.031*
Advanced Math	.057	.167	.236
	.037*	.108	.128
High School Math Grades	.218	.056	.090
	.377	.099	.146
High School Sci. Grades	.010	.100	.082
	.014*	.153	.116
Educational Expectations	−.112	−.133	−.053
	−.175	−.184	−.080*
Occupational Expectations	.010	.016	.009
	.252	.443	.222
College Control	−.024		
	−.014*		
College Grades	−.042	−.007	−.080
	−.072*	−.014*	−.155
R²	.348	.352	.283

---

[a] Analysis is based on SPSS subprogram regression option Pairwise Deletion. The number of cases for blacks in white colleges ranged from 98 to 126; for blacks in private black colleges 296–367; and for blacks in black public colleges 332–434.

[b] The top coefficients are the unstandardized values, and the bottom coefficients are the standardized (beta) coefficients.

* Coefficients are less than 1.5 times their standard error.

black students' college majors using data from the National Longitudinal Survey of High School Seniors.

The two variables affecting black students' college major choice most strongly in this study were occupational expectations (.341) and sex (.213). Columns 1–5 show that both these variables have a significant indirect (Columns 1–4) and direct (Column 5) effect on college major. The positive regression coefficients for these variables indicate that students with high rather than low occupational expectations, and black males more so than black females, select majors in the biological, natural, and technical sciences.

Other variables significantly related to major field choice for the total sample of black students are high school math (.135) and science (.124) grade performance, having taken advanced high school math courses (.125), college racial composition (− .122), and college grade performance (.097). It is also interesting to note in Table 9.1 that college racial composition (i.e., attending a TWI) has a significant negative effect on black students' college major. This means that, among the present sample of blacks, students who attend TWIs are less likely to major in the biological, natural, and technical sciences than are their peers who attend TBIs. This finding was also reported in previous descriptive studies by Thomas, Alexander, and Eckland (1979) and Trent (1983).

Tables 9.2 and 9.3 present the results of separately analyzing the regression model for black males and black females and for blacks in public and private TBIs and in TWIs. Beginning with sex comparisons, the standardized values (the bottom coefficients in the table, which are appropriate for comparisons among variables within groups) in Table 9.2 show that occupational expectation most strongly influences the independent variables on major field choice for black males (.196) and for black females (.390). This is consistent with the hypothesis that early career interests and expectations are of primary importance in influencing students' college major choice. However, the unstandardized values in Table 9.2 (the top coefficients) show that the influence of occupational expectations on college major is twice as strong for black females (.014) as for black males (.007). Also, high school math (.178) and science (.043) grade performance and having taken advanced high school math (.202) significantly affect the major field choice of black females but not of black males. Thus Sells' 1976 and Fox's 1976 hypothesis regarding the critical "filtering role" that high school math preparation plays in sorting students into different career tracks appears more applicable to black females than to black males.

Another interesting sex difference in Table 9.2 is that the negative effects of attending a TWI on majoring in the natural and technical sciences are significant for black females but not for black males. Finally, comparing the R^2 values in Table 9.2 shows that the independent variables are three times more effective in explaining the college major selection process for black females ($R^2 = .31$) than for black males ($R^2 = .11$). An important question, which might be answered by replicating this study on additional samples of black males, is whether the comparatively low percentage of variance explained for black males and the lack of significance of some of the independent variables for black males are due to the limited number of black males participating in this study or to the unique characteristics of this particular sample of black males.

Table 9.3 presents parallel regression equations for black students enrolled in TWIs and in public and private TBIs. Three observations should be noted regarding these results. First, the model is somewhat less effective in explaining the college major selection process for blacks in public TBIs ($R^2 = .28$) than for blacks in private TBIs ($R^2 = .35$) and in TWIs ($R^2 = .35$). Second, the positive and significant effect of sex across all three equations shows that the black female disadvantage in majoring in the biological, natural, and technical sciences exists among black students in all three types of colleges. However, the unstandardized values suggest that the female disadvantage regarding enrollment in these majors is twice as great among blacks in TWIs (.323) and in public TBIs (.309) than among blacks in private TBIs (.144).

Descriptive data presented elsewhere (Thomas 1983) revealed distinct and traditional sex patterns for the present sample of blacks. These data showed that black females relative to black males showed a greater childhood interest in reading, cooking, and sewing but less interest in building and repairing and in working on science projects. Also, black females more often than black males aspired to be teachers and showed a greater interest than black males in careers that enabled them to help people. In addition, they were less likely to participate in high school science clubs or take advanced high school science or to view themselves as highly competitive in comparison to black males. These findings are useful in explaining the positive effects of sex on college major, which favors black males and indicates a disadvantage for black females. In addition, these observations suggest that the career aspirations and choices of black females are strongly affected by traditional sex-role socialization.

A third and final observation in Table 9.3 is that the influence of high academic performance in high school math on majoring in the natural and technical sciences is three times as great for black students in TWIs (.218) as for blacks in private TBIs (.056) and public TBIs (.090). Previous comparisons of the present sample of blacks and whites who participated in the study showed that black students reported lower grades in high school math than did whites. This observation and the importance of high school math performance for black students' access to math and science majors in TWIs may explain the relatively lower enrollment of black students in these majors in TWIs.

Summary and Conclusions

This study's findings clearly suggest that the process of choosing a college major for the present sample of black students is a relatively deliberate process that begins long before the point of college entry. The study shows that early career interests and occupational expectations, the descriptive status of sex, and high school course and academic preparation are important variables that influence black students' selection of a college major. Thus, as was hypothesized, noneconomic factors are more important variables in determining black students' major field choice than are economic factors.

A second observation that the study makes fairly obvious is that, in studying students' career orientations and aspirations, taking sex differences into consideration and examining students in different educational environments is important. Significant differences were found for males and females and for blacks in TBIs and in TWIs.

Third and finally, additional studies on the nature of race and sex socialization and on the college major selection process of black males are needed, given the low proportion of variance explained in the present model for black males and the importance of socialization for career attainment implied in this study and in previous research.

References

Admissions Testing Program of the College Board National College-Bound Seniors.
    1983   Princeton, N.J.: Admissions Testing Program.
Brown, F., & Stent, M.D.
    1977   *Minorities in U.S. Institutions of Higher Education.* New York: Praeger.

Cebula, R.J., & Lopes, J.
  1982 Determinants of student choice of undergraduate major field. *American Educational Research Journal, 19,* 303–312.

Davis, J.
  1966 *Undergraduate Career Decisions.* Chicago: Aldine.

Fox, L.
  1976 Women and the career relevance of mathematics and science. *School Science and Mathematics, 26,* 347–353.

Koch, J.V.
  1972 Student choice of undergraduate major field of study and private internal rates of return. *Industrial and Labor Relations Review, 26,* 680–685.

Lederer, D.A.
  1983 *Determinants of Womens' Choice of Undergraduate Major.* Manuscript, University of Delaware, Newark.

Sells, L.W.
  1976 *The Mathematics Filter and the Education of Women and Minorities.* Paper presented at the annual meeting of the American Association for the Advancement of Science, Boston.

Thomas, G.E.
  1980 Race and sex group equity in higher education: Institutional and major field enrollment statuses. *American Educational Research Journal, 17,* 171–181.

Thomas, G.E.
  1981 *Student and Institutional Characteristics as Determinants of Prompt College Graduation for Race and Sex Groups.* Report No. 313. Baltimore: Johns Hopkins University, Center for Social Organization of Schools.

Thomas, G.E.
  1983 *Understanding the Major Field Choice and Career Aspirations of Black College Students.* Atlanta: Southern Education Foundation.

Thomas, G.E., Alexander, K.L., & Eckland, B.K.
  1979 Access to higher education: The importance of race, sex, social class and academic credentials. *School Review, 87,* 133–156.

Trent, W.T.
  1983 *Race and Sex Differences in Degree Attainment and Major Field Distributions from 1975–76 to 1980–81.* Baltimore: Johns Hopkins University.

Chapter 10

FACTORS RELATED TO THE
POSTBACCALAUREATE CAREERS
OF BLACK GRADUATES OF
SELECTED FOUR-YEAR
INSTITUTIONS IN ALABAMA
Rhoda B. Johnson

This study's major objective was to examine the factors related to the postbaccalaureate career attainment of black graduates from four selected four-year Alabama institutions (a private, traditionally black institution, or TBI; a public TBI; a private, traditionally white institution, or TWI; and a public TWI). The study addressed two general questions: What are the actual career attainment levels of the black graduates, and what are the best predictors of career attainment — the characteristics of the graduates or the characteristics of the academic institutions? More specifically, the study examined the effect of college control (public–private), college racial composition (TBI–TWI), college grade average, and parents' socioeconomic status on educational attainment, occupational status, income level, and job satisfaction. Although a career means much more than a job or occupation, this study limited its analyses to those aspects of career attainment that could be most effectively evaluated and measured. The graduates' lifestyles, for example, were not examined.

In order to measure the impact of the independent variables (parents' socioeconomic status, college racial composition, college control, and graduates' grade average) on the dependent variables (occupational status, yearly income, job satisfaction, and additional education), questionnaires were mailed to a random sample of 1974–1978 graduates from the private and public TBIs and the public TWI; and the 24 black graduates of the private TWI. After follow-up mailings, 210 usable questionnaires were returned, a 65% overall return rate. Response rates by institutional

This chapter is based on a previously published research monograph by Rhoda B. Johnson: *Factors Related to the Postbaccalaureate Carrees of Black Graduates of Selected Four-Year Institutions in Alabama.* Atlanta: Southern Education Foundation, 1982.

characteristics were private TBI, 57%; public TBI, 63%; private TWI, 54%; and public TWI, 77%.

The data were analyzed using multivariate techniques. Since this study used both descriptive and inferential statistics, cross-tabulations were also included and discussed. Multiple regression was used to analyze the relationships between the dependent variables and the independent or predictor variables to determine if a significant amount of dependent variable variance could be explained by the set of predictor variables. The F-test was used to determine if the amount of variance explained was statistically significant.

The unstandardized regression coefficient, or b, was also computed. The unstandardized regression coefficient is the change in the dependent variable attributable to a unit change in the independent variable. The standardized regression coefficient, or beta, the fraction of the standard deviation of the dependent variable determined by the independent variable, was also reported. The statistical significance of the regression coefficient was measured using the standard errors of b weights. The regression coefficient must equal at least 1.96 times the standard error of b before the coefficient can be considered statistically significant.

Major Descriptive Findings

Graduates were more likely to be single than married; an overwhelming majority listed Alabama as their residence at 16 years of age (44% of private TBI graduates, however, came from other states); approximately 60% had three or more siblings; and the majority of their parents had less than a college degree.

Some characteristics that tended to differentiate the graduates were spouses' and mothers' education and racial composition of graduates' high schools. While the majority of spouses were at least college graduates, spouses of private TBI graduates were more likely to have a college or advanced degree. The mother's educational level is highest for students who attended the private TBI (29% have a college degree or more) and the public TWI (28% have a college degree or more). The private TBI and private TWI graduates were more likely to have attended a predominantly white high school (47 and 46%, respectively) as compared to 35% of the public TWI and 24% of the public TBI graduates.

The decision to attend college was likely to have been made in high school, but TWI graduates were more likely to report deciding in elementary school or earlier. This finding implies that the parents of TWI graduates may have played a large role in their decision to attend college, since the decision was made so early.

The university that granted the baccalaureate was the "first choice" for over 66% of the graduates. If the institution that granted the undergraduate degree was not the "first choice," then the choice was likely to have been a TBI. The exception was the private institution graduate whose "first choice" was more likely to be a TWI. The reasons for attending the college that granted the degree were numerous, but the reason rated as "very important" by the largest percentage of graduates was the "reputation" of the institution. Another important factor appears to be "closeness to home." If graduates are allowed to attend the institution of their choice, it is likely to be one close to home. Financial assistance was also rated as "very important" by a substantial percentage of graduates. A significantly greater percentage of TBI graduates indicated that "family and friends attending" the institution and "a large black population" played a role in their decision to attend the TBI.

While education was the most popular academic major (32% for TBIs and 23% for TWIs), other fields were also popular. TBI graduates were likely to have majored in business (22%), social sciences (19%), and natural sciences (11%). The most popular fields for TWI graduates were social sciences (18%), humanities (17%), and natural sciences (14%). Although the black graduates were majoring in the fields of study that have been traditional for blacks, they were also majoring in less traditional fields, such as natural sciences, humanities, and business.

While grade averages in major fields of study were similar, overall grade averages for TWI and TBI graduates were significantly different. Chi-square (x^2) was used to determine that the observed difference between TBI and TWI graduates' overall grade averages was statistically significant. TBI graduates were more likely to have A to $A-$ averages (12% compared to 1%), and TWI graduates were more likely to have C to $C+$ averages (45% compared to 29%). These findings indicate that TWI graduates did well in their major fields of study but less well in distribution requirements; 27% of TWI graduates had A to $A-$ averages in majors, but only 1% had A to $A-$ overall averages. This finding is important, since overall grade average is the first major factor that differentiates TWI and TBI graduates.

Graduates were asked to rate the main sources of information about jobs. The top two sources for TBI graduates were career placement offices (3.61) and faculty members (3.88); the main sources for TWI graduates were career placement (3.74) and fellow students (3.56). The two statistically significant differences between TBI and TWI graduates were that TWI graduates were more likely to rate fellow students as main sources of job information, and TBI graduates were more likely to rate recruiters as main sources of information.

These findings suggest that students at TBIs may have greater access to recruiters than black students at TWIs because recruiters interested in black employees are more likely to go where blacks are concentrated. The importance of the job information of fellow students suggests that black TWI graduates may have taken advantage of a broader range of occupational information available at the TWIs because of the diverse student population. TWI graduates may also trust the information of fellow students more than they trust other sources.

The significant correlation between college preparation and number of job offers suggests that graduates may feel that their colleges prepared them well if they received a number of job offers. The number of job offers was significantly correlated with overall grade average. The rating of how well college prepared the graduate did not appear to be related to overall grade average, however.

The correlations also provide additional support for the decision to include selected variables in the multivariate analyses. To understand more about the relationship between the variables, correlations are presented that indicate the best single predictors of overall grade average, job status, income level, and job satisfaction. Overall grade average was best predicted by TBI public and TWI public ($r = .21$ and $-.24$, respectively, $p < .05$). The best single predictor of occupational status of first job was overall grade average ($r = .20, p < .05$). The best predictors of first yearly income were first-job status and parents' socioeconomic status ($r = .32$ and $.20$, respectively, $p < .05$). Both present yearly income and present-job status were best predicted by first income and first-job status. Additional education was also significantly correlated to present-job status ($r = .29, p < .05$).

The graduates are employed full-time and are pursuing careers in the professional and technical fields or in managerial and administrative positions. Only a small percentage of graduates were unemployed and looking for work. This finding may, of course, be overly positive, given the fact that unemployed graduates may be less likely to return questionnaires. Over 70% of the graduates worked for professional and related services (e.g., offices of physicians, hospitals, health services, elementary or secondary schools, colleges and universities, and accounting services) or government agencies. Construction and manufacturing industries employed 21% of the natural science majors; 40% of humanities majors worked for communication (e.g., radio broadcasting and television) and entertainment industries (e.g., theater and motion pictures); and 30% of business majors were employed in a business-related field.

Major Inferential Findings

The best predictor of first-job occupational status was overall grade average. Each point increase in overall grade average is equal to a 7-point increase in occupational status. The best predictors of present-job status were first-job status and additional education. Obtaining additional education meant a 1-point increase, and each 10 points of first occupational status were equal to 4.6 points in additional status for the present job.

The finding that overall grade average was the best predictor of first-job occupational status is a particularly important one, given the previous finding that TWI graduates were less likely to have an A or B overall grade average. While there may be an advantage to graduating from a TWI, the tendency of black graduates to receive C to C+ overall grade averages may negate the positive impact of a TWI degree.

Starting annual incomes for the graduates were relatively low, even for the South. With the exception of natural science majors, over 40% of the graduates made less that $10,000 a year on their first full-time job. The best predictors of first yearly income were overall grade average and parents' socioeconomic status. For graduates earning $10,000 to $17,000 a year, an A average rather than a B average was worth $648. Each point increase in parents' socioeconomic status was worth a $39 increase in yearly income.

The best predictors of present income level were first yearly income and occupational status. Since the occupational status index is based on the incomes of occupations, in addition to prestige ratings, this finding is not surprising. The relationship between present income and additional education is unclear, since many graduates are still in graduate school or advanced training programs. The relatively low income levels for the graduates may also reflect the fact that many are also in school while they are employed. The reported data, however, reflect the incomes of only those graduates who indicated that they were employed full-time. The fact that many graduates are obtaining additional education may indicate that they are not satisfied with their present income levels.

The findings suggest that the best predictors of job satisfaction were present yearly income and grade average in major. The higher the yearly income and the higher the grade average in major, the higher the satisfaction level with the present job. Impressions gained from reading comments from graduates about their satisfaction with life since graduation indicate that many graduates were not satisfied because they were not working in their major field. These results suggest that graduates who did well in their major areas may be more competent, or at least feel more competent, in their jobs. This competence may be rewarded by employers, and graduates may feel more satisfied with their jobs.

Policy Implications

Although there may be some advantages to receiving a degree from a private institution or TWI, the major factor affecting initial entry into a career was overall grade average. Given the importance of overall grade average, the general distribution requirements should be reviewed. What is it about TWI general distribution courses that make them so difficult? Is it course content, class size, or the lack of emphasis placed on them by academic advisers? Since college emphasis is likely to be placed on major requirements, understanding how employers evaluate the grade averages of prospective employees might be beneficial. If employers are more concerned about overall grade averages than major grade averages, universities and colleges should be the first to know and should relate this information to their students.

Based on the research in the area, it must be concluded that a complex relationship exists among the following variables: characteristics of graduates, characteristics of undergraduate institutions, parents' status, and postbaccalaureate career attainment. Receiving a college degree does seem, however, to be crucial to higher occupational status and higher income levels. Employers appear to use the degree as an indicator of a particular worker's potential performance or value. The current retrenchments from the goals of equal access to higher education may mean that the current trend of upward mobility for blacks could quite easily become a trend toward downward mobility. Policymakers, who are concerned that the progress made over the past decades not be jeopardized, must make sure that any changes in the higher education systems provide, at the least, comparable access to education for black students.

PART 4

Social and Psychological Dimensions
of the Learning Environment:
Experiences of Blacks on College Campuses

It is well known that the past decade has witnessed a phenomenal increase in black student enrollment in colleges and universities. For black students to persist and graduate is yet another matter. During the college years, students search for self-awareness; they want to know who they are, what to value, and what to believe in. Many experience more independence than ever before and must make decisions that determine whether they will persist to graduation, transfer to another institution, fail academically, or simply drop out. When their experiences are overlaid with new relationships with people of other races, the college years become enormously complicated.

The chapters in this section address situations that bear on this theme. Yvonne Abatso in Chapter 11 describes an experiment designed to determine variables that help students to cope with their environment. In Chapter 12, Walter Allen contrasts the demographic characteristics of black students who are attending TWIs and TBIs and describes how they feel about their institutions. James Blackwell, in his study of graduate and professional students, sheds light in Chapter 13 on networking and mentoring, phenomena that have been part of the informal structure of graduate and professional education for years. The focus of growing research interest, these practices merit study as valuable resources for black students.

Chapter 11

COPING STRATEGIES: RETAINING BLACK STUDENTS IN COLLEGE

Yvonne R. Abatso

Astin's 1968 classic study identified four particular college environmental variables that differentiated among institutions — the peer, classroom, administrative, and physical environments. Baird (1980) used perceptual measures to obtain social and psychological information about college environments from the people with whom students interact — other students, faculty, administrators, and staff. It appears that the undergraduates' attitudinal and behavioral changes may depend greatly on the kind of institutional interactions they experience. Pace and Baird (1966) found that the overall college environment influenced students' general evaluations of their progress and development during college, whereas participation in small subcultures, such as academic and peer groups, influenced most specific attitudes and behavior.

Another perceptual approach to assessing learning environments used essays written by black and white students to develop an instrument that was administered to samples of black and white students. The results indicated differential dimensions of the university environment as viewed by black and white students; black students assessed the university more negatively. The white dimensions were an impersonal academic atmosphere, administrative neglect, social interaction, racism, non-classroom-related activities, and attempts at communication. Similarly, other researchers (Tucker & Yates 1976; Webster 1977) have found racial differences in the perception of various aspects of the college learning environment.

These findings suggest the merit of studying aspects of the campus's psychosocial environment as perceived by students in relationship to the problem of alarmingly high attrition for black college students. Tinto

This chapter is based on a previously published research monograph by Yvonne R. Abatso: *Coping Strategies: Retaining Black Students in College.* Atlanta: Southern Education Foundation, 1982.

(1975) has suggested the need for a research design that permits understanding the interaction of factors that contribute not only to dropping out but also to staying in. Many previous studies have demonstrated the obvious, namely, that student academic achievement is positively related to whether they continue in school. However, recent research shows that this is not the only variable influencing attrition, since there is a higher-than-predicted attrition rate among scholastically high-achieving students (Astin 1973). Rossman and Kick (1970) discovered findings of perhaps greater relevance for black students: that moderate commitment to a particular college along with high academic competence characterized persisters as compared to dropouts, who displayed low competence and low commitment.

Persistence, then, can be conceptualized both as an outcome of personal characteristics and as a result of a process of interactions within the college's academic social system. Scott (1971) and Spady (1971) found that individual perception of integration into the college's social system related most directly to persistence. Dropouts perceived themselves as having less social interaction than did college persisters. Dropping out, then, appears to result at least partially from a lack of congruence between the individual and the institution's social climate.

This investigation was based on a multidimensional conceptual framework that included personality–expectational variables, achievement variables, and social interactional variables.

Purpose of the Study

This research study, building on previous studies, was designed to address three interrelated inquiries:

1. To discover if there existed a coping personality, that is, identifiable personality traits, expectations, and attitudes related to higher academic achievement and attrition. Fundamental to this inquiry was the hypothesis that academic achievement was a mediating factor in retention for black students.

2. To discover if there are patterns of interaction between black students and the college's academic–social system that are associated with higher retention for blacks. Since personal attributes account only partially for persistence and attrition, the college environment was explored, using the black student's perception of it as a frame of reference. Interaction with various aspects of the institution was assessed in an attempt to understand the way such involvement affects the retention behavior of black students.

3. To discover if coping strategies relevant to the process of mastering academic requirements facilitate achievement and persistence for black students in higher education.

The following hypotheses were proposed:

1. A personality syndrome associated with high academic coping for black college students consists of certain personality variables. Self-concept of ability, locus of control, and expectation of success and failure are the most important discriminators, in that order, between high and low copers.

2. High achievement, along with positive interaction with the college environment, will contribute to a discriminating function that distinguishes students who persist in college from those who drop out.

3. Teaching coping strategies to an experimental group will lead to higher achievement and retention rates than those of a control group.

Research Design

The research plan consisted of a longitudinal in-depth survey and an experimental design. Since the highest attrition rate occurs after the freshman year, the study focused on entering students for 16 months. The entire freshman class of 265 students from a small, private, traditionally black liberal arts university in the South was administered self-report battery Number 1 during freshman orientation week. The battery consisted of the following variables and instruments:

I. Student Information Form, which assessed the following personality variables and collected background, education, and demographic data.

   A. Self-Concept of Ability (Brookover Self-Concept of Ability Scale 1965).

   B. Locus of Control (Gurin's Adaptation of the Rotter Internal/External Locus of Control Scale).

   C. Expectancy of Success and Failure (Mehrabian Achievement Motivation).

   D. Perception of the Opportunity Structure (Landis & Scarpitti Awareness Scale of Limited Opportunities 1965).

   E. Coping (Student Information Questionnaire—Part II, Abatso 1980). This variable was operationalized as behavior related to how students attempt to master the academic demands of the classroom, namely, the conditions that they set up and the ways in which they attempt to learn and study.

    F. Verbal Ability (California Achievement Test, Form 19, Vocabulary and Reading Comprehension).

Recent previous research indicated that self-esteem and conformity were not crucial to this inquiry, but they were included in the battery.

  II. 1980 Freshman Follow-Up Form. A second self-report form was given to the 1980 freshman cohort of 265 students at the start of the sophomore year. It included two versions, one for on-campus returnees and another for those who transferred or dropped out of school. Achievement was measured by a student's total grade point average on a four-point scale at the end of the freshman year or at the time of dropping out.

 III. The study's experimental component (Hypothesis 2) was designed to determine if coping strategies would improve achievement and retention for those identified early in the freshman year as low copers. The Student Information Questionnaire — Part II, administered during freshman orientation week, identified three coping groups: low, middle, and high. From among the low copers, an experimental group was exposed to 12 one-hour weekly sessions of intervention. A control group did not receive any treatment. At the end of 12 weeks, the questionnaire was again given to the experimental and control groups.

Results

A Coping–Retention Personality

The low and high groups differed both quantitatively and qualitatively in the strategies they reported using. Qualitatively, low copers used fewer strategies and frequently attempted individual action without soliciting the aid of others when confronted with academic difficulty. They reported minimal or no contact initiated with instructors of classes in which they were experiencing difficulty. A frequent response to poor grades was to "shake it off and make an *A* next time," without suggesting a concrete, workable plan for accomplishing that objective. Because they did not adhere to study schedules, they admitted that they abandoned all time-management attempts and simply studied when they felt like it. In spite of this behavior, low copers held unrealistic grade expectations, thereby setting themselves up for intense disappointment.

In contrast, high copers maintained a larger repository of specific strategies from which to select, depending on the situation. They reported more problem-solving behavior, greater initiative and active engagement of the environment, frequent contact with teachers, and greater use of available assistance and resources. Neither group showed much familiarity with the productive use of group study.

No significant differences occurred among the three coping groups in their expectations as evidenced by their initial freshmen expectancies about achievement, rank in class, or advanced degrees. Nor was there a significant difference among the coping groups on the Mehrabian Instrument of *N* achievement motivation. However, there was a significant difference between low and high copers on the Verbal Ability Scale of the California Achievement Test, indicating that students with higher verbal ability were also higher copers. Given differences in verbal ability and knowledge about study advice, all students, including low copers, shared similar expectations about academic performance and educational aspirations. Clearly, these expectations were unrealistic for low copers. In fact, low copers held the highest expectations about rank in class and advanced degrees, followed by the high copers and then the middle copers. These students all expressed high expectations and aspirations.

It had been hypothesized that three personality variables would discriminate the high copers from the low copers. However, only one of these personality attitudes, locus of control, significantly separated the two groups. The high copers, who demonstrated a greater sense of internality, expressed more self-accountability and control over the events in their lives. These were students who believed that their own efforts greatly influenced what happened to them as compared to students who perceived outcomes to be influenced more by external persons and events.

There were important differences between low and high copers in three dimensions of personality investigated. Self-esteem, conformity, and perception of the opportunity structure proved to be significant discriminators between the groups. Whereas neither group had very low self-esteem, was excessively conforming, or perceived the opportunity structure as extremely closed, high copers revealed a higher sense of confidence and satisfaction in themselves. This is an interesting finding because often there is relatively little differentiation in global self-esteem among black students on entry into the same college.

Low copers expressed hope for the highest academic performance and more advanced degrees. This apparent discrepancy may indicate internalization of the necessity for education and advanced degrees as an instrument of upward mobility and the quality of life they desire, but it also includes the uncertainty of one's ability to obtain them. The low copers were more external in their locus of control, indicating the importance of external factors in shaping outcomes and events. Low copers may compensate for their lower self-esteem by espousing excessively high expectations. Since they also hold to a more closed view of the opportunity structure, their attitudes combine with higher externality and greater conformity to mediate feelings of self-esteem, resulting in a lower sense of adequacy and self-satisfaction.

In contrast, the high coper's responses were more consistent throughout, expressing high self-esteem and a sense of autonomy over their lives, less need to conform, and a view of the opportunity structure as being more open to them.

Academic–Social Interaction on Campus

Through the use of discriminant analysis procedures, those particular factors of college environment positively associated with retention were identified as support from the college administration, satisfaction with personal study habits, and satisfaction with campus dormitory and food services. A student's perceived support from the administration was a discriminator between those who persisted and those who dropped out. More students who expressed greater satisfaction with administration representatives and policy persisted at the university.

Satisfaction with personal study habits also discriminated among the two groups at less than the .05 level. Somewhat unusual was dissatisfaction with dormitory and food service as a discriminator. Less satisfied students persisted, while those expressing greater satisfaction dropped out. Other school environment factors were not significant discriminators between returnees and nonreturnees.

A discriminant analysis run on retention status included all major variables in the study—personality–expectancy, achievement, and academic–social interactional variables. One personality variable, locus of control, contributed to this set, with returnees displaying an internal locus of control. This sense of control over the events in one's life powerfully influences retention. Returnees appear to put greater emphasis on their own efforts to succeed. Throughout the analyses, high final grade point averages characterized the persisters. When dropouts were asked why they did not return, two major reasons emerged: academic problems and financial problems.

In the total discriminant analysis, finances replaced study habits as a discriminator, with returnees showing moderate satisfaction with their financial status. Students with the greatest financial problems dropped out; those with the fewest problems enrolled elsewhere; and those at a moderate level remained at their original college.

Satisfaction with dormitory and food services again separated the groups, with persisters expressing less satisfaction (but obviously not leaving in spite of it), and dropouts expressing more satisfaction (but not staying because of it). The range for both groups was between sometimes satisfied and seldom satisfied. So even though it emerged as a statistical discriminator, its meaning, if any, is unclear.

Perception of the administration as supporting a student's academic learning and development also discriminated among the returnees and non-returnees, with the returnees perceiving the administration as upholding and promoting their academic growth interests.

As predicted, high achievement, along with a pattern of campus interaction that perceives the administration as supporting growth and development, enhanced retention. A moderate level of financial satisfaction is necessary to retain black college students.

Experimental Study–Teaching of Coping Strategies

Two major questions were of concern — did teaching coping strategies result in higher achievement, and did participants in the experimental group have higher retention rates in the university? A positive relationship developed between precoping and postcoping scores (preintervention and postintervention). For those who were taught strategies, there was a stronger relationship upon completion between their skill level and their final grade point average than was true before intervention. The teaching sessions significantly affected postcoping skills regardless of their entry-level coping skills. However, quite expectedly, the higher the precoping level, the higher the achievement level, since students would initially bring more effective study skills to bear on mastering course content.

No significant differences occurred between the experimental and control groups in achievement after controlling for the effect of precoping. Since postcoping skills do strongly relate to grade point average, it would appear that a longer intervention period is necessary. The limitation of only 12 weekly sessions and the time lag involved in becoming proficient at a newly learned skill at least partially could explain the lack of statistical significance found in relationship to achievement. Seventy percent of the experimental group persisted at the university, compared to 45% of the control group. Although the significance level was greater than .05, it represented an important trend, particularly when coupled with a similar trend found in achievement.

Summary and Discussion

Coping strategies did relate to achievement, and final achievement significantly influenced retention, but they did so in concert with school environment factors that reflected on an institution's highest commitment to its black students — administrative support of their academic growth and development. Students who persisted displayed personality attitudes that gave them a sense of control over the events in their lives. The more students knew how to interact successfully with their college environment, the more one could expect them to continue pursuing their academic goals, given financial resources. Recommendations for institutions of higher education enrolling black students include the following:

1. An institution of higher education wanting to retain black students should make a commitment to their academic development, from the highest levels of the administration down to those who represent and translate administrative policy and intent to students, faculty, and staff. The commitment should express itself in a self-study of every aspect of campus life that has an impact on black freshmen.

2. The commitment should extend to developing financial resources for those with extreme need who otherwise would of necessity drop out.

3. The selection of faculty teaching black freshman students should take into account the positive effect of teacher rapport and relationships as instruments of teacher effectiveness. Since students experiencing academic difficulty often are reluctant to approach faculty, overtures by faculty may assist a freshman to use available campus resources.

References

Astin, A.W.
1968 *The College Environment.* Washington, D.C.: American Council on Education.

Astin, A.W.
1973 Student persistence: Some stay, some don't — why? *College and University, 48,* 298–306.

Baird, L.
1980 *Understanding Student and Faculty Life.* San Francisco: Jossey-Bass.

Haan, N.
1963 Proposed model ego functioning: Coping and defense mechanisms in relationship to I.Q. change. *Psychological Monographs: General and Applied, 77,* 1–23.

Pace, C. R., & Baird, L.
1966 Attainment patterns in the environmental press of college subcultures. In T. M. Newcomb & E. K. Wilson (Eds.) *College Peer Groups: Problems and Prospects for Research,* pp. 215–243. Chicago: Aldine.

Pantages, T., & Creedon, C.
1978 Studies of college attrition. 1950–1975. *Review of Educational Research, 48.* 49–101.

Rossman, J. E., & Kick, B. A.
1970 Factors related to persistence and withdrawal among university students. *Journal of Counseling Psychology, 17,* 56–62.

Scott, J.
1971 *A Study of the Relationship Between Students' Personal Perception of Environment Press and Attrition in a Two Year College.* Ph.D. dissertation, University of Missouri, Columbia.

Spady, W.
1971 Dropouts from higher education: Toward an empirical model. *Interchange, 2,* 38–62.

Tinto, V.
1975 Dropouts from higher education: A theoretical synthesis of recent research. *Review of Educational Research, 45,* 89–125.

Tucker, M. B., & Yates, F.
1976 Success expectations and preferences for individual and collaborative learning among black and white college students. *Journal of Negro Education, 45,* 295–305.

Webster, D.
1977 *A Comparison of Problems Perceived by Minority and White University Students.* Washington, D.C.: ERIC ED148 985.

Chapter **12** COLLEGE IN BLACK AND WHITE:
BLACK STUDENT EXPERIENCES
ON BLACK AND WHITE
CAMPUSES
Walter R. Allen

Over the past 25 years, black student patterns of college attendance
have shifted so that the majority now attend traditionally white institutions.
Sizable numbers of black students also continue graduating from traditionally black colleges and universities. Previous research shows that black
students on white campuses are disadvantaged relative to their white peers
in terms of persistence rates, attainment of aspirations, academic achievement levels, enrollment in advanced degree programs, and psychosocial adjustment levels. Compared to their peers on white campuses, black students
on black campuses generally have lower family socioeconomic status,
poorer academic backgrounds, and higher college grade point averages.
Unlike black students on white campuses, these students report less anx-
iety–alienation, show greater relative academic gains, and have higher persistence rates. It appears that black and white campuses represent
qualitatively different educational environments for black students, with
each having positive as well as negative consequences.

This research compares black student characteristics, experiences, and
outcomes on black and white campuses. The study's purpose is to examine
connections between black student background factors, institutional context, and interpersonal relationships and student adjustment/achieve-
ment/aspiration levels. The study includes 16 campuses nationally, 8 of
which are traditionally black: Morgan State University (Baltimore),
Jackson State University (Jackson, Mississippi), Florida Agricultural and
Mechanical University (Tallahassee), North Carolina Agricultural and
Technical University (Greensboro), Texas Southern University (Houston),

This summary is excerpted from a report in preparation for the Southern Education Foundation monograph series. The research was funded by grants from the Southern Education Foundation, the Ford Foundation, and the Charles S. Mott Foundation.

North Carolina Central University (Durham), Southern University (Baton Rouge), and Central State University (Wilberforce, Ohio). The remaining 8 campuses are traditionally white: University of Michigan (Ann Arbor), University of North Carolina (Chapel Hill), University of California (Los Angeles), State University of New York (Stony Brook), Arizona State University (Tempe), Memphis State University, University of Wisconsin (Madison), and Eastern Michigan University (Ypsilanti).

To date, three data collections have been made on these campuses. In 1981, cross-sectional data were collected from black undergraduate and graduate–professional students attending the traditionally white universities. In 1982, data were collected from first-year black undergraduate and graduate–professional students on the white campuses in preparation for a longitudinal study. In 1983, cross-sectional data were collected from black students attending the traditionally black universities. A longitudinal component was incorporated, thus effectively combining the cross-sectional and longitudinal data collections into a single operation for the black schools.

The research design involved research collaborators on each participating campus. Research collaborators were paid an honorarium for assisting with the data collection. Research collaborators and their students were granted access to the data for purposes of writing for scholarly publication and presenting at professional meetings as an additional incentive to participate in the study. Data were collected using mailed questionnaires, which students returned to the University of Michigan for coding and computer tabulation. Questionnaires focused on student family background, prior educational experiences, current educational experiences, and personal attitudes. The self-administered questionnaires took 20 to 30 minutes to complete. Selection of students for participation in the study was random, guided by lists of currently enrolled students supplied by the various university registrars' offices. For each campus, a systematic random sample was drawn, and selected students received the questionnaire and four follow-up mailings. The 1981 data collection included 695 undergraduate and 353 graduate–professional students, for an overall response rate of 30%. The 1982 data collection included 902 undergraduate and 407 graduate–professional students, for an overall response rate of 45%. The 1983 data collection included 833 undergraduate and 247 graduate–professional students, for an overall response rate of 25%. Procedures to increase the 1983 response rate are currently under way. At the same time, the first follow-up data collection on the 1982 student sample is in progress.

Overview of Research Findings: Undergraduate Students

For clarity's sake, this summary of research findings from the National Study of Black College Students is organized into two categories: findings from the traditionally white institutions and findings from the traditionally black institutions.

Traditionally White Institutions (1981 Sample)

College Adjustment and Academic Performance

The sample consisted of 240 males (35%) and 455 females (65%), who represented the various levels of enrollment — 27% freshmen, 23% sophomores, 25% juniors, and 25% seniors. The students were single (88%), childless (90%), and between 19 and 21 years old (61%). Overall, the students' adjustment to university life seemed awkward and generally unsatisfying. Nearly 62% reported little or no integration into general student campus activities. In addition, 45% reported that campus extracurricular activities did not adequately reflect their interests.

The majority of students were doing relatively well academically; 10% reported grade point averages (GPAs) of C (2.0) or less, and approximately 45% reported GPAs of $C+$ (2.76) or higher. However, fewer than 3% reported GPAs above $B+$ (3.5), a significant shift from the 37% with $B+$ averages in high school. One-third of the students set their ultimate educational goal at the bachelor's degree level; another third aspired to master's-level degrees; and the final third sought terminal, professional (M.D., J.D., or D.D.S.) or doctoral degrees. While educational goals expressed by students were evenly distributed, occupational aspirations were uniformly high. Nearly 85% expected to move into upper-level, white-collar professional and administrative positions.

Student Backgrounds

The backgrounds of black students in this national study suggest that popularized stereotypes bear little resemblance to actual characteristics of black college students across the country. Sixty-five percent of students in the sample grew up in two-parent households. Only 15% were from families with annual incomes of $8,000 or less. Nearly half were from families with incomes above $21,000 per year. The pursuit of education appears to have been encouraged and practiced in these students' families, as evidenced by parents' high educational attainments and the even higher attainment of their siblings. Twenty-eight percent of the respondents' fathers, 29% of their mothers, and 39% of their siblings attended college.

High School Education Experiences

Black students in this study entered college with established records of high academic achievement. Over half (67%) reported high school GPAs of *B* or better. Of all students, 37% reported GPAs of *B* + (3.5) or better. Over half the students ranked in the top 10% of their graduating class, with over one-fourth ranking in the top 5%.

The high school years did not, however, prepare these students for the reality of being a racial minority in school settings. Fewer than 17% attended high schools where black enrollment was 10% or less. On the contrary, over half these students attended black majority high schools (60% or more black) prior to entering their respective universities. The shift in school racial composition from high school to college was significant, since, apart from those at Memphis State University, black students in this sample represented less than 10% of the total student enrollment on their respective campuses.

Campus Interpersonal Relations

On entering college, these students were forced to cope with the unfamiliar situation of being in a minority, not in a majority as they were in high school. We see considerable evidence of social adjustment difficulties, which undoubtedly have negative consequences for black student outcomes. Half the students pointed to lack of money and inadequate high school preparation as the most serious barriers to more black students being admitted and deciding to attend the university. Seventy-nine percent of the students believed there were inadequate numbers of black students at their universities. As for seeking black faculty and/or staff to aid in easing adjustment problems, these students encountered additional problems. Black student contact with black faculty and staff was at best limited. Sixty-seven percent of the students reported little or no exposure to black faculty and staff. Most students expressed the need for an increased number of black faculty and staff.

Of necessity, black students must rely on white students and professors for help in making their adjustment to campus life. In this connection, a majority (80%) of the black students reported that white peers only sometimes showed high regard for their academic abilities. However, over half (87%) also reported that white students sometimes or often avoided interacting with them socially outside the academic halls. Just under two-thirds (59%) reported that white students treated them as equals. Academic competition among students at participating universities was reportedly intense. Nevertheless, a majority reported that this competition either did not affect them or was positive in its effects.

In the area of race relations, black students did not fare well. Fifty-eight percent reported having experienced at least one incident of racial discrimination. Of this group, 60% cited racial insults and negative racial attitudes as the most common forms of discrimination encountered.

More than 60% of the black students characterized general black student relations with white faculty (60%) and white staff (63%) on their campus as negative. However, 83% reported good to excellent personal relationships with white faculty, 88% with white staff, and 80% with white students. Thus, the view was one of generally poor race relations on the campus, although these students claimed to maintain positive relationships as individuals with whites on the campus in question. Interesting patterns were apparent in black students' evaluations of their largely white faculties. Eighty percent reported professors as evidencing some difficulty in relating to them, and 80% also reported that professors commonly avoided interacting with them outside class. While a significant portion of the students reported professors as encouraging them to pursue advanced studies (43%) and demonstrating concern about their success (51%), over half expressed doubts concerning professorial fairness in evaluating black student academic performance.

There appear to be three major classes of problems and difficulties most commonly faced by black students at these white universities. Twenty-one percent reported academic problems, 28% referred to problems of cultural adjustment or feelings of social isolation, and 18% reported problems with racism.

Campus Support Services

Black students' evaluations of university support services were largely positive. With respect to finances, most identified parental earnings and grants-in-aid as major sources of funding for college. Twenty-one percent of the students reported not having received any financial aid from their universities. Roughly a third judged their financial aid as adequate. A higher proportion (45%) appeared satisfied with the caliber of academic advising received, although a third expressed dissatisfaction. Three-quarters of the students found campus remedial, tutorial, and academic services somewhat helpful. Similarly, half the students identified some campus office, program, or organization as having been particularly helpful to their academic and/or social adjustment.

Even though evaluations of support services were largely positive, 75% of the students knew of other black students who left the university for reasons other than graduation. Among the reasons cited, the majority (70%) reported either lack of money or academic problems as the reasons students left.

Student Attitudes

Black students in this study exhibited high self-concept. On most points of evaluation, mean scores were above average. The points evaluated were leadership ability, self-confidence, popularity, physical well-being, community perception of the student, closeness with family, high school teachers' evaluations, popularity with the opposite sex, and professors' evaluations. On all points, well over 50% of the student sample rated themselves as above average or high.

Summary and Conclusion

Black students in this study entered college with established histories of academic achievement, measured by high school GPA and rank in graduating class. These black students came from high schools where blacks were the majority. They entered universities where blacks were a decided minority. At these universities, they received, at best, limited exposure to black faculty and staff primarily because so few blacks are employed in such positions.

Students reported relatively good relations with their white peers in the classroom. Outside the academic walls, however, they had little or no interaction with the same white students. There was intense academic competition among students at these universities. For the most part, black students reported either being unaffected by this competition or being positively motivated as a result.

Students reported frequent exposure to racial discrimination. In general, students reported fairly poor relationships with white faculty, staff, and students on their campus. These relationships were rated good to excellent when the students evaluated them in terms of their personal interactions with white faculty, staff, and students.

The relationship between white professors and black students was variable. Students reported white faculty as having difficulty relating to them and tending to avoid interacting with black students outside class. Most students believed that white faculty members were concerned about their success but felt that they sometimes evaluated black student academic performance unfairly.

Socially, black students were at a severe disadvantage. Even though black organizations sponsored activities, over half the students reported, at best, infrequent participation in such activities. The students called overwhelmingly for recruiting and admitting more black students.

Most students were reasonably satisfied with the amount of financial aid received. However, over a third felt that the quality of other support services (e.g., academic advising) was less than satisfactory. The students' educations were mostly financed by their parents or by the students' own incomes. Despite obvious problems, black students in the sample clearly possessed high perceptions of "self."

Higher education is oriented around two fundamental assumptions. First, it is assumed that students will enter college with adequate preparation and sufficient self-motivation to ensure their ability to take maximum advantage of the opportunities afforded for learning and advancement. Second, it is assumed that universities will provide optimal settings (in academic and social–psychological terms) for talented minds to find ample opportunity to develop to their fullest potential. Therefore, under normal circumstances, one expects to find symbiotic relationships between students and their universities. The relationship should be one in which each feeds the needs of the other to the mutual benefit of both. It is evident from these and other data that black students in this sample were not achieving such satisfactory relationships with their universities. This disjuncture occurs sufficiently often to cause great concern.

In looking for plausible explanations of this seeming disjuncture between black students and their universities, we are forced to admit that the implied partnership, while real, is an unequal one. That is, while black students bear some responsibility for how they fare at these universities, theirs is not the pivotal role. The educational missions of these public universities charge them with responsibility for developing and implementing strategies that provide for the effective education of the nation's (and their respective state's) diverse population. Since these universities are the vehicles through which students matriculate, ultimate responsibility and resources for making this transition by black students (and all students, for that matter) a smooth one rests with the institution and its officers, faculty, and staff.

The task confronting interested researchers, practitioners, and policymakers at this point is to identify factors and formulate strategies that will help improve the educational experiences and outcomes of black students in higher education. Clearly, a tremendous gap exists between black student needs on white campuses, as revealed in this research, and the currently existing policies and programs at the respective universities. Without continuous effort, long-term investment of resources and sincere commitment, traditionally white universities will not reverse the patterns of declining enrollments–rising attrition rates that result in reduced numbers of black students attending and graduating from the nation's colleges.

Traditionally Black Institutions (1983 Sample)

The sample consisted of 388 male (44%) and 497 female (56%) students spread across all the college levels — 12% freshmen, 19% sophomores, 27% juniors, and 40% seniors. These students were mainly single (88%) and childless (83%). Most came from families with four children or less, and 61% came from stable, religious, low-income families. The modal income was less than $8,000 per year, and the median income was approximately $16,500.

About one-quarter of the parents (fathers, 23%; mothers, 27%) had at least a high school diploma, while 34% of fathers and 41% of mothers had some college education or a college degree. Siblings were equally well educated — 69% had some college education or a college degree.

Sixty percent of the students in this study attended relatively large high schools. Only about 40% attended schools with 700 or fewer students. Fourteen percent attended schools with 700 to 1,000 students; 18% attended schools with 1,000–2,500 students; 6% attended schools with 2,500–3,500 students; 5% attended schools with over 3,500 students.

While most of the students attended integrated high schools, only 21% attended schools where blacks were a definite minority (less than 20% of the school's population), and only 11% attended schools where blacks were a definite majority (more than 60%). The others went to schools where blacks constituted between 21 and 60% of the population, while 28% could not estimate the percentage of blacks in their schools.

The students reported being fairly well prepared academically for college. Ninety-four percent rated the quality of education they got up to high school as either excellent (13%), very good (37%), or good (45%). Only 6% thought their precollege preparation was poor or very poor (0.1%). Ninety-five percent reported being in the upper 50% of their senior class. However, only 9% of these students reported being in the upper 5% at graduation. Eighteen percent said they were in the upper 10%, 23% in the upper 20%, and another 23% in the upper 30%. Only 5% reported being in the lower 50% of their senior class in high school. These ranks compared favorably with the 67% who reported that their high school teachers would evaluate them to be average, above average, or high compared to others in their respective senior classes. Specifically, 26% thought they would be rated high, and 41% thought they would be rated above average, while only 27% thought they would be rated below average by their high school senior class teachers. The model and median high school GPA was 3.00, and the average was 2.95. The GPA for females was 3.00, whereas that for males was 2.89. This difference is statistically significant (t = 2.59, p = .009, df = 743).

While students in this study showed high academic aspirations, their choice of school was predominantly determined by the geographic location of schools (probably proximity to current residence). Nineteen percent of the students chose a school to attend because of its location, 16% because of the programs offered, 15% because of financial considerations, and another 15% because they preferred a black setting. Irrespective of the reasons for the choice of school, it was extremely important for 78% and very important for 17% to get a college degree. This commitment and aspiration to education was buttressed by the students' responses on how far they intended to go educationally. Specifically, fewer than 1% intended to stop before getting at least a bachelor's degree. About one-third (31%) wanted to get at least a bachelor's degree, another third (34%) a master's degree, 16% a professional degree, and 17% a Ph.D. These students were highly motivated, as evidenced by 61% wanting to be recognized as the top person in their field. They were also quite self-confident; 35% rated themselves high in self-confidence, another 35% above average, and 26% as average. Only 4% of the students felt they lacked self-confidence. This pattern was followed closely by the students' self-rating of personal leadership abilities. Sixty-three percent said they were either high (26%) or above average (37%) on this trait. Seventy-five percent of these students rated themselves as high or above-average people, generally speaking.

In retrospect, the students who participated in this study came from stable, low-income families, which nevertheless had consistent and pervading commitments to education. The students attended fairly large, integrated high schools, and about 20% were a definite minority in such schools. The students considered the quality of education received in high school as very good, and they were characterized by very high educational aspirations, self-confidence, and leadership abilities. However, only a relatively small percentage of these students graduated near the top of their senior high school class. Interestingly, the major determinant of college choice was location rather than the school's academic reputation. Other important determinants were programs offered, financial considerations, and preference for a black setting. In the following section, the experiences of these students in traditionally black colleges are examined.

College Experience

Students reported a very cordial relationship at college with all faculty (black and nonblack), all students, and all staff, though to a lesser extent with nonblack staff. Specifically, 96% of the sample rated their relationships with black students as excellent or good. Ninety-four percent rated their relationships with black faculty as excellent or good, whereas 85% had an excellent or good relationship with black staff. With regard to nonblack personnel, 75% of the students had an excellent or good relationship with nonblack students, 85% with nonblack faculty, and 70% with nonblack staff.

This very positive relationship is further supported by the report that only 19% experienced any form of racial discrimination on the campus, compared to 81% that did not. Also, 64% of the students were either satisfied or very satisfied with social life in the university, as against 20% who were not. Surprisingly, only 26% felt, to a considerable extent, part of the campus life with regard to student activities and government. Thirty-four percent did not feel a part of the campus life at all or only to a limited extent. Similarly, 37% of the students participated in extracurricular activities sponsored by student organizations, such as fraternities or sororities, professional organizations, and clubs. This may be partly explained by the finding that campus activities reflected the interest, to a considerable extent, of only 28%. Twenty-nine percent reported that their interests were not reflected in those activities, while 43% said that their interests were only represented to some extent. It is also possible that many students did not participate in student activities because of lack of funds, especially as most of the students came from low-income families.

Academic Environment

The academic environment was fairly relaxed in these black colleges. Nine percent of the students reported that the academic competition was extremely intense, while 26% thought it intense. As regards attitudes toward the level of academic competition on campus, 13% felt very positive, and 46% felt positive. Eight percent expressed negative feelings about the level of competition. It is not clear, though, whether students who felt very positive were happy with the generally low level of competition because it was low or because they considered it sufficiently high. Similarly, it is difficult to say whether those with negative feelings desired increased competition or found the current level of competition to be excessively high.

Probably because of the low level of competition, nearly half (46%) of the students spent only 10 hours or less per week in studying, compared to 39% and 33% who spent 11 hours or more per week on recreational activities and dating, respectively.

The students were generally satisfied (60%) with the academic advising received. Thirty-one percent found tutoring services either helpful or very helpful, while 25% found these only marginally helpful or no help at all. Well over a third of the students (40%) did not use tutorial services, presumably because they did not need to.

The median and average college GPA for these students was 2.74. The average for males was higher (2.77) than for females (2.71), though not significantly so. Thus, it appears that females experienced greater performance decreases from high school to college than did males.

The major categories of problems reported were those academic in nature (22%) and those associated with adjustment to college life (23%). These problems were handled by either seeking help (43%) from counselors and professors or by working harder (22%). Perhaps the inadequate management of time and academic pressures may explain the problems with academic performance, which in turn explain the fairly low cumulative GPAs.

The most frequent personal problems encountered by students in this sample related to interpersonal relationships (e.g., with friends, dating, and courtship). These were handled mainly by seeking help (38%) from others, such as friends, family, or counselors, or by working them out alone themselves (43%).

Even in this black college environment, and despite a relatively relaxed atmosphere, as many as 40% of the students reported having seriously considered leaving the university. More important, their reasons were neither academic, cultural, or social. The most important reasons were financial (14%) and miscellaneous (61%), which spanned a whole range of subjects. For example, one student felt disillusioned because he was recruited to play basketball, and yet, for two years in a row, he had not been part of the basketball team. Many complained about the poor living conditions, poor and nonchalant administration, homesickness, and the fact that theirs was mainly a black environment.

Summary and Conclusion

There seems to be a need to help students in traditionally black colleges manage their time more efficiently and hence improve their academic performance. One way to do this is to increase the academic competition within and between schools. This will, it is hoped, help make the students spend more time studying than they do at present and improve their study habits. It may also help to recruit more students who were in the top 10–20% of their graduating high school class. In other words, the traditionally black colleges will have to compete more effectively with white colleges for the top students in the nation's high schools.

According to Fleming (1984), black colleges provide environments that facilitate intellectual development and growth. One would thus expect better academic performance in these colleges than the sample in this study indicates. There was, in fact, a decrease in mean GPA from high school to college, despite the high self-confidence and academic aspirations reported by these students.

Is it possible that, although the students eschewed immediate racial discrimination by choosing and attending black colleges, they remain painfully aware of the vicissitudes of the society in which they live and hope to work? Are they painfully cognizant of the disadvantages and obstacles with which they will have to contend? And is it possible that these considerations engender a sense of hopelessness or despondency in students that prevents them from giving their best effort in college?

There is some evidence in this study to suggest that these questions may be answered affirmatively. An examination of the responses to statements about the situation of black people in the society reveals some important student concerns. For example, 76% felt that attempts by black people to "fit in" and do what is proper have not paid off. Thirty-three percent felt that being qualified did not ensure their getting a job. Sixty-seven percent thought that the conservative upsurge indicated no end to racial discrimination in this country, and 63% felt that the best way to overcome discrimination was through pressure and social action. Thirty-five percent felt that those who are not doing well are working hard but are not getting any breaks in life.

However, 77% felt that the future is promising for the educated black. Thus, the black student goes to college because he or she believes that the educated black is better off than the noneducated black. Once in college, however, the apparent futility of hard work and the plight of those who have gone before tend to demoralize the student and mitigate against high academic persistence and performance. It may well be that, as Gurin and Epps (1975) conjectured, the most successful black students will ultimately be those who are able to reconcile a firm belief in their abilities to determine their own futures with an astute understanding of the reality that there exist many institutional arrangements in the society that discriminate against blacks, handicap their chances in life, and are beyond their personal control.

General Summary

Preliminary results from the National Study of Black College Students reveal that black students attending traditionally black and traditionally white institutions differ in terms of characteristics, experiences, and outcomes. In most respects, the revealed differences parallel findings from earlier studies. Students on black campuses have lower socioeconomic status and weaker precollegiate educational backgrounds; however, compared to students on white campuses, they have higher college GPAs, higher self-confidence, and better psychosocial well-being. The general picture that emerges shows students on white campuses in a more favorable light when traditional academic and status achievement indicators are consulted. Students on black campuses are viewed more favorably when emphasis is placed on measures of social–psychological health, identification with the black community, and involvement in extracurricular activities. Future analysis of these data will attempt more detailed examination of the points of similarity and difference in black student experiences at traditionally white versus traditionally black institutions.

References

Fleming, J.
1984   *Blacks in College: A Comparative Study of Student Success in Black and White Institutions.* San Francisco: Jossey-Bass.
Gurin, P., & Epps, E.
1975   *Black Consciousness, Identity and Achievement.* New York: Wiley.

Related Reports (available on request)

Allen, W., Bobo, L., & Fleuranges, P.
1984   *Preliminary Report: 1982 Undergraduate Survey of Black Students Attending Predominantly White, State-supported Universities.* Ann Arbor: National Study of Black College Students, University of Michigan.
Allen, W., Daughtry, D., & Wilson, K.
1982   *Preliminary Report: Winter 1981 Study of Black Undergraduate Students Attending Predominantly White, State-supported Universities.* Ann Arbor: National Study of Black College Students, University of Michigan.
Allen, W., & Nweke, W.
1985   *Preliminary Report: 1983 Survey of Black Undergraduate Students Attending Historically Black, State-supported Universities.* Ann Arbor: National Study of Black College Students, University of Michigan.

Chapter 13

MENTORING AND NETWORKING
AMONG BLACKS
James E. Blackwell

In recent years, a significant body of literature has developed about mentoring and its importance for the development of a protégé's career. Little or none of it has focused on the black population. Until the early 1970s, most literature on this subject dealt exclusively with mentoring as it applied to white males. With the entry of larger numbers of minorities and white women into graduate and professional schools and with their token representation in professional occupations, many researchers began to devote special attention to the experiences of white women with role modeling and mentoring processes. This interest is reflected in the works of A. Epstein (1969), C. Epstein (1971, 1973), Fowler (1982), Kanter (1977a, 1977b), Kanter and Epstein (1970), Levinson (1978), Lynch (1980), Moore (1982), Phillips-Jones (1982), Shapiro, Haseltine, and Rowe (1978), Speizer (1981), and Taylor and McLaughlin (1982).

These and related studies have attempted to bring conceptual clarity to our understanding of mentoring as a process and to differentiate it from other roles that are less intense in character, such as those of "sponsors," "advisers," "guides," and role models (Levinson 1978; Shapiro *et al.*,1978). Other researchers have attempted to explain mentoring and to specify its functions, delineate specific characteristics of mentoring, and address the problems associated with selection as a protégé (Collins & Scott 1978; Fowler 1982; Klopf 1982; Levinson 1978; Lynch 1980; Moore 1982).

With respect to characteristics attributed to mentors, it is generally agreed that mentors and protégés are most frequently of the same race and sex and that mentors are usually older, have greater experience, seniority, and influence, and occupy high-level positions of power (Levinson 1978; Lynch 1980; Roche 1979). Approximately 15 mentor functions have been

This chapter is based on a previously published research monograph by James E. Blackwell: *Networking and Mentoring: A Study of Cross-Generational Experiences of Blacks in Graduate and Professional Schools* Atlanta: Southern Education Foundation, 1983.

identified in the literature. They include training and advice, emotional support and advocacy, performing developmental roles, socializing the protégé into the profession's expectations, and assisting the protégé to obtain positions or facilitating the protégé's upward mobility in the professional world. Inasmuch as mentors often attempt to "reproduce themselves" in their protégés and because they expend so much time, social energy, and resources in the development of the protégé, and because of the protégé's myriad expectations about the mentor, the mentor–protégé relationship is extremely complex and emotionally charged. Due to the enormity of role requirements and mentor expectations, it is difficult to characterize many persons as true mentors. True mentoring may be rare; instead, individuals perform functions that are oriented toward that end but that are, in fact, substantially less intense than true mentoring.

As suggested by the terms "old boy networks" and, more recently, "old girl networks," networking is in some ways an extension of mentoring processes. Again, as increasing numbers of white women attempted to move into professional occupations during the late 1960s and early 1970s, a more systematic body of literature began to emerge that focused on their problems (Green 1982; Javonovich & Tanguay 1980; Pancrazio & Gray 1982). As early as 1950, Homans's seminal work, *The Human Group*, identified a number of social conditions pertinent to the development of viable social networks.

Several years later, Granovetter (1976) argued that network analysis necessitated understanding what he called "acquaintance volume," "network density," and "network ties." *Acquaintance volume* refers to social contacts, the number of people known by a person; it separates social isolates from persons who are more integrated in a social world. *Network density* measures the ratio of people's actual ties to the number of theoretically possible ties, given the size of the acquaintance volume. *Network ties* refer to the social bonding between two or more actors.

Examination of factors associated with the recruitment, enrollment, and progression of black students through graduate and professional schools (Blackwell 1981, 1982) raised a number of questions about mentoring and networking. Only during the 1960s was a concerted national effort mounted to attack the ubiquitous problem of the underrepresentation of blacks in graduate and professional schools and in professional occupations (Blackwell 1981). Subsequently, a plethora of studies on retention revealed that an unusually large proportion of black students were not progressing through college with anticipated speed, that attrition was particularly high among black students, and, consequently, that the potential pool of matriculants for graduate or professional school was limited. For those blacks who did enroll in graduate or professional school, important questions were raised about the quality of life, about their relationships with white professors (since black professors were either absent or present only in token numbers), and about degrees of social isolation black students experienced when no critical mass of black students was enrolled in their institutions (Blackwell 1981). Essentially, then, these conditions raised doubts about the presence of role models, exposure to and participation in a mentoring process, and students' ability to establish and benefit from viable social networks.

From these conditions, the research problem that emerges is the perceived salience of mentoring and networking for the experiences of black students while enrolled in graduate or professional school and the degree to which mentoring and networking are important contributors to subsequent career development and occupational advancement.

Hypotheses

This exploratory study seeks to illuminate a number of pertinent issues related to the experiences of black Americans with mentoring and networking during and subsequent to their graduation from a graduate or professional school. Seven preliminary hypotheses were delineated for testing.

1. Black student participation in the mentor–protégé relationship varies by time and by the location of the institution in which graduate or professional training was received.

2. The younger the person, the less likely is participation in the mentor–protégé relationship.

3. Blacks who received undergraduate degrees from northern, traditionally white institutions (TWIs) are less likely to participate in the mentor–protégé relationship than are blacks who received undergraduate degrees from traditionally black institutions (TBIs).

4. Blacks who attended a traditionally black graduate or professional school are more likely to have participated in the mentor–protégé relationship than are blacks who graduated from a traditionally white graduate or professional school.

5. In general, blacks are less likely to have participated in a mentor–protégé dyad and more likely to have been involved in a relationship that was less intensive than mentoring.

6. Blacks who did participate in a mentor–protégé relationship will show greater career advancement than those who did not have this experience.

7. Strong network ties are as effective in facilitating career advancement as is participation in a mentor–protégé relationship.

Method

Universe and Sampling Frame

Inasmuch as the membership rosters of black professional organizations were not available for developing a study universe, an alternative arrangement for selecting a sample had to be determined. A snowball sample was selected from rosters of black professionals who had attended three national conferences and from nominations of black professionals made by other black professionals who resided in six regions of the United States. In addition, interviews were conducted with third-year law school students enrolled in a southern TBI and in a traditionally white law school in the Northeast. This combination of sources of possible participants yielded 956 names from which a 22% sample, comprising 226 names, was randomly selected. Three mailings, plus interviews with representatives of the law school class of 1983, generated a 66% response, or 157 respondents. Data collection occurred between June and September 1982.

Description of Instrument

Respondents were mailed a 57-item, precoded and pretested instrument, which consisted of 39 closed and 18 open-ended questions. The items sought (1) general background characteristics; (2) information concerning transfer or movement between black and white institutions; (3) occupational data; (4) a networking scale; (5) information that produced a mentor scale; (6) characteristics of role models; (7) qualitative and quantitative data about the relationship between the respondent and the "most important person" while in graduate or professional school and in subsequent career development; and (8) special comments. Questionnaire items facilitated stratification of the sample among those dimensions critical to testing the seven hypotheses.

Characteristics of Respondents

More than seven-tenths of all respondents were male, and about three-tenths were female. This imbalanced sex ratio reflects the continuing disparity in this society between the proportion of men and women who obtain professional or graduate degrees. The respondents ranged in age from 24 to 85, a distribution that facilitated cross-generational analysis. However, the largest single group of respondents (45.5%) was born between 1941 and 1950. This range suggests that the median age of respondents was about 40 years and, consequently, that most were already well established in their careers. Three-fifths were married, slightly more than one-fifth were single, about one-eighth were divorced, and about one-tenth were either separated or widowed. Although 33 states and 2 foreign nations were listed as places of birth, 59% of the respondents were born in one of 18 southern and border states. Of persons born outside the South, the most frequently mentioned places of birth were, in descending order, New York, Ohio, and Illinois.

Respondents were almost equally distributed among the four types of undergraduate colleges from which their baccalaureate degrees were received. Specifically, 27.5% received the baccalaureate degree from private TBIs, 26.8% from private TWIs, 22.9% from public TBIs, and 22.9% from public TWIs. Not unexpectedly, a significantly large proportion of the respondents received their graduate or professional degrees from TWIs. This situation is explained by the relatively few TBIs that offer professional degrees and programs of doctoral study, which in turn swelled the number of blacks seeking these degrees at TWIs. Almost 80% of the respondents graduated from a private or public TWI. Only 9.2% of the respondents received a graduate or professional degree from a private TBI, and only 11.3% from a public TBI. Again, inasmuch as only six TBIs offer doctoral degree programs, only two have traditionally offered professional degree programs in medicine and dentistry, only six provide degree training programs in engineering, and only four do so in law and pharmacy, it is not unexpected that the majority of blacks would be graduates of TWIs (Blackwell 1981).

With respect to the highest degree earned by the respondents, about one-half reported the Ph.D. or the Ed.D. Physicians (M.D. degree) accounted for 11%, lawyers for 8.4%, dentists for 4.5%, and professionals with a baccalaureate degree for 12.3% of all respondents.

Nonrespondents

Approximately 30% of potential participants failed to respond to the mailed questionnaire. It is impossible to specify such important descriptive characteristics of the nonrespondents as age, year of college graduation, year of graduation from graduate or professional school, and institutions from which they received their degrees. Even though assuming gender from given names is risky, examining given names indicates that 34% of the nonrespondents were women and 66% were men. Examining the rosters and lists of names provided by informants showed that 4 nonrespondents held the Doctor of Optometry degree, 4 held the Doctor of Social Work degree, 8 were dentists, 18 were lawyers, 15 were physicians, 6 were engineers, and 13 held either the Ph.D. or Ed.D. degree. Physicians, dentists, and lawyers accounted for 58% of all nonrespondents—a fact that might reflect a general disinclination to respond to social research or mailed surveys.

Variables

The variables selected for analysis reflect observations arising from analyzing the literature on factors associated with mentoring and the conditions or situations that affect degrees of networking. Specifically,

1. Sex is a dichotomous variable used as a measure of mentoring and of degrees of networking.

2. Education is a trichotomous variable that refers to the kind of degree received. Bachelor's and master's degree holders were characterized as "lower-level professionals" and coded 1. Ph.D. or Ed.D. degree recipients were labeled "graduate degrees" and coded 2. M.D., D.D.S., LL.B., or O.D. degree holders were labeled "higher professional degrees" and coded 3.

3. Type of undergraduate college was coded as follows: 1 = private and TBI; 2 = private and TWI; 3 = public and TBI; and 4 = public and TWI.

4. Type of graduate or professional school was coded in the same manner as type of undergraduate institution.

5. Institutional location or region was a dichotomous variable. TBIs were coded 1, and northern TWIs were coded 2. All jurisdictions outside the District of Columbia and 18 southern and border states were treated as northern states.

6. Age, labeled COHORT, was computed from the year in which the undergraduate degree was obtained. Recipients of a baccalaureate degree prior to 1950 were coded 1; those between 1950 and 1959 were coded 2; those between 1960 and 1969 were coded 3; and those between 1970 and 1983 were coded 4.

7. Occupation was scaled along the dimensions suggested in the Blau–Duncan Index of Occupational Status (Blau & Duncan 1967,

pp. 22–23; Reiss 1961). Because of the small numbers in some occupational categories, recombinations of occupations reported by the respondents produced five occupational groupings: (1) code 1 was assigned to physicians, dentists, lawyers, judges, engineers, salaried bankers and managers, and self-employed proprietors; (2) code 2 was assigned to college presidents, high-level academic administrators, deans, and college professors holding the rank of assistant professor or above; (3) code 3 was given to other administrative personnel in universities, such as affirmative action officers, special assistants, directors of special admissions, and similar positions; (4) code 4 was given to students (third-year law students); (5) code 5 was given to all others.

8. *Mentor* was not predefined for the respondents. This variable was computed as a composite index based on items identified as characteristics or functions of mentors. It assumed that all persons identified as "the most important person during graduate or professional school" may not have functioned equally in executing presumed or perceived mentoring behavior. It also assumed that there are different degrees or levels of mentoring (Shapiro *et al.* 1978). Based on the literature review, 23 items were selected as critical to the mentoring role. Ten items were double weighted because of their perceived value in the mentoring process. The maximum score from weighted items was 60 (6 × 10) plus 39 points (3 × 13) from the nonweighted items, or a maximum possible score of 99 points. An assessment of frequency distributions generated a trichotomized mentoring scale. Hence, persons with a score of 75 to 99 were called "mentors" and coded 1. Persons scoring 66 to 74 were called "sponsors" and coded 2. Persons scoring 0 to 65 were called "advisers, teachers, or peers" and coded 3. The mentor variable was called SCALE.

9. Postgraduate/Professional Functions (PGPF) refers to the kinds of functions provided by the various levels of mentors for the protégé/ex-student following graduation. This variable was computed on a summed scale constructed from 20 subcomponents of one item. Responses were weighted from 1 to 5, for a maximum of 100 points on the scale.

10. The network variable, called "NET–2," represents a composite index computed from 19 possible responses in a single item. Scores ranged from 1 to 3, which represented degrees of importance attached to the item. A maximum score of 57 points was possible on this scale (3 × 19). Hence, this trichotomized scale indicates that a score of 38 to 55 represents a "strong" network; a score of 31 to 37 indicates an "adequate" network; whereas a score of 21 to 30 means a "weak network."

11. A variable called "Ties," which followed Granovetter's (1973, p. 1360) formulation, was computed from responses on four items: amount of time spent with most intimate friends, friends as a source of companionship, friends providing emotional support, and friends as good for mutual confiding. As suggested by the degree of importance attached to each response, ranging from 1 to 3, the maximum score possible was 12. A score of 9 to 12 represented "strong" ties, a score of 6 to 8 "adequate" ties, and a score of 1 to 5 "weak" ties.

12. Again, following Granovetter's formulation, "acquaintance volume" refers to the average number of people the respondent knew during each semester while in graduate or professional school. The median number of persons respondents knew per semester was 30.3.

The Statistical Package for the Social Sciences (Nie *et al.* 1975) was used for data analysis. Reliance was largely on descriptive statistics, the Chi Square test of significance, and the Pearsonian Correlation Coefficient. A confidence level of .05 was established as acceptable.

Findings

Role Models

As a result of black underrepresentation on faculty and administrative staffs of colleges and universities (Blackwell 1981; Pruitt 1981; Thomas 1981), it was assumed that few blacks served as role models for black students in graduate or professional school. The relative shortage of black faculty was confirmed by the fact that 39.5% of all respondents stated that no blacks taught in any capacity in their institutions. However, 42.8% reported that blacks were teaching full-time in their departments, while about 1 in 12 stated that blacks were hired exclusively as adjunct professors to the department. Not unexpectedly, blacks in full-time positions were more frequent in the TBIs than in the TWIs. In TWIs, blacks tended to be present only in token numbers, quite frequently as adjunct department members.

Yet slightly less than one-fifth of the respondents stated that they did not have a role model. Even fewer said that they had at least one role model, but more than two-thirds claimed two or more role models during their graduate or professional school careers. Importantly, white professors in the major field were reported more than two and one-half times as often as black professors in the major field as the respondent's role model. In fact, total black professors in the field and in clinical programs and black professors outside the respondent's major did not equal the number of white persons specified as role models. Only when community professionals and persons outside the academic community itself are added to the list of blacks does the number of blacks serving as role models exceed the absolute number of whites characterized as role models.

However, a role model is not necessarily the same person who becomes a mentor. Approximately one-third of the persons respondents identified as "my most important person" during graduate or professional school were not identified as role models.

Mentors

Data analysis revealed that mentoring is rare in the academic world. Among participants in this study, only about one in eight persons score sufficiently high on the mentor SCALE to be classified as having had a mentor during graduate or professional school. More than three times as many persons had "sponsors"; fewer, but still more than three times as many persons were aided during graduate or professional school by "advisors, teachers, or another peer." No evidence was found to support the hypothesis that black student participation in the mentor–protégé relationship varies by time and the location of the institution in which the graduate or professional training was received. Mentoring was not significantly correlated with age cohorts as defined by the age variable.

However, when age groups were collapsed and dichotomized in terms of the time frame within which the highest professional degree was awarded (i.e., pre-1960 and post-1960), the relationship is significant between mentoring and the time during which the highest professional degree was received. Only in this sense can the opposite hypothesis be accepted, that the younger the person, the more likely is participation in the mentor–protégé relationship. Otherwise, that hypothesis is rejected. Nevertheless, it is worthwhile to note that 6.9% of persons who received their undergraduate degree during the pre-1950 period, 10.3% of those in the 1950–1959 period, 14.5% of those in the 1960–1969 period, and 15.9% of those in the post-1970 period had mentors. More than one-half of all persons in the pre-1950 period, compared to slightly less than one-third of those in the post-1970 period, regarded advisers, teachers, or friends as their most important persons while in graduate or professional school.

The hypothesis was not confirmed that blacks who received their undergraduate degrees from northern TWIs were less likely to participate in the mentor–protégé relationship than were blacks who received their undergraduate degrees from TBIs. Although the respondents were about evenly divided in terms of the location of their undergraduate institutions, they were indistinguishable with respect to the degree of mentoring experienced during their graduate or professional education. Neither is the hypothesis supported that blacks who attended a black graduate or professional school were more likely to have participated in the mentor–protégé relationship than were blacks who received their training at a TWI. Nevertheless, examining the descriptive statistics suggests that important though not statistically significant relationships may be observed regarding degrees of mentoring and the graduate or professional school's racial composition. For instance, a higher percentage of blacks attending TWIs than those attending TBIs had mentors. Further, a higher percentage of black TWI graduates had "sponsors" than the 37.3% of blacks who received their degrees from TBIs. More than half the TBI graduates, compared to one-third of black TWI graduates, had "advisors, teachers, or friends" as their most important persons during this phase of their lives. Hence, the hypothesis is confirmed that blacks are more likely to have participated in a relationship that is less intensive than mentoring, such as sponsor–student, adviser–student, or, perhaps, a peer relationship.

This analysis showed particularly strong support for the hypothesis that blacks who participated in the mentor–protégé relationship would show greater advancement with respect to career development. In other words, persons in higher-status occupations rank higher on the mentor scale than persons in lower-status occupations. Further, rank on the Mentor SCALE is significantly correlated with rank on the Postgraduate Professional Function (PGPF) scale.

As suggested in the literature, mentors are regarded as persons having significant power and influence not only in the respondent's academic department but within the university and the profession as well. About three-fourths of persons characterized as mentors were perceived as having "some" or a "great deal" of power and influence. About the same proportion was regarded as enjoying the respect of colleagues and students.

The most important person to blacks in graduate or professional school, either mentor, sponsor, adviser, teacher, or peer, was a white male. White females accounted for 8.5% of persons so characterized; therefore, white persons represented more than one-half of all persons identified by blacks as their "most important person" during their graduate or professional school experience. Black males and black females accounted for a total of 42.6% of their "most important persons." The remainder of such persons were found among other ethnic groups.

The "most important person" tended to be older than the respondent. About one-fifth were slightly older; a third were 10 to 19 years older; and slightly more than one-fourth were 20 or more years older. Approximately one in six of them were about the same age as the respondent, while only 2.6% were younger. Hence, this research confirms assertions previously cited that mentors tend to be older than protégés.

Networking

This research defined networks as a process of information sharing and exchange that facilitates the construction of important contacts for attaining present and future goals. They involve relationships characterized by a high degree of reciprocity and mutual trust and by varying degrees of intimacy and self-confidence (Moore 1982; Moses 1980). Although no hypotheses were advanced with respect to the salience of networks for graduate or professional experience, with the exception of their influence on occupational advancement, this research tested several hypotheses.

For instance, a significant relationship was observed between rank on the acquaintance volume (AV) scale and rank on the education scale. Specifically, the higher the score on the AV scale, the higher the rank on the education scale. A high and statistically significant correlation also existed between the racial designation of the institution from which the graduate or professional degree was received and rank on the AV scale. Not unexpectedly, blacks were more likely to know more students per semester if they attended a TBI than if they attended a TWI. This situation holds in both private and public TBIs. However, blacks who attended public TWIs had a higher AV score than did blacks who attended a private TWI. The reverse was true with respect to those who attended a private TBI, 71.4% of whom scored high on the AV scale, compared to the 55.6% of blacks who attended public TBIs who scored high in acquaintance volume. The differences observed may be explained by a greater degree of intimacy, due to small size, found at private TBIs in comparison to a higher overall volume of black students enrolled in public TBIs, and to a higher degree of social isolation at private TWIs when compared to a larger critical mass of black students at public TWIs.

Significant gender differences occurred in distribution on the networking scale (NET–2). Women are more likely to have strong networks than are men. Over half the women and only 27.4% of the men scored strong on NET–2. By contrast, more than half the men and only a fifth of the women scored "adequate" on this scale. More than one-third of the men and only a fifth of the women scored "weak" on NET–2.

Age is also significantly correlated with networking. The younger the person, in terms of how recent the degree, the stronger the social network or the higher the rank on NET–2. Further, networking is stronger among blacks who attended public graduate or professional schools than among those who attended private graduate or professional schools. Network strength may reflect a larger critical mass at public institutions from which to select a larger or more viable acquaintance volume. In turn, more extensive networks are established. This finding is particularly complex, since one might also assume that the small-world syndrome that operates when blacks are in low numbers in high-prestige positions might be conducive to establishing strong networks. That situation did not appear to exist among this study's participants.

Networking was significantly related to rank on the AV scale and to race of the graduate or professional school. Hence, the higher the acquaintance volume and the greater the number of blacks who were graduated from TBIs, the stronger the networks established. Further, black friends are more likely to facilitate the career advancement of black graduates of graduate or professional schools than are white friends.

This research did not support the hypothesis that strong network ties are as effective in moving persons through and up in the system of professionals as is participation in the mentor–protégé dyad. The relationship between the Ties scale and the Index of Occupational Status is not within the boundaries of acceptability.

Discussion

As this research shows, mentoring is not as widespread as many persons might imagine. Only one in eight respondents scored sufficiently high on the mentor scale to be categorized as a participant in a mentor–protégé relationship. One explanation for this situation might be the serious underrepresentation of blacks in faculty roles in graduate and professional schools and the unwillingness of a significantly larger number of white faculty to select blacks as protégés. The fact that some white males do perform mentoring functions twice as often as black males may reflect their willingness to serve in this role, but it also indicates the absence of a sufficient number of blacks in the institution or the department or a relative paucity of blacks who are viewed as sufficiently influential to perform mentoring roles.

Even though 11 out of 12 blacks in this study did not have mentors during their graduate or professional school experience, they believed uniformly that mentors were of immense importance to them. Mentors were not only invaluable for helping blacks "maneuver in the system" or for providing timely and sound advice and information; they were critical for helping blacks understand how the system of graduate or professional education works and for promoting their upward mobility or advancement in the occupational structure.

The majority of respondents reported satisfying relationships with professors. Nevertheless, these relationships, however cordial and friendly, were situationally constrained by time and role expectations and rarely endured beyond the academic environment. A few reported less-than-desirable relationships with professors because of what they described as "racial hang-ups of white professors" or white professors who did not respect the intelligence of black students. Given these observations, it is not unexpected that black graduates of TWIs tend to regard these institutional experiences as nothing more than a kind of rite of passage that was necessary to move into the world of professionals. Surprisingly, many had similar attitudes toward the TBIs from which they received their graduate or professional degrees.

This research also confirmed the need for considerably stronger social networks among blacks that will follow them after graduate or professional school experiences. A significant number of the study's participants reported a high degree of social isolation even when a substantial number of blacks were attending their institutions. A major problem was a pattern of blacks avoiding one another and a failure to extend themselves to one another in order to establish friendly relationships. Persons who were more aggressive or who were members of formal or informal organizations seemed substantially more successful in building networks than were less assertive individuals. Other problems are evidenced in the following statement by the first black to desegregate a southern TWI law school during the early 1950s:

It is probably more difficult to succeed today than it was in the 1950s. It is probably more difficult to form the kinds of relationship that facilitate success in a graduate or professional school because of a number of reasons. First, there is a kind of interpersonal gestalt that operates today. So many white students are so concerned about "self" that they will not extend themselves to be helpful to black students. Second, many black students do not know how to reach out to each other; yet, they need each other. Sometimes black students will read "race" into situations that have nothing to do with race. If they were a part of a network with people who are honest with them, those friends could help them look at the situation with a more objective view and not see race where it is unimportant. Third, it is even more important for black students to have networks that enable them to expand out into the whole graduate or professional system, to share information, to create alliances between or with white networks that are of mutual benefit to black networks. I also think that the post-graduate networks . . . are critical. They are critical for information sharing, for the development of important resources and to render it easier to advance goals and careers.

Finally, although drawing generalizations beyond what was observed for this particular sample is inappropriate, a few implications are clearly warranted from this study. First, the need still exists to increase the number, proportion, and distribution of blacks in faculty and administrative positions in institutions of higher learning. Second, a substantially larger number of black students should participate in a rewarding mentor–protégé relationship, and they in turn should perform mentoring functions to subsequent generations of students of all races. Third, widening black student access to graduate or professional schools or enrolling a critical mass of black students within a specific institution or department is not sufficient. The overall quality of institutional life should foster the establishment of viable social networks that facilitate learning, contacts, and network ties; that help advance or promote the career development of participants; and that encourage them to help create a more just and humane society for others. Fourth, it seems evident that institutions of higher learning still have a social responsibility to create a more positive learning environment by helping to provide the atmosphere in which interracial contacts between faculty and students and faculty and administrators of all races are not superficial. Further, the environment should permit working and mentoring and learning that is not constrained by boundaries of race, ethnicity, or sex.

References

Blackwell, J. E.
  1975 *The Black Community: Diversity and Unity.* New York: Harper & Row.
Blackwell, J. E.
  1981 *Mainstreaming Outsiders: The Production of Black Professionals.* Bayside, N.Y.: General Hall.
Blackwell, J. E.
  1982 Demographics of desegregation. In R. Wilson (Ed.), *Race and Equity in Higher Education,* pp. 28–70. Washington, D.C.: American Council on Education.
Blau, P., & Duncan, O. D.
  1967 *The American Occupational Structure.* New York: Free Press.
Collins, E., & Scott, P. B.
  1978 Everyone who makes it has a mentor. *Harvard Business Review* (July–August), 89–101.
Epstein, A.
  1969 The network of urban social organization. In J. C. Mitchell (Ed.), *Social Networks in Urban Situations,* pp. 116–132. Manchester: Manchester University Press.
Epstein, C.
  1971 *A Woman's Place.* Berkeley: University of California Press.
Epstein, C.
  1973 Positive effects of the multiple negatives: Explaining the success of black professional women. *American Journal of Sociology, 78*(4), 912–925.
Fowler, D. L.
  1982 Mentoring relationships and the perceived quality of the academic work environment. *Journal of National Association of Women Deans, Administrators and Counselors* (Spring), 27–33.
Granovetter, M.
  1973 Strength of weak ties. *American Journal of Sociology, 78* (May), 1360–1380.
Granovetter, M.
  1976 Network sampling: Some first steps. *American Journal of Sociology, 81–86,* 1287–1303.
Green, M. F.
  1982 A Washington perspective on women and networking: The power and the pitfalls. *Journal of National Association of Women Deans, Administrators and Counselors* (Fall), 17–21.
Homans, G.
  1950 *The Human Group.* New York: Harcourt, Brace and World.
Javonovich, J., & Tanguay, S. L.
  1980 Networking. *Journal of Placement* (Fall), 30–34.

Kanter, R. M.
　1977a　*Men and Women of the Corporation.* New York: Basic Books.
Kanter, R. M.
　1977b　Some effects of proportions on group life: Skewed sex ratios and responses to token women. *American Journal of Sociology, 82,* 965–990.
Kanter, R., & Epstein, C. F.
　1970　Encountering the male establishment; Sex limits on women's careers in the professions. *American Journal of Sociology, 75(6),* 965–982.
Klopf, G. J.
　1982　The case for mentors. *The Educational Digest, 1(4)* (January), 34–35.
Levinson, D.
　1978　*The Seasons of a Man's Life.* New York: Ballantine Books.
Lynch, S. M.
　1980　The mentor link: Bridging education and employment. *Journal of College Placement* (Fall), 44–47.
Moore, K. M.
　1982　The role of mentors in developing leaders for academe. *Educational Leader, 63* (Winter), 23–28.
Morris, L. O.
　1979　*Elusive Equality: The Status of Black Americans in Higher Education.* Washington, D.C.: Howard University Press.
Moses, K.
　1980　Networking. *Black Enterprise, 11* (September), 29–34.
Nie, N. A., Hull, C. H., Jenkins, J. G., Steinbrenner, K., & Bent, D. H.
　1975　*The statistical package for the social sciences* (2d ed.). New York: McGraw–Hill.
Pancrazio, S. B., & Gray, R. G.
　1982　Networking for professional women: A collegial model. *Journal of National Association of Women Deans, Administrators and Counselors* (Spring) 10–19.
Phillips-Jones, L.
　1982　*Mentors and Protégés.* New York: Arbor House.
Pruitt, A. S.
　1981　*Black Employees in Traditionally White Institutions in the Adams States: 1975 to 1977.* Atlanta: Southern Education Foundation.
Reiss, A. J.
　1961　*Occupations and Social Status.* New York: Free Press.
Roche, G. R.
　1979　Much ado about mentors. *Harvard Business Review* (January), 14–28.
Shapiro, E. C., Haseltine, F. P., & Rowe, M. P.
　1978　Moving up: Role models, mentors and the patron system. *Sloan Management Review, 19(3),* 51–58.

Speizer, J. J.
     1981 Role models, mentors, and sponsors: The elusive concepts. *Signs* (Summer), 6: 692–712.
Taylor, I., & McLaughlin, M. B.
     1982 Mentoring freshmen women. *Journal of National Association of Women Deans, Administrators and Counselors* (Winter), 10–15.
Thomas, G.E. (Ed.)
     1981 *Black Students in Higher Education: Conditions and Experiences in the 1970s.* Westport, Conn.: Greenwood Press.

PART 5

The Significance of Financial Aid for Black Students in Higher Education

Perhaps second only to the quality of public school preparation is the need for financial assistance in assuring black student entry and success in higher education. Black families are concentrated at the lowest rung of the economic ladder, making scarce the resources to enable their children to go on beyond high school. Among the measures that *Adams* states include in their plans for desegregation is the provision of financial aid. This, in addition to aid provided by the federal government, is examined in Chapter 14 by Jerry Davis and Kingston Johns.

Cameron Fincher approaches the concept of finances from an entirely different but equally critical perspective in Chapter 15. In examining the effectiveness of Title III of the Higher Education Act of 1965, he focuses on the pervasive lack of funds that has characterized traditionally black colleges since their founding. In calling for the disestablishment of segregated systems of public higher education, the *Adams* criteria require the states to strengthen the role of TBIs. Although Title III is a piece of federal legislation, its impact, as analyzed by Fincher, is critical to the success of desegregation efforts.

Chapter **14**   FINANCIAL ACCESS TO
POSTSECONDARY EDUCATION
FOR MINORITY–POVERTY
STUDENTS: A LOOK AT THE
RECENT PAST AND A VIEW OF
THE FUTURE
Jerry S. Davis and Kingston Johns, Jr.

During the turbulent years of the 1970s, a growing uncertainty developed about the potential health and well-being of higher education for the remaining decades of this century. Some educators viewed with considerable alarm the probabilities of shrinking enrollments as the number of traditional-age students declined; the threat that rising tuitions and other costs posed to student demands for higher education; the increased interinstitutional competition for students that might occur with estimated shortages in the number of qualified applicants; and the myriad other perennial problems that institutions must confront, such as handling faculty demands for increased salaries, repairing or replacing deteriorating physical plants, and securing financial support from public and private sources.

But other educators looked at the future more optimistically, noting, for example, that enrollments might not fall too far if traditional-age students were replaced by older or "adult" students who wished to be retrained to meet new employment demands. They noted further that tuition revenues could be allocated to the general improvement of teaching and the quality of education, thus making postsecondary education more attractive in spite of its increased costs.

Outlining these fundamentally opposing viewpoints about the future of postsecondary education, the Carnegie Council of Policy Studies in Higher Education (1980) expressed its judgment about the future by

This chapter was commissioned for this volume by the Southern Education Foundation, Atlanta, Georgia.

stating: "We do not expect a fast or slow fadeout for American higher education. We expect it to continue to move forward in response to both national and individual aspirations" (p. 97).

Since the Council's report was published, however, new threats to higher education's potential have appeared. Federal resources, in the form of support for financial aid programs, have declined in both absolute and relative terms, thus creating more difficulty for students and their families to meet educational costs. A variety of commissions, study groups, and other associations have expressed concern about the general losses of quality in postsecondary education, thus raising questions about the value of the higher education experience to students and society. And, although the potential decline in enrollments of traditional-age college students has been offset by the growth in attendance of "adult" and other students enrolled on a less than full-time basis, concern exists that this attendance may soon reach a plateau if costs continue to rise and the value of education continues to be questioned.

Within the context of growing uncertainty about the future of higher education, this chapter examines the special financial problems that minority–poverty students have faced and will continue to face in gaining access to postsecondary education.

Access to financial aid resources has always been the key to the minority–poverty student's ability to enroll in college. Student access to financial aid resources is decreasing in both relative and absolute terms. Furthermore, the costs of attending college, as well as the costs of attending other forms of postsecondary education, are growing at a rate that outpaces inflation and increases in personal income. At the same time, widely publicized concerns about the quality and consequent value of postsecondary education may have suppressed parental and student willingness to make the sacrifices they have always made to matriculate and graduate. These trends do not bode well for future enrollment of minority–poverty students.

Unfortunately, for whatever reasons, the "quality of education" issue is all too frequently counterpoised, in the eyes of the public and public policymakers, by the issue of providing low-income students with access to postsecondary education. Too few observers seem to believe that our nation can afford quality of education and equality of access to education at the same time. This attitude continues to stand in the way of minority–poverty students at a time in our history when access is perhaps more important than ever.

Changes in Access to Postsecondary Education

Before looking to the future of postsecondary education and the minority–poverty students' potential participation in that future, briefly examining the most immediate past will be useful.

A study prepared for the National Commission on Student Financial Assistance (NCSFA 1983, pp. 31–36) revealed that, between 1974 and 1981, college participation rates for all persons age 18 to 24 increased slightly, from 26.4% to 28.0%. The participation rate for all white students grew from 26.3% to 28.2%, while the participation rate for black students increased by only 1.5%, from 22.2% to 23.7%. However, family incomes influenced participation rates for white and black students in very different ways. For example, *dependent* white students from families with incomes below $12,000 increased their participation rates from 24.5% in 1974 to 32.6% in 1981. Dependent black students from similar family income circumstances experienced a *decrease* in education participation rates, from 30.4% to 24.2%.

In another study, based on other sets of data (Davis & Johns 1982), the authors found that, between 1966 and 1981, the nation made strides in enrolling low-income freshmen in its colleges, strides that peaked, for most types of institutions, in the late 1970s. Those data, the authors noted, clearly documented "the fact that financially handicapped students have been and continue to be underenrolled in higher education. This is especially true for those students from the lowest-income strata" (p.28).

Between 1974 and 1981, the probability that the lowest-income students would receive a financial aid award remained fairly constant. However, low-income students were more likely to receive a *smaller* award in 1981 than in 1974. Although black students were more likely than white students to receive an aid award in both 1974 and 1981, black students were more likely to receive a *smaller* award, but white students were more likely to receive a *larger* award in 1981 than 1974. The median award to white students rose from $1,832 to $1,987, but the median award for black students fell from $1,896 to $1,668. One explanation for the precipitant decline in black students' median award sizes is that black students became more likely to attend community colleges than four-year colleges. Between 1974 and 1980, enrollment at two-year schools nearly doubled, but enrollment at four-year colleges increased by only 12%. By 1978, a black college student was 20% more likely to be enrolled in a two-year college than was a white student; a Hispanic student was 60% more likely to attend a two-year college than was a white student (NCSFA 1983, p. 34).

Data to chart the changes *precisely* in patterns of access to financial aid and postsecondary education for low-income or minority–poverty students are, as the researchers for the National Commission and others have noted, not available. Nevertheless, a variety of data bases show, to one extent or another, that access to both aid and education has declined during the 1980s after significant increases during the 1970s. Reasonable observers may disagree about the extent to which access has declined, for whom, and under which circumstances, but they do not disagree that the situation is worse now than it was in the latter years of the preceding decade.

Explanations for the worsening situation abound, but most explanations for the declining access include the following: (1) Inflation has combined with recent years' recessions and has led to greater inequality in the distribution of family income (e.g., the number of families living below the poverty line increased by 40% between 1973 and 1981); (2) tuition costs versus a share of discretionary income have increased drastically; and (3) amounts of average aid awards, especially for low-income students, have not increased as fast as the tuition those students must pay.

The Continuing Value and Need for Postsecondary Education

A study by the U.S. Bureau of the Census (1983) demonstrated that individuals who obtain college degrees can still expect substantial increases in lifetime earnings. For example, 22-year-old males with four-year college degrees were expected, in 1979, to earn 37% more in their lifetimes than were similar males who had only completed high school. Female baccalaureate degree holders were expected to earn 35% more than female high school graduates.

A postsecondary education continues to provide a means of dramatic upward socioeconomic mobility. For example, a study of 1981 graduates of all types of postsecondary institutions in Pennsylvania (Davis 1983) found that in 57% of the cases, working alumni (and only 5% were unemployed) from families with incomes below $12,000 earned more in their first year after leaving school than their parents earned. About 39% of the alumni from families with incomes in the $12,000 to $18,000 income interval were already earning more than their parents earned.

With the shift of the nation's economy from an industrial base to an information and service base, no reason exists for believing that the value of a postsecondary education will decrease. Postsecondary education and training will provide their beneficiaries with access to better-paying jobs in this new economy, and those unfortunate enough to have been denied such experiences must increasingly confront what is now called "structural unemployment," that is, unemployment that is a dual function of the skills the unemployed possess and the absence of jobs that require those skills.

Even if postsecondary education were no longer considered a path to, or a requisite for, employment and better earnings, other values are derived from the educational experience. These values are very likely to remain extant to both individuals and society. For example, college-trained individuals are better-informed citizens who are more likely to participate in community affairs. In the domain of family life, college affects the selection of marriage partners and tends to delay marriage and reduce the birth rate; but, at the same time, it increases the thought, time, energy, and money devoted to child rearing. As consumers, college-educated people get greater returns than others from given income levels. They are more likely than others to be oriented toward the home and the nurturing of children. College-educated persons save more, cope better with life's practical problems, and are healthier (Bowen 1977).

Since the present and future economic, social, political, and individual benefits derived from postsecondary education are significant and substantial, it is crucial that no segment of our population be denied access to it.

Past and Recent Trends in Financial Aid

As noted above, financial aid has always been the key to minority–poverty students' access to postsecondary education, and as further noted, these students have experienced real losses in access to aid in the 1980s. But the authors recognize that minority–poverty students must surmount other, nonfinancial barriers to postsecondary education before attending college.

These barriers include (1) the academic barrier—students may not have the appropriate high school preparation, or they may not have achieved the appropriate degree of success in their high school programs; (2) the attitudinal barrier—students and their parents may not recognize the value of postsecondary education or know that ways exist for attaining it; and (3) the geographic barrier—students may live too far, in distance or commuting time, from an institution that they can afford or are able to attend (Ferrin 1970).

Although these barriers are substantial and, to one degree or another, inhibit the access of minority–poverty students to postsecondary education even when access to financial aid is present, in the absence of available aid, the financial barrier will certainly prove insurmountable. Quite simply put, in the presence of available aid, some minority–poverty students may not achieve access, but in the absence of available aid, all are certain to be denied access. Therefore, charting the recent changes in student access to financial aid and examining the trends one can expect in the near future are extremely important.

Between 1970–1971 and 1980–1981, available financial aid from all sources, in current dollars, grew by 284%, from $4.5 billion to $17.3 billion. Between 1977–1978 and 1980–1981, available aid grew by 56%, from $11.1 billion to $17.3 billion. However, between 1980–1981 and the 1983–1984 academic year, available aid decreased by 7%, from $17.3 billion to $16.1 billion (Gillespie & Carlson 1983, p. 5). After a dramatic increase in the 1970s, a decrease has been experienced in this decade. We should note that much of the recent loss in available aid occurred in losses of Social Security Administration and Veterans Administration benefits, which declined from $3.621 billion to $1.308 billion. These losses are particularly important to minority–poverty students because they receive awards from these programs in aggregate amounts disproportionate to their numbers.

Another major change in financial aid has occurred in the types of aid made available to students. As recently as 1975–1976, over 80% of available aid was received in the form of grants and educational benefits. In 1983–1984, only 48% of the available aid was in the form of grants or educational benefits. Put another way, between 1975–1976 and 1983–1984, available grant–educational benefits dollars decreased by 49%. During this same time period, available loan dollars increased by 138%, and available work–study dollars increased by 19%. Therefore, more of the aid received by students continues to be in the form of "self-help" aid (Gillespie & Carlson 1983, p. 6).

Average financial aid per full-time equivalent (FTE) student peaked in 1981–1982 at $2,003; since that time, it has shrunk to $1,778, or by 11.2%. In constant (inflation-adjusted) 1982 dollars, the peak year was 1980–1981, when the average aid per FTE student reached $2,210. Since that peak year, average aid has fallen to $1,693, a 30.5% reduction (Gillespie & Carlson 1983, p. 14).

At the same time that average aid per FTE student was decreasing by 30.5% in constant 1982 dollars, constant-dollar attendance costs were increasing at private universities by 14.7%; at private four-year colleges by 11.8%; at public universities by 10.7%; at public four-year colleges by 10.5%; and at community colleges by 4.4% (Gillespie & Carlson 1983, p. 20). These data illustrate two major points. Costs have outpaced available financial aid in recent years, but costs have increased less at community colleges than at other institutions. The latter point clarifies why more minority–poverty students have turned to community colleges than to other colleges and universities.

The nationwide picture of financial aid trends can be summarized as follows: (1) After dramatic growth in total aid from all sources during the 1970s, total available aid has decreased in current and constant dollars during the 1980s; (2) the decline in available aid dollars has been especially acute for grant aid and educational benefits; and (3) average aid per FTE student declined in the 1980s as costs were increasing sharply.

The relationships between college costs and available aid are extremely important to minority–poverty students, who, by definition, have no available income to spend on education. Nevertheless, we must note that college costs as a percent of available personal income for all students have increased during the 1980s. This relationship is important, because increasing costs create greater financial burdens for all students and also sharpen the demand for limited financial aid dollars. As this demand increases, minority–poverty students face greater competition from other less financially handicapped students, who also seek financial aid.

The Future of Financial Aid

Given the current conservative mood of Congress and the nation at large, the demands on public sources of funds, and the ever-growing federal budgetary deficits, we cannot expect the current decline in available financial aid to be reversed soon. This is especially true at the federal level, where the administration's budget requests are consistently below the levels of fiscal year 1984.

Some evidence exists that state governments may provide more financial aid to offset partially losses at the federal level. State appropriations are unlikely to replace federal losses, however, and that growth at the state level will meet the increased demands for financial aid is very unlikely.

The National Association of State Scholarship and Grant Programs (NASSGP 1983) reports that, between 1977–1978 and 1983–1984, state-supported, need-based, grant program aid to undergraduates grew by 47%, from $715.6 million to $1.05 billion. Aid from these programs in the 19 *Adams* states increased by 50% during the same time period, from $159 million to $238.6 million. During the 1977 to 1984 period, however, college costs in the *Adams* states increased so much that the increased grant dollars, about $79.6 million, would have covered the cost increases for only

46,000 students enrolled at four-year public institutions in all 19 states. So the dramatic, and laudable, increases in state funding of grant programs were absorbed and exceeded by increased costs.

During the late 1970s, all states that previously had not established guaranty agencies to enhance their citizens' access to long-term, low-interest loans through the Federal Guaranteed Student Loan Program (GSLP) established such agencies. These agencies have expanded student access to loan capital from private sources. In 1981, however, the federal government restricted access to these GSLP loan monies by charging students a 5% origination fee and by requiring students from families with incomes above $30,000 to demonstrate financial need in order to establish eligibility. The administration currently proposes requiring all loan applicants to demonstrate financial need in order to establish eligibility for a loan. This latter proposal would not have a direct impact on low-income borrower's access to loan money, as all would demonstrate financial need. Nevertheless, this restriction for middle- and upper-middle-income borrowers would cause the demand for financial aid money to shift from the Guaranteed Student Loan Program (GSLP) to those other programs that also serve low-income students. Thus, the competition for limited aid dollars would widen.

States have also expanded their support of financial aid programs by establishing work–study programs for their students. As of this writing, 12 states have their own work–study programs, and another 8 states are considering implementing new ones (NASSGP 1983, p. 2). These work–study programs will expand student access to part-time, term-time, and full-time summer employment, especially in the private sector of the economy. However, increased employment for minority–poverty students, many of whom must take remedial courses or reduced course loads to compensate for academic deficiencies, does not represent a viable alternative to grant funds.

The Washington Office of the College Board (February 1983, p. 4) reports that Representative Paul Simon (D-Ill.), chairman of the House Subcommittee on Postsecondary Education, put forward for consideration four major goals for reauthorization of the Higher Education Act:

1. Simplify the student aid system.
2. Retarget aid on the neediest.
3. Reestablish a more appropriate balance between grant and loan programs.
4. Allow institutions greater flexibility in administering the aid programs.

As expected, in an election year, no reauthorization occurred. Congress was simply too busy with other activities. But Mr. Simon's hearings could prove to be especially important preliminaries to the 1985–1986 session, when Congress again takes up the matter.

Meanwhile, "the era of dramatic increases in student aid has passed" with "less help . . . available for students and their families to pay college expenses" (Gladieux 1982–1983, pp. 13, 18). At the same time, and as outlined earlier, tuition and fee increases appear to be greater than the inflation rate. Costs as a percentage of disposable personal income per capita are advancing at a faster pace. Under these circumstances, forecasting any immediate changes in the less-than-satisfactory enrollment patterns of low-income and minority students is unrealistic.

The quality of education — or the lack of quality — became a major topic for discussion and debate and for certain new initiatives in several states in 1983–1984. Although it is much too soon to assess the effectiveness of any changes in the educational system across the country, enough movement has occurred to merit considerable public attention. The nation is faced with huge fiscal problems and a record federal deficit; we see no logical reason to look for any short-term growth in federal student aid program appropriations.

Another issue that troubled many educators was the rapidly escalating use of "no-need" scholarships or merit awards without regard to need; these were used chiefly as recruiting tools to attract academically strong students, probably at the expense of other, less talented applicants, especially low-income and minority students.

Who are the needy? Who got the money? Has it done any good? These and other fundamental questions continue to disturb those interested in, and concerned about, worthy and deserving students.

Additional factors are noteworthy. The characteristics of college students are changing, as are their periods of enrollment. More students are part-time, more are women, more are minorities, and more are older. A widely diversified student population has served to complicate an already overburdened financial aid delivery system — a system mainly administered manually and generally immersed in a flood of paper. But new technological developments are under way, and a distributed data-processing structure linking all the people with all the programs may not be too far off. This is an encouraging situation because existing practices and procedures have not always worked well for disadvantaged financial aid candidates.

Conclusion

In a May 1983 *U.S. News & World Report* special supplement, "What the Next 50 Years Will Bring," Marvin Cetron of Forecasting International stated: "What you learn as a young person will not be enough to carry you through a lifetime of work" (p. A26). Increasingly, skilled workers will be at a premium in an economy whose strength is based on high technology. More than ever before in our history, education, training, and retraining will be vital to the individual's success and satisfaction in the market place. Yet low-income and minority students as a group typically fail to participate fully in these activities.

Noting that the future will bring more special programs for the most able students, *U.S. News & World Report* quotes Cetron further: "College will not be made available in the future for mediocre students because it will be too expensive" (p. A42). Again, too many low-income and minority students possess less-than-competitive academic credentials, and they have inadequate resources with which to pay college costs.

While most predictions about the nation's economic well-being in the next decade are positive, a high rate of unemployment is expected to persist among the undereducated. And, historically, the undereducated are black, Hispanic, and poor.

In a free society, the goal is more education for more people, not less education for fewer people. Adequately funded student financial aid programs can contribute to that goal.

References

Bowen, H. R.
   1977   *Investment in Learning: The Individual and Social Value of American Higher Education.* San Francisco: Jossey–Bass.
Carnegie Council on Policy Studies in Higher Education
   1980   *Three Thousand Futures: The Next Twenty Years for Higher Education.* San Francisco: Jossey–Bass.
Davis, J.S.
   1983   *What Our Alumni Have Done: A Study of the Employment and Educational Activities of Pennsylvania State Grant Recipients One Year After Completion of Their Undergraduate Programs, Spring, 1982.* Harrisburg, Pa.: Pennsylvania Higher Education Assistance Agency.

Davis, J. S., & Johns, K.
    1982 Low family income: A continuing barrier to college enroll-
          ment? *Journal of Student Financial Aid* (February), vol. 12, no.
          1, p. 5–11.
Ferrin, R. I.
    1970 *Barriers to Universal Higher Education.* New York: College
          Entrance Examination Board.
Gillespie, D. A., & Carlson, N.
    1983 *Trends in Student Aid: 1963 to 1983.* Washington, D.C.:
          Washington Office of the College Board.
Gladieux, L. E.
    1982– The future of student financial aid. *College Board Review, 126*
    1983   (Winter), 18.
National Association of State Scholarship and Grant Programs.
    1983 *15th Annual Survey Report, 1983–84 Academic Year.* Har-
          risburg, Pa.: Author.
National Commission on Student Financial Assistance.
    1983 *Access and Choice: Equitable Financing of Postsecondary
          Education.* (Report No. 7) Washington, D.C.: Author.
U.S. Bureau of the Census, Current Population Reports, Series P–60, No. 139.
    1983 *Lifetime Earnings Estimates for Men and Women in the United
          States: 1979.* Washington, D.C.: GPO.
U.S. News & World Report
    May 9, What the next 50 years will bring – A special supplement.
    1983
Washington Office of the College Board
    1984 *Update from Washington* (February), 4.

Chapter **15**   A STUDY OF TITLE III's
IMPACT ON TRADITIONALLY
BLACK INSTITUTIONS
Cameron Fincher

The enactment of Title III of the Higher Education Act of 1965 publicly acknowledged the national role that traditionally black institutions (TBIs) play in education beyond the high school. Although poorly funded and vaguely expressed, Title III left no doubt about the federal government's intent to recognize TBIs as national resources and to provide symbolic, if not substantive, forms of institutional support. Reenactment of Title III in the Educational Amendments Act of 1972 and other extensions of the original act have not altered the basic thrust of federal policy, and despite the doubt cast upon Title III by several evaluations, its institutional support to TBIs should be obvious.

The premises on which a survey of Title III's impact has been conducted are quite simple. At the time of the survey, Title III was under attack by the General Accounting Office. A nationally released report had concluded that no assurance could be given that Title III was meeting its objectives to strengthen developing institutions. Given Title III's original intent, the emphasis that it had placed on institutional management, and evaluations stressing the importance of institutional leadership, the Southern Education Foundation quickly funded a study to seek the informed opinions and beliefs of institutional management and/or leadership. The crucial premise, therefore, was the expectation that presidents of TBIs would be unusually well informed about Title III's effectiveness and that their perceptions of success or failure would be valuable information in further deliberations at the national level.

The speed with which the Southern Education Foundation funded that survey was not matched by its implementation. Survey questionnaires

This chapter is based on a previously published research monograph by Cameron Fincher: *A Study of Title III Impact on Historically Black Institutions.* Atlanta: Southern Education Foundation, 1980.

could not be mailed until late summer, and they may have reached Title III presidents at the most inopportune time imaginable. Questionnaires were mailed to 103 TBIs on the assumption that each was receiving Title III funds and with careful efforts to distinguish traditionally black from predominantly black colleges. Not all TBIs received Title III funds, however, and the survey would have been improved had it included at least some of the later-established, predominantly black colleges that did receive Title III funds.

The low response rate by Title III presidents was understandable but nonetheless disappointing. Efforts to contact the nonrespondents by phone were unsuccessful in retrieving 57 questionnaires; thus, the analysis of survey results was based on 38% of the original 103 questionnaires. Later contacts with some of the nonrespondents suggested that several recently appointed presidents did not believe themselves sufficiently informed to complete the questionnaire. One or two presidents passed the questionnaire along to other administrators, who were reluctant to accept responsibility for its completion.

Examination of the returned questionnaires gave good reason to accept their contents as both significant and credible. Survey findings were then interpreted not as a representative sample of Title III presidents but as the viewpoints of a particularly important group of institutional leaders and spokespersons. Collectively, their institutions educated almost 45% of the national enrollment in TBIs. Many of the responding institutions were among the most prominent in the nation, and no evidence of geographic or institutional bias could be detected through comparisons of responding and nonresponding institutions. The survey report was thus written with the conviction that the responding presidents were among the most knowledgeable spokespersons that TBIs could claim and that their expressed opinions and beliefs concerning Title III effectiveness were undoubtedly consequential.

Survey Findings and Conclusions

Survey results underscore the assistance that Title III has given the responding institutions in carrying out the mission traditionally assigned them. Title III funds have permitted these institutions to fulfill roles and responsibilities that easily could have lagged without the financial and moral support TBIs require. The responses of Title III presidents clearly imply that the missions of their institutions have been broadened or consolidated and that the range or scope of their educational service has been improved. It is appropriate to conclude from survey findings that Title III has effectively reached an appreciable number of smaller, developing institutions that are outside the mainstream of higher education but that are capable of making a substantial contribution.

Institutional Management

Although its funding priorities have varied, Title III has given better assistance to institutional planning and curriculum development than to faculty development and improved services. Over one-half the responding presidents replied that the major emphasis of their Title III programs has been institutional planning and/or curriculum development, while less than 10% believed that such an emphasis was less than average.

The emphasis given by Title III programs to institutional planning has assisted in developing long-range plans, improving management information within the institution, and establishing institutional research as a much-needed management tool. Responding presidents also pointed to improvements in data processing, budgeting, and fiscal accountability. Title III funding was less successful, they believed, in helping their institutions with overall institutional development, personnel selection, and salary or wage administration, but a majority of presidents reported the effectiveness of Title III efforts in upgrading administrative staffs through workshops and seminars.

Other attempts to increase institutional effectiveness through employing new administrators, reassigning personnel to new responsibilities, or developing administrative support along technical or semiprofessional lines were variously reported by Title III presidents but did not impress them as outstanding. Responding presidents did endorse, however, the use of Title III funds for consultative services of a professional or technical nature and for on-site visits to other campuses for observational purposes.

Some of the responding presidents had received personal benefits from Title III in the form of training or supervised experience, but few indicated a high degree of involvement in Title III as proposal readers, consultants, or evaluation team members. Whenever Title III presidents reported such involvement, they believed it to be a valuable and job-related experience, but, as a group, they did not perceive themselves as beneficiaries of Title III in a direct or personal sense.

Program Improvement

Responding presidents did not doubt the effectiveness of Title III in improving their academic programs. At least two-thirds of the group believed that Title III funding had been of substantial assistance in strengthening established major fields through the addition of new courses. An even larger proportion of the group was pleased with the use of instructional media made possible through Title III funds, and almost as many presidents appreciated new major fields or areas of specialization that such outside funding had permitted. Academic programs at their institutions had been improved, they believed, through various forms of interdepartmental and interinstitutional cooperation, but many presidents doubted that the exchange of students and the provision of field trips and other cultural experiences had improved academic programs directly. Two out of three presidents did not think that the exchange of students had helped at all.

Title III presidents did not doubt the effectiveness of Title III funds in improving the quality of instruction within their institutions, but improvement appeared to be more evident in program development than in assistance to individual faculty members. Although an appreciable number of faculty had received some kind of direct support under Title III, only half the responding presidents believed that faculty workshops and seminars were highly effective, and at least a fourth regarded National Teaching Fellows as being of no help at all. Improving academic programs through acquiring instructional equipment, supplies, and materials was more obvious to responding presidents than were faculty efforts to update their teaching and/or classroom skills. In much the same manner, Title III presidents reported an appreciation of consultants for special projects funded under Title III but did not regard the effectiveness of such consultants as outstanding.

Student Services

Title III projects to improve student services were variously appreciated by the responding presidents and, like faculty development efforts, may have been a matter about which the presidents felt some ambivalence. They appeared most to appreciate such student services as reading labs, career counseling, and academic advisement, but responding presidents were also aware of limitations in most student services as they were currently provided. When asked which specific student services would not have been available without Title III funds, responding presidents identified counseling services and basic skills programs more frequently than any other student service.

Almost one of four presidents expressed dissatisfaction with the effectiveness of financial aid advisement in their institutions. Title III funds had not contributed significantly to improving this particular service, they believed, and other presidents may have been equally dissatisfied with the improvement of testing services, efforts to improve speech communication, and the development of student computational skills. In brief, responding presidents appreciated the assistance in student services provided by Title III funds, but few presidents were thoroughly pleased with the quality of student services in their institutions.

The Overall Value of Title III

In addition to various questions about Title III's effectiveness in improving institutional functions and operations, the survey sought the presidents' informed judgment about the general value of the act and its implementation. An impressive majority of respondents gave Title III a high rating in comparison with other 1960s legislation. Virtually all the presidents agreed that Title III had been effective in making higher education more accessible to minority students. Their opinions were divided, however, on the effectivenes of specific programs fostered under Title III.

A majority of responding presidents did not regard consortia as highly successful. They concluded that direct institutional support was a more satisfactory funding arrangement, and several presidents responded that their institutions had avoided membership in consortia as such. Membership in a consortium, nonetheless, was a more frequently reported form of interinstitutional cooperation than were bilateral agreements with an assisting university. A majority of Title III presidents reported a bilateral agreement with a public university at some time in the years of Title III funding, while less than a third reported a similar agreement with private universities. Well over half the institutions had used private consulting agencies, and almost as many had used freelance consultants, on Title III projects.

When asked to judge Title III's cost effectiveness, a majority of presidents responded that the cost effectiveness had indeed been significant. They agreed that Title III had been instrumental in improving the financial stability of their institutions, but they would have preferred greater funding under more predictable circumstances. At least 3% of the responding presidents doubted the effectiveness of Title III funds in improving their institutions' financial stability. Title III funds did constitute a large portion of the institutions' general expenditures budget, and almost half the presidents reported that their current Title III funds were less than during the previous year.

Responding presidents appreciated the difficulties they believed inherent in administering Title III and rated the performance of federal officials as adequate. Nevertheless, a fourth of the presidents believed that federal officials had done a poor job of informing potential recipients about funding, and at least 4 of 10 presidents believed that processing Title III applications had been handled poorly. Some of the presidents also expressed displeasure with the monitoring of Title III grants. Responding presidents, who would have preferred better assurance of continued support, strongly favored multiple-year funding. Less than a majority of the presidents believed, however, that payments should be made directly to assisting agencies. In much the same manner, they did not believe that the federal government should exercise better control over assisting agencies.

Within their institutions, responding presidents rated the performance of Title III project directors higher than they did that of Title III coordinators. Almost two-thirds rated the performance of their project directors superior or excellent, and no president rated a project director's performance poor. The performance of Title III coordinators, to the contrary, was often rated inadequate. A reason for the less favorable rating may lie in the federal requirement that there be a Title III coordinator. Given the smallness of grants, a full-time coordinator's salary may have been a luxury that many institutions could ill afford.

Title III's overall value to TBIs as a group is clearly acknowledged by presidents responding to the survey. Although too small to produce institutional changes of great magnitude, Title III funding has been instrumental in significant institutional changes. Title III itself is seen by many TBI presidents as an effective means of institutional support at a time when such support was crucial.

General Implications

When asked for the most valuable expenditure of Title III funds in their institutions, at least one-third of the responding presidents identified administrative development projects or activities. It is distinctly possible, therefore, that Title III has been of greatest service to TBIs by aiding the continued professional and personal development of institutional leaders. Despite the inconsistencies of funding policies and priorities under Title III, funds have been available to institutional leaders for institutional development. The use of these funds has not depended on theories of institutional development, and use has not required consistent, coherent rationales for administrative and faculty development. Thus, Title III might be successful because it has been a means of sustaining or enhancing ongoing functions and has been a way in which new functions could be initiated where gaps or deficiencies obviously existed. Administering funded projects is immediately and directly relevant to administrative development.

If later studies should verify that the primary benefits have been indirect, such findings should not lessen Title III's overall impact. They may well substantiate the possibility that Title III has provided funds for problem solving or experimental purposes to a group of institutions that greatly needed such funds for the experiential learning that would result. Title III monies have given the appearance of discretionary funds at a time when such funds were virtually nonexistent. To state the matter differently, Title III has permitted some degree of administrative problem solving or experimentation, and administrators have learned from the experience in a way that does not depend on the success of solutions or on experimental results. Using Title III funds has made institutional leaders more knowledgeable in many ways, and the implications of that particular outcome should be more evident with continued development of TBIs.

PART 6

The Employment of Blacks in Traditionally White Institutions

The *Adams* criteria call for assurance that the number and proportion of blacks in the ranks of employees in traditionally white public colleges and universities will be increased. These increases must include employment in positions requiring a master's degree as well as in those requiring a doctorate. These increases are expected both in academic and administrative positions where there has been no tradition of such presence, as well as in nonacademic positions that were not as restricted.

We might hope that race discrimination was all that we had to worry about. But the academic marketplace has also been biased against women, a fact that influenced the Center for Law and Social Policy, as Counsel for the Women's Equity Action League, to join in the *Adams* litigation and call for the enforcement of Title IX of the Civil Rights Act of 1974. In 1977, the Department of Health, Education, and Welfare (HEW) was ordered in *Adams* v. *Califano* to institute enforcement proceedings. Hence, the research reported by Anne Pruitt in Chapter 16 examines the extent to which white colleges and universities increased employment of blacks by race and gender.

BLACK EMPLOYEES IN
TRADITIONALLY WHITE
INSTITUTIONS IN THE
ADAMS STATES, 1975 TO 1977
Anne S. Pruitt

The goal of this research was to describe and analyze the status of
black employees in traditionally white institutions (TWIs) of higher education in eight states (Arkansas, Florida, Georgia, North Carolina, Maryland,
Oklahoma, Pennsylvania, and Virginia) affected by the *Adams* v. *Califano*
desegregation case and to identify patterns of change in that status over a
two-year period, 1975–1977. The object was to use the Equal Employment
Opportunity information system (EEO–6) to construct longitudinal records
on the employment of black workers in order to show relationships between
employment variables such as race, sex, and salary and primary occupational activity. A further purpose was to analyze the status of black
employees to show relationships between employment variables and institutional types, such as flagship institutions and community colleges, and the
selectivity of institutions. This research was viewed as an opportunity to
provide baseline data for longitudinal studies of black employment in
Adams states.

The employment of blacks in white colleges and universities is not new.
They have long served as cooks, janitors, yard men, and menial laborers,
just as they have in the labor force in general. The struggle for equal
employment opportunities has been most protracted in the academic, administrative, and managerial realms. The *Adams* guideline ordering the
employment of minorities in all sectors of colleges and universities was an
unusual historical event, mandating the influx of a new group into the work
force of the higher education system.

This chapter is based on a previously published research monograph by Anne S. Pruitt: *Black
Employees in Traditionally White Institutions in the Adams States, 1975 to 1977.* Atlanta:
Southern Education Foundation, 1981.

Rationale

Jurisdictional control, admission requirements, and institutional type are important criteria for profiling schools. All schools in this research are publicly controlled. With respect to admission requirements, institutions can be separated into selectivity levels. This concept, generated by Astin's 1977 research, advanced the view that institutions of higher education form a hierarchy based on estimates of the average admission test scores of their entering freshmen. In describing the public hierarchy, Astin used 1,326 institutions in the United States and divided them into three levels of selectivity each among two-year colleges, four-year colleges, and universities. Astin reported that selective institutions spend in excess of three times more per student than do the least selective four-year and two-year colleges. Also, educational and general expenditures, value of buildings, land and equipment, and library expenditures increase with selectivity. One of the questions explored in this research is whether or not a patterned relationship exists between institutional selectivity and black employment.

Quantitative analysis of black employment status is important because of considerable question about whether the employment criteria are strong enough. This is of special concern in the case of faculty. Fairfax (1978) notes that HEW permitted the states to submit plans without deadlines but with commitments to do better eventually. Furthermore, the states have adopted national criteria for hiring blacks into positions that require the doctorate. Yet national data on faculty by earned degrees in the 1970s show that the master's degree is the highest earned degree for large numbers of faculty members.

Atelsek and Gomberg (1978), studying new faculty in 10 selected fields, point out that, of the 10,000 faculty hired in 1976–1977, only 49% of those hired at public four-year colleges had the doctorate degree or were within two years of earning it. When asked about preference for the doctorate, only 67% of four-year colleges and 8% of two-year colleges responded positively. This preference was even lower in nonscience fields. The one strong point in the *Adams* employment criteria mandates the states to adopt as a goal hiring blacks in positions that do not require the doctorate and hiring them at a level equal to the state's percentage of blacks who earn masters' degrees. Although EEO–6 report forms do not specify degree levels required for various positions, a quantitative analysis, such as the one reported here, provides a basis for examining this matter at some future date.

Quantitative analysis of employment by race and sex derives from additional considerations. Gurin and Pruitt (1977) argue that

> typical presentations of sex and race differentials in wages and occupational position have contributed to, rather than corrected, the erroneous picture of black women as having an edge in the market. . . . This has occurred because sex and race discrimination have been treated as totally separate phenomena. (p. 89)

To separate faculty employment from all other employment recognizes the distinctive process that takes place in the academic marketplace. It is characterized by a system of collegiality that includes three facets of special importance to the consideration of blacks: data regarding the pool, the "old boy" network, and the prestige of prospective faculty members and the hiring institutions. Although affirmative action guidelines have been designed to publicize openings more widely and to make the recruitment process more open, observation suggests that "old boy" networks still affect the process to a considerable degree. Assigning greater weight to individuals who have been nominated than to those who apply is a common practice. Caplow and McGee (1958) argue that these "networks of influence" are decisive in assuring the placement of students for research and graduate education, and hence for hiring, once the degree is earned. As a consequence, nominations by prestigious professors from prestigious universities carry the greatest weight.

Despite the fact that some believe that the current process in faculty recruitment deviates from the Caplow–McGee emphasis on collegial influence and consensus, observation suggests that it still remains a system over which faculty exert control in a way far different from the control exerted in hiring nonfaculty; also, it is a system into which blacks have not had the same entrée as whites. Promotion and tenure are even more collegial than recruitment. They are greatly influenced by political and economic forces affecting higher education. Although this project did not examine the processes of faculty hiring, promotion, and tenure, the dynamics are sufficiently distinctive to call for separating the faculty and nonfaculty groups for analysis.

Analyzing faculty and nonfaculty by institutional type raises another issue. On the one hand, it could be argued that flagship institutions, being the most prestigious, are also the most visible to enforcement agencies. Under court order, they, rather than community colleges, for example, would tend to make the greatest progress in hiring blacks. On the other hand, the percentage of black students enrolled could shift attention in the direction of community colleges. In 1978, 44% of black students in TWIs were enrolled in community colleges (National Advisory Committee on Black Higher Education and Black Colleges and Universities 1980). Because the credentials required for employment at such institutions are not as stringent as those at the four-year colleges and universities, community colleges could be expected to lead the way in employing blacks.

The following questions directed this project:

1. For the years 1975 and 1977, what was the status of black employees regarding primary occupational activity, salary level, length of annual contract, rank and tenure, and source of funding for salary (*a*) for all eight states? (*b*) for four states selected on the basis of the following factors: percentage of blacks in the population; amount of progress in hiring blacks; change in the hiring of blacks; and presence of a diverse, longstanding community college system?

2. How were faculty and nonfaculty race and sex groups dispersed across institutional types?

Design

Data on the employment of blacks by TWIs were retrieved from computer tapes prepared by the HEW Office for Civil Rights (OCR) for the years 1975 and 1977. Four types of institutions were identified, using a modification of the classification system set forth by the Carnegie Commission on Higher Education (1973): (1) flagship institutions; (2) doctoral-granting institutions; (3) comprehensive universities and colleges; and (4) two-year colleges. All institutions were assigned a selectivity score, according to Astin's coding system, which yielded 232 institutions. An overall analysis of black employment in all eight states was conducted for the base year 1975, then compared with 1977. Each POA (Primary Occupational Activity) was examined for salary levels and presence of blacks. These data were reported by sex, and all were compared with similar data for white employees.

Four states were selected for more intensive analysis. In order to determine how the changes observed in the initial analysis were dispersed across institutional types and between the sexes and races, stepwise discriminant analyses were performed. For this analysis, employees were categorized as faculty or nonfaculty and were analyzed according to the variables of institutional type, selectivity, race, sex, and year of employment.

Limitations. The project's major limitation is that it relies on secondary analysis of statistical reports. A related problem was missing data. Some states provided totals only, without disaggregating data by lines. Only those institutions that completed the EEO–6 forms were included. Also, there is the inevitable difference among institutional respondents in the way they categorize employees.

Analysis of Black and White Employment in the Eight States

POA Analysis: 1975

In 1975, TWIs in the eight states under study employed 188,993 individuals, of whom 84.5% were white, 13.4% were black, and 2% were other minorities.

9–10 Month Contract

Faculty. Females constituted 26.5% and blacks 2.9% of faculty on 9–10 month contracts. White males dominated this group both in numbers and salary level. Both black and white males clustered at a higher salary than females. Females were more prominent than males at the lowest salary level. Analysis by race indicated that 22% of whites were at the highest salary levels, but only 10% of blacks were.

11–12 Month Contract

Executive, Administrative, Managerial, and Professional Nonfaculty. White males were divided almost evenly at all but the lowest salary level. In comparison, black males and white females clustered at the lowest levels. Almost 88% of the employees at the lowest salary level were black males, black females, or white females, but only 10% of those at the highest level were from these three subgroups. White males dominated the higher-paying executive–managerial positions.

Faculty. Faculty on 11–12 month contracts were even more dominated by white males. While 11% of black females earned salaries at the highest levels, 55% of white males did. Only 12% of white males earned less than $10,000 annually, but 40% of black females were in that group.

Secretarial–Clerical, Technical–Paraprofessional, and Skilled Crafts. This employee category was 73% white and 14% black. Over 90% in the secretarial-clerical positions were female. Yet, even here, white males held a higher percentage of the higher-paid positions. Technical–paraprofessional positions were evenly divided between males and females, although there was a large number of black females at the highest salary level. White males held 88% of the skilled crafts positions, blacks 9%, and females 4%. Thus, although all four subgroups clustered at the lowest salary levels, white males dominated the skilled crafts positions.

Service–Maintenance. All four subgroups clustered at the $5,000 to $8,000 salary level. Again, the salaries of white males were more often at the top two salary levels (44%), and black females were the lowest paid.

Full-time Faculty by Rank and Tenure

Tenured. In 1975, only a little over 1% (404) of tenured faculty were black, and less than 19% were female (4,909). More than 4,000, or 23% of white males, and less than 100, or 40% of black males, were tenured with less than associate professor rank. Among tenured female faculty, however, 49% of white females and 76% of black females held less than associate professor appointments. In contrast, 38% of the white males were full professors, compared to only 15% of the blacks and 17% of the white females. Both sex and race differences emerged. Forty-nine percent of tenured black females were at the instructor–lecturer–other rank.

Nontenured, On Track. In 1975, this group included only 4% blacks. White females made up 27% of this group, in contrast to black females, who were at 2%. As with tenured faculty, black females clustered at the instructor –lecturer level, while the other three groups were at the assistant professor level.

Other Faculty. In 1975, other faculty (neither tenured nor on the tenure track) accounted for 13% of all black and white faculty. There were almost twice as many males as females, and blacks made up 6% of the group. All four subgroups clustered heavily at the instructor–lecturer–other rank. Comparing these percentages with tenured faculty, this category contained twice as many black men and four times as many black women. Compared to nontenured, on-track black faculty, the percentage of black men was the same, but twice as many black women were in this category.

Temporary and Part-Time Employees

Temporary employees included 10% blacks (4% black males and 6% black females) and 47% females. Faculty made up the bulk of this group

(70%) and represented 29% of all faculty. Most of these faculty members were nontenured and not on track (95%), and blacks were a larger percentage (8%) here than in any other faculty group. In addition, among executive–managerial and professional nonfaculty employees, the majority of each subgroup (except for black males, who were split evenly between the two positions) were in professional nonfaculty positions.

POA Analysis: 1977

By 1977, employees in the TWIs of the eight state systems had increased by 5%. Black faculty were now 1.6% of the group, a decrease of 0.2%, although their total numbers did increase slightly. More substantial was the increase in the percentage of other minorities from 2% to 2.4%, which represented a numerical increase of 20.6%.

9–10 Month Contract

Faculty. Of faculty with 9–10 month contracts, 3.2% were blacks (a 0.3% increase). White males represented 71% of the group and clustered at the highest salary levels. White females and black females both clustered at the middle salary range. Forty-one percent of white males were at the highest salary levels, but only 24% of black males, 17% of white females, and 8% of black females were at those levels. Only 8% of white males were at the bottom of the scale, compared to 36% of black females.

11–12 Month Contract

Executive, Administrative, Managerial, and Professional Nonfaculty. By 1977, although the total number of employees in this category had increased by 8% and the number of blacks had increased by 5.6%, the percentage of blacks had decreased by 0.2%. The percentage of white males had decreased and that of white females had increased. In the main, white males clustered at the highest salary level, black males at the middle, and both white females and black females near the bottom. White males dominated the higher-paid executive–administrative positions. The percentage of all subgroups at the lowest level had decreased substantially; however, the percentages of those at the highest level had not changed to any great extent, except for black females, whose percentage at that level doubled and whose actual number increased from 13 to 33 (2.5 times).

Faculty. The percentage of black faculty remained at just under 4%, and females still made up about 23%. Although all four subgroups made progress in salary levels, black females lagged behind. They had the largest percentage of individuals at the bottom of the salary scale and the smallest at the top. Females in general fell behind males; they clustered at the middle, while white males clustered at the highest level, with black males just below them.

Secretarial–Clerical, Technical–Paraprofessional, and Skilled Crafts. In 1977, this category consisted of 2.5% more blacks than in 1975. It was still made up of 73% females. The group's male and female composition had not changed. Although all four subgroups had made progress up the salary scale, clearly it was white males who profited the most.

Service–Maintenance. Although this category decreased by 1%, white females and black females both increased 1%. White males continued to head the salary scale, and, although black males and all females clustered at the middle level, the difference between them was clear. Only 46% of white females were still at the middle level, compared to 60% of black males and 71% of black females. Finally, while the percentage of white males at the top had increased from 11% to 27%, it had increased only a few points for each of the other subgroups.

Full-time Faculty by Rank and Tenure

Tenured. Tenured faculty reflected some major differences by both race and sex. Tenured faculty represented 54.4% of all full-time faculty (a 3% increase) and included only 1.8% blacks (a 0.3% increase, although their number increased by 26.7%). The number of females had increased by 10.3%. White males clustered at the professor rank, black males and white females at the associate professor rank, and black females at the assistant professor rank. Black females, however, had made the most progress, increasing from 8% to 20% at the full professor rank and decreasing from 49% to 25% at the instructor–lecturer–other level.

Nontenured, On-Track Faculty. Nontenured, on-track faculty decreased by 9.6% between 1975 and 1977, while the percentage of blacks within the category increased by 0.6%. All but black males and females declined in percentage in the instructor–lecturer–other level. This decline suggests that more blacks were leaving before promotion and tenure. There were 23 fewer blacks at the associate professor level in 1977 than in 1975, a 43.4% decrease.

Other Faculty. In general, other faculty continued to remain at the in-structor–lecturer–other rank. The number of individuals in this category increased by 3.6%, but the percentage of blacks decreased by 0.5%.

Temporary and Part-time Employees

Temporary employees increased by 6.3%, but the percentage of blacks hired as temporary employees decreased by 2% (their number decreased by over 13%). The percentage of both black males and black females in these positions decreased by 4%. The percentage of blacks in executive, ad-ministrative, managerial, nonfaculty professional positions also decreased. Overall, the largest percentage increase occurred among white females (2%), the increase coming primarily from secretarial–technical–skilled crafts positions. They also decreased by 4% in faculty positions, although their number actually increased.

New Hires

New Hires was a category added to the EEO–6 reporting form in 1977, and the data, therefore, have no 1975 equivalents for comparisons. In 1977, the largest proportion of new hires was in secretarial–technical–skilled crafts positions, with the service–maintenance POA accounting for 45% of the blacks. Only 4.8% of the blacks went into faculty positions. Where blacks are concerned, the executive, administrative, managerial, and pro-fessional nonfaculty category shows 2.3% more females than males.

Analysis of Selected States

Findings on four selected states — Arkansas, Florida, Georgia, and Maryland — are summarized here individually along the lines of the analysis of all states.

Arkansas

In 1969, Arkansas completed a plan for desegregating its higher educa-tion system. Cobb (1979) points out that Arkansas officials moved swiftly to develop the plan. The process was nearly devoid of disruptions caused by local preferences or federal guidelines and did not meet with the public outrage found in many other *Adams* states.

In 1975, Arkansas employed only 8,990 in higher education, of whom 11% were black. It also had the smallest percentage of blacks in its population. Yet the percentage increase in black professional employment was the largest. By 1977, the total number of employees in Arkansas had grown by 54.9%. The number of black employees had increased by 8%, although their percentage of total employees had actually decreased by 1.1%.

In 1977, 18.4% of all black and white employees were new hires. Eight percent of those in the executive category and 4% of those in the faculty category were black. The executive category also included 71.2% females, and the faculty category included 33.4% females.

The data show that Arkansas increased the number of blacks in all professional positions. For example, the number of blacks in executive, administrative, managerial, and professional nonfaculty positions increased from 88 to 133. Although the numbers are small, they represent a 33.8% increase in two years, and increases of similar scope can be found in the other categories.

Florida

In 1975, TWIs in Florida employed 34,112 individuals, of whom 15% were blacks. By 1977, Florida employed 7% more people. Black employees still made up 15% of the group, although this actually represented a 0.2% decrease in two years. In that same period, a 0.9% increase in the number of other minorities occurred. The 7% increase was distributed across all categories, so none of the subtotals showed any notable change.

New hires in 1977 represented almost 6% of all employees, and blacks were 15% of the group. Nontenured faculty made up 32%, with 9% black. Executive and professional nonfaculty made up 12%, with 9% black. These data suggest encouraging trends, since blacks in both categories had rarely constituted more than 7%.

A large percentage of minority employees, expected because of the large and diverse community college system, was not found. In fact, there were decreases in the number of blacks in executive, administrative, managerial, and professional nonfaculty positions and in temporary faculty, who make up about one-third of all faculty. While the percentage of blacks in faculty positions did increase, the numbers were still minuscule.

Georgia

Blacks in 1976 accounted for 27.2% of Georgia's population, the largest percentage of blacks in any of the states analyzed in this report.

In 1970, OCR notified the Board of Regents of the University System that the state had failed to desegregate its dual system of higher education (Haynes 1979). Instead of submitting a plan, the Board of Regents replied that the state had made great strides in that direction during the 1960s. To the contrary, OCR, in its 1973 response, noted that blacks constituted only 0.006% (30 of 4,857) of the faculty members at the TWIs and that no black faculty were located in any of the system's two-year colleges. Unlike the process in Arkansas, the process of compliance in Georgia had been characterized by one disruption after another.

In 1975, TWIs in Georgia employed over 23,000 persons, of whom 18% were black. Males accounted for 53%. Eight percent of the black workers were male, and 10% were female.

By 1977, Georgia's TWIs had hired 7% more workers. Data indicate a 4% increase in the number of blacks, who were found overwhelmingly in the full-time, 11–12 month contract category. The increase took place primarily in the secretarial and service POAs, while the executive and faculty categories changed very little.

New hires constituted 12% of all employees for 1977, and blacks made up 18%. The percentage of blacks ranged from 56% of all new hires in the service–maintenance category down to 5% in the faculty category. The percentages of blacks in the executive, administrative, managerial, and professional nonfaculty categories were similar to the 1975 percentages of blacks already in these categories.

Because Georgia had the largest percentage of black population of any state under analysis, it could be expected that Georgia had the largest pool of potential employees and, as a consequence, would have increased the proportions of blacks. The data presented above indicate that such was not the case. Specifically, in 1975, Georgia employed a percentage of blacks in professional positions similar to that of the other states, and this percentage did not increase substantially during the two years under consideration.

Maryland

Of the eight states examined, Maryland showed the greatest changes in black employment. Employees totaled 15,182 and consisted of 87% whites, 11% blacks, and 2% others. This was in a state that, in 1975, had a 20% black population. By 1977, the total number of employees had increased by 2%, but the number of blacks had increased by only 0.3%

Although faculty employed on 11–12 month contracts shrank by 17% in the two-year period, more striking is the 51.7% decrease in the number of blacks. By contrast, the percentage of white males increased. Among temporary and part-time employees, blacks decreased in number by 12%. The percentage of blacks as temporary faculty decreased by almost 1%, but their number decreased by 36. The number of executive–professional nonfaculty increased by 27%, while the percentage of blacks in the POA decreased slightly, although their actual number increased by three.

New hires accounted for almost 7% of all employees, and 18% of them were black. Specifically, black professionals accounted for 15% of the executive–professional nonfaculty positions, 2% of the new tenured faculty, and almost 5% of the nontenured faculty. These new hires, however, did not counteract the cuts in number.

Maryland either made no progress in hiring black employees or actually cut their number by a percentage unparalleled by the general cutbacks in its work force. This is particularly true in the faculty positions, where, for example, the number of blacks in full-time, 11–12 month contract faculty positions was cut by nearly 52%. At the same time, although tenured faculty increased by 256, this number included only 5 blacks.

Discriminant Analysis

Over the two-year period, black employment increased by 0.2%. The percentage for black men decreased by 0.3%, but for black females, it increased by 0.4%. In order to determine how these changes were dispersed across institutional types and between the sexes and races, discriminant analyses were performed. Considering institutional types, the results show that, by race, after selectivity was controlled, community colleges were more likely to hire blacks in nonfaculty positions, after the relative proportions of black faculty were accounted for.

When the sexual dimension was considered, the above conclusion was modified: After controlling for selectivity, community colleges were more likely to employ black women than were flagship and doctoral schools. The important group proportion that distinguished between the four institutional types appeared to be black women.

Conclusions

In 1975, higher education in these eight states was big business, employing nearly 189,000 individuals in TWIs. By 1977, this number had jumped to more that 199,000 — a 5% increase in two years. Yet employment of blacks increased by only 0.2%. For black men, the percentage actually decreased by 0.2%, but for black women, it increased by 0.4%.

In every POA, white males predominated at the highest salary levels and black women at the lowest. For blacks, the change in relative POA share was greater in nonfaculty than in faculty positions.

When the opportunity came in 1977 to hire new workers, 85% of those hired were white. Most of the blacks hired were in secretarial–clerical, technical–paraprofessional, and skilled crafts positions. Only 8.7% of blacks hired were appointed to the faculty. Black males who were tenured faculty members clustered in 1977 at the associate professor level, a step up since 1975. Those who were nontenured but on-track shrank in percentage at the associate professor level. Although those who were classified as "other" remained at the instructor–lecturer level, their relative employment share decreased, as did their share of the temporary and part-time positions.

For black females, a tenured faculty position meant an assistant professorship, for they predominated at this level. Yet, in the two-year period, they did make the greatest progress at the professor rank and the greatest decrease at the instructor–lecturer rank. In nontenured, on-track appointments, they decreased at both the instructor and associate professor levels. In the category of "other" faculty, as compared with tenured and nontenured, on track, they were found in much larger numbers and at the lowest level: instructor–lecturer.

The number of white female faculty increased in tenured and nontenured, on-track appointments and in the ranks of "other" faculty. The largest percentage increase in the temporary and part-time category occurred among white females, who were hired in secretarial–clerical, technical–paraprofessional, and skilled crafts positions. While the white female percentage of temporary and part-time faculty decreased, their numbers increased.

The primary gainers were white males. They clustered at the rank of professor and increased in all other categories, with the exception of the lowest: instructor–lecturer. Their numbers increased in the category of "other" faculty and in temporary and part-time employees.

By sex, the two-year period saw more gains for men than for women. Analysis of year-round, full-time employees in 1977 revealed that income was lowest for minority-race women. When POAs were examined, women workers were in the majority as clerical workers but held only a small fraction of the skilled crafts jobs, a large percentage of the service maintenance jobs, and less than half the professional and technical jobs.

Arkansas, the smallest employer of workers in its higher education system, documented the greatest increases in proportions of blacks hired. Blacks did not fare as well as might have been expected in Florida, whose community college system could have provided employment opportunity for those without the doctorate. The number of black employees in Georgia did not reflect its relatively larger black population. And Maryland, with two years in which to increase the number of blacks employed, actually cut back in several POAs.

Postscript

In the years since this research was completed, the author has corresponded with the EEOC and the OCR for the purpose of securing the 1979 EEO–6 computer tape. Although a tape was purchased in August 1982, it contains serious flaws. This information was transmitted to the OCR, with requests for assistance in securing a tape that could be used. In June 1983, the author was told that EEOC's records are confidential and that only aggregated data by states, not individual institutional records, could be provided.

When asked about the data dissemination policy for research purposes, OCR replied that it has no policy that forbids issuing data to researchers. It does require, however, that certain procedural safeguards be followed before the data can be released.

Safeguards were applied in this research. In creating the data files, FICE (Federal Interagency Committee on Education) codes were used to identify TWIs in eight states so that they could be pulled off the tape and used to create a new file that corresponds to institutions for which Astin selectivity codes are available. The institutions were then grouped according to the Carnegie Classification System. No institution was identified in the final report.

Hence, the analysis reported above ends at 1977. Data have been published, however, in the aggregate, and from these one can glean some information about participation rates.

Data for the nation as a whole show that, in 1979, TWIs employed about 10,000 black full-time faculty. Blacks constituted 2.4% of all full-time faculty in these institutions. Blacks were more numerous in public TWIs (2.7%) than in private TWIs (1.4%) (Hill 1983). Thus, the employment picture did not change.

Policy Implications

One of this study's most significant contributions is its implications for public policy. For example, the importance of the federal government's role with respect to improving job opportunities is well established. Traditionally, our federal policy stance has been that public interest in the employment of its citizenry is justified when it encourages, or its absence prevents, greater output and a higher standard of living, a higher quality of goods and services, long-term social and economic growth, or a more dynamic and adaptable economy. When compared with right to work in general, the federal government's role in supporting fair employment practices and affirmative action has been *ad hoc.* Absence of a coordinated, systematic policy is evident in the finding that black employment in TWIs in the *Adams* states was minuscule as late as 1977.

This research's most obvious contribution is the baseline data for trend studies. It also provides statistical support for the widely held belief that public and institutional policies are inadequate to achieve substantial increases in the numbers and proportions of black employees, academic and nonacademic, in the higher ranks and higher salaried positions in TWIs in the *Adams* states. During the period covered by this study, minority faculty were being appointed in significant though insufficient numbers, but their prospects are diminished for the next two decades. In the late 1970s, institutions that were expected to be least vulnerable to enrollment declines were research universities, selective liberal arts colleges, and public two-year colleges. Moreover, the eight states in this study were among those whose enrollment trends relative to the national average were expected to be average or better. The implications that follow are set forth with this scenario of retrenchment and creeping conservatism in mind.

1. The *Adams* guideline on employment should be strengthened to include definite timetables and goals. The states should be advised of patterns of progress as well as deficiencies in their plans, of the required corrective steps to be undertaken, and of the costs or sanctions involved in noncompliance.

2. As in the private sector, public colleges and universities should be targeted for compliance review. The NAACP Legal Defense and Educational Fund has recommended that senior officials of the Office of Federal Contracts Compliance Programs, EEOC, and the Justice Department should be informed of the need for an overall coordinated strategy for combating racial discrimination in public colleges and universities.

3. States should be required to justify racial disparities in salary, tenure, and promotion and to set forth specific remedial steps to eliminate these disparities.

4. State legislators must work for increased funding in order to enlarge the pool of black academic and professional workers, to recruit them, and to provide for their continuing professional development.

5. Colleges and universities must become more creative in designing ways to continue the flow of high-quality young black faculty into their ranks. Given current retrenchment measures, blacks are being blocked by faculties composed mostly of white men who are tenured-in.

6. State systems must require all their institutions to target blacks for employment. Over the past two decades, public community colleges have constituted the fastest-growing segment of postsecondary education—a fact that may account for their hiring large numbers of blacks. Community colleges, however, might not sustain such growth in the future. They are now at the mercy of taxpayer revolts and criticisms from neighboring institutions because of invasion of turf.

7. More pressure must be placed on the Congress to fund doctoral fellowship programs (such as The Graduate and Professional Opportunity Program) and postdoctoral fellowship programs in order to enlarge the pool of blacks with the doctorate or appropriate additional preparation, especially in fields in which they have been underrepresented.

8. With federal legislation now providing for portable fellowships, blacks should be counseled to apply and use the awards at prestigious research universities.

9. More blacks ought to be counseled to secure preparation in the skilled crafts through vocational education and apprenticeship training.

10. Blacks seeking faculty positions should be warned of the increasing ratio of part-time to full-time faculty. State plans under *Adams* should not be allowed to target a disproportionate number of blacks for these positions.

11. A national agency or association in the field of graduate education should prepare annually a compendium of blacks earning masters' and doctorate degrees. It would provide information now lacking regarding the pool.

12. Faculty members who teach black graduate students must assume a greater mentoring role in which they stress the importance of research and writing and other kinds of scholarly productivity.

Suggestions for Further Study

The data base assembled for analysis in this study provides a valuable resource for secondary analysis. For example, discriminant analyses that exclude community colleges are needed. Studying black employment in executive and managerial positions by institutional type would be useful. Special attention should be directed to the disaggregation of data on black women and black men in nonfaculty positions in the various types of schools. The paucity of information about the black woman academician demands more research focused on this group.

The growth of part-time employment in academe in general is reflected in the TWIs analyzed in this study. Although it is a desirable option for certain classes of workers, it can be a dead end (Tuckman 1978). Research is needed on the trend toward using blacks in large numbers in low-level positions at TWIs in the *Adams* states.

As the monitoring of desegregation in public higher education continues, a longitudinal study should be set in motion. As biennial reports are received, the computer program and files used in this report can form the basis for future analyses.

Analysis is needed in which a parity index, based on the population of sex–race groups in each state, is calculated. Also, direct rather than stepwise discriminant analysis would allow one to compare what the string of variables entered into the analysis statements looks like when all variables are included. Moreover, determining the rate of wage increase of those hired and the rate at which workers move up through the institutional hierarchy would be useful. Studies have begun to appear (e.g., Fleming, Gill, & Swinton 1978; Smelzer & Content 1980), but more is needed on the arrangements that influence the recruiting, hiring, and promoting of blacks in TWIs.

References

Astin, A. W.
  1977 New measures of college selectivity. *Research in Higher Education, 6,* 1–9.
Atelsek, F. J., & Gomberg, I. L.
  1978 *New Full-time Faculty 1976–1977: Hiring Patterns by Field and Educational Attainment.* Higher Education Panel Report No. 38. Washington, D.C.: American Council on Education.
Caplow, T., & McGee, R. J.
  1958 *The Academic Marketplace.* New York: Basic Books.
Carnegie Commission on Higher Education
  1973 *A Classification of Institutions of Higher Education.* Berkeley, Calif.: The Commission.

Cobb, H. E.
    1979 A plan for the desegregation of public higher education in
          Arkansas: An analysis. In L. L. Haynes, III (Ed.), *An Analysis
          of the Arkansas–Georgia Statewide Desegregation Plans.* Wash-
          ington, D.C.: Institute for Services to Education.
Fairfax, J.
    1978 Current status of the *Adams* case: Implications for the educa-
          tion of blacks and other minorities. In College Entrance Ex-
          amination Board, *Beyond Desegregation: Urgent Issues in the
          Education of Minorities.* New York: The Board.
Fleming, J. E., Gill, G. R., & Swinton, D. H.
    1978 *The Case for Affirmative Action for Blacks in Higher Educa-
          tion.* Washington, D.C.: Howard University Press.
Gurin, P., & Pruitt, A. S.
    1977 Counseling implications of black women's market position,
          aspirations and expectancies. In *Conference on the Educational
          and Occupational Needs of Black Women.* Washington, D.C.:
          National Institute of Education, Department of Health, Educa-
          tion, and Welfare.
Haynes, III, L. L. (Ed.).
    1979 *An Analysis of the Arkansas–Georgia Statewide Desegregation
          Plans.* Washington, D.C.: Institute for Services to Education.
Hill, S. T.
    1983 *Participation of Black Students in Higher Education: A Statisti-
          cal Profile from 1970–71 to 1980–81.* Washington, D.C.: Na-
          tional Center for Education Statistics.
National Advisory Committee on Black Higher Education and Black Col-
leges and Universities.
    1980 *The Black Higher Education Fact Sheet #1: Did You Know...?*
          Washington, D.C.: The Committee.
Smelzer, N. J., & Content, R.
    1980 *The Changing Academic Market: General Trends and a Berkeley
          Case Study.* Berkeley, Calif.: University of California Press.
Tuckman, H. P.
    1978 Who is part-time in academe? *AAUP Bulletin, 64,* 305–315.

PART 7

Summary and Conclusions

Chapter **17** HIGHLIGHTS OF THE STUDIES
AND SOME POLICY INITIATIVES
Anne S. Pruitt

The crisis that prompted the *Adams* litigation (summarized in Chapter 1) was one among many in the continuing pursuit of equal educational opportunity. In 1974, when the Department of Health, Education, and Welfare (HEW) approved the desegregation plans of eight states, we had precious little research — if indeed we had any — on the impact of desegregation on higher education. As a consequence, studies reported in this volume contribute to the examination of an unusual phenomenon that can be likened in its uniqueness to the Land Grant Act, the GI Bill, and the National Defense Education Act. While those pieces of legislation targeted all of higher education, *Adams,* a federal court order, focused on a select group of states with one characteristic in common — a dual system of segregated public higher education. It forced changes in long-held values, mores, habits, practices, and, indeed, a way of life. It challenged long-held beliefs about who should go where to college. It challenged stereotypic thinking about racial inferiority and traditional views of appropriate roles for men and women. Although it targeted public colleges and universities, it produced the inevitable ripple effect that led to changes in the private sector as well.

In introducing this publication, we argued that our earliest priorities had to do with access. Yet, we noted that a broad range of issues relevant to equity in educational opportunity had to be examined.

In the chapters that followed, 19 authors, sensitive to the education of black people and higher education in general, summarized their research and addressed what they believe to be the policy implications for access, aspirations and career choices, social and psychological dimensions of college and university campuses, financial aid, and employment in postsecondary education. They used research designs that enabled them to examine some of the nuances in the education of blacks that might not be apparent in the use of traditional schema. They disaggregated data that often mask variables unique to blacks. They designed studies to respond to the rhetoric about what is taking place under desegregated conditions. Taken together, their explorations suggest that black students in the public higher education systems of the *Adams* states are an endangered species. Operationalizing *Adams* amounts to window-dressing, for although it may increase access, it may fall short of ensuring completion of baccalaureate or professional and graduate degrees, and the employment of black people in both academic and nonacademic ranks. Access apart, attention must be paid to the conditions under which students study, and to the antecedents — such as educational preparation, values, and family socioeconomic condition — that they bring to the college gates.

Access and Progression

Counting the number of black undergraduates enrolled in TWIs, Brazziel and Brazziel presented data that showed how much and where black student enrollment increased. Parity, however, was an illusive goal. They discovered a concurrent decrease in TBI enrollment, leading them to ask whether a zero-sum game was being played at the expense of TBIs.

It is no news that the higher education system is hierarchical, such that one's life chances are often influenced by the type of college attended. As a result of the broader options available under *Adams,* it then became important to examine the choices that black students were making. Grigg showed that in Florida, community colleges, enrolling blacks in large numbers, were channeling them in such a way that they were not achieving access to baccalaureate and graduate and professional degrees. The implications of his results for other states with well-developed community college systems are clear. Thomas and Braddock reported that family background, grades, and racial composition of the high school influenced enrollment in white versus black colleges.

The relative effectiveness of black and white colleges has been debated for some time. TBIs have shouldered the lion's share of attending to the higher education of this country's black leadership. Yet by traditional measures — such as endowment, number of library volumes, and faculty with Ph.D. degrees — they were regarded as substandard. To be sure, they have even been referred to as "invisible colleges." These institutions have countered with the contention that they had accepted black students — despite their own substandard status and despite students' weak academic backgrounds — and had educated them to the point where they could earn graduate and professional degrees from the nation's most outstanding research universities. They argued that they were more effective than TWIs and that their students persisted and graduated at a higher rate than those who entered TWIs.

Studies reported in this volume do not permit a categorical response to these views. In fact, the findings are mixed. Nettles and his colleagues found that black students in southern and southern border states get higher grades at TBIs but that those grades are still below par. Whites earn higher grades at both TBIs and TWIs. Although black students are more satisfied at TBIs, their retention rate is lower than at TWIs. Hart, however, using institutions spread over a wider geographical area, concluded that both eastern prestigious institutions and TBIs were effective in seeing blacks through to graduation. Unlike Nettles, he noted that effectiveness was influenced in large measure by the presence of black faculty. In somewhat the same view, Blackwell's examination of graduate and professional education underscored the centrality of institutional commitment, financial aid, and the presence of black faculty to the production of blacks with terminal degrees.

Highlighting conclusions like these can oversimplify the richness of the results reported by these researchers. They do provide encouragement for supporters of both types of institutions, and they confirm how important it is to conduct qualitative as well as quantitative research into questions of access and progression. Variables involved in persistence are complex and require the concerted attention of college and university officials, parents, counselors, teachers, and school officials alike.

Aspirations and Career Choices

Pursuing the need to go beyond the questions of access, exploration by Epps and Jackson of occupational goals and educational attainment suggests that for black males, the school influence is becoming as important as it is for black females. We must look to the schools to play a major role in educational and occupational attainment of these young people.

Thomas's report on major field choices of blacks demonstrates that general cultural expectations affect choices. This includes both their early experiences at home and their high school curricula.

Speculation about the influences on career outcomes of attendance at TBIs versus TWIs was enlightened by Johnson's research. The match between student needs and institutional environment is more important than institutional differences in career opportunities. Both types of institutions provide access. The major factor affecting initial entry into a career was overall grade point average. The fact that blacks attending TWIs earn lower grades carries considerable support for previously reported findings that blacks must be helped to excel in course work. Moreover, the student network seems to be used much more heavily in TWIs than in TBIs, an interesting commentary on coping at TWIs.

Social and Psychological Dimensions of the Learning Environment

Abatso's research suggests that coping skills can be improved. Although she identified low-coping and high-coping personalities that predispose students to variations in college persistence, she demonstrated that strengthening coping skills can lead to higher achievement and retention rates. Allen's inquiry into how black students feel about their experiences on black and white campuses reveals considerable variation. Blacks at TWIs seem to be much more successful in cognitive areas than their counterparts at TBIs. Yet, as suggested by Nettles, attendance at TWIs may be taking a greater psychic toll. Those at TBIs are not achieving as well academically, in large measure because of the lack of competition. However, they do not feel the stress of discrimination and racism described by their counterparts at TWIs. Blackwell's study of black graduate and professional school students identifies networking and mentoring as significant mechanisms in improving the quality of campus environments.

Financial Aid

The prospect that financial aid will decline in the face of Reagan administration budget-cutting initiatives poses the most devastating roadblock to increasing access of black students to higher education. The Davis and Johns chapter, although not restricted to the *Adams* states, makes the point that minority students will continue to face this most unsurmountable of barriers. Hardly a chapter that precedes their work — from Part 2 on access and progression through Part 3 on aspirations to Part 4 on the college environment — fails to identify the impecunious position of black families and therefore their inability to see their children through college. Even those identified as middle class and those who send their children to more prestigious, selective institutions need financial assistance. Thus, achieving equity in education is compounded by financial inability to meet increasingly high costs.

The values of institutional financial support referred to by Brazziel and Brazziel in Chapter 2 is supported by Fincher's research. If enhancement of TBIs is to remain a central dimension of *Adams* guidelines, the values to program improvement, institutional management, and student services, affirmed by TBI college presidents, is essential. Of course, federal funds are not the only resources. The states must continue to be partners in this joint undertaking.

Employment

Over and over again, research reported in this volume called for the hiring of more blacks in the faculty and administrative ranks of institutions in the *Adams* states. Blackwell notes the significance of their presence in graduate and professional schools, as do Nettles *et al.* and Hart in their studies of institutional effectiveness. As the work by Pruitt demonstrates, however, little progress was made in the first two years in which *Adams* states reported on their hiring practices. At the present time, creeping conservatism, resulting in weakened attention to affirmative action, will surely limit any improvement in the future.

Policy Initiatives

In sum, access remains an urgent concern. Not only must we continue to monitor progress but we need also to investigate the structural, procedural, and motivational variables that mitigate against enrollment. Increasing the number of blacks with baccalaureate, doctoral, and professional degrees is another continuing concern. Unlocking the secrets to success in graduation rates will surely contribute as well to our understanding of affirmative action issues involved in employment of blacks in academe.

Among the policy initiatives to come out of these executive summaries are the following:

1. TBIs must be enhanced with additional state and federal funds.

2. The concept of racial balance should be replaced with the concept of cross-racial enrollment.

3. Enrollment at TBIs must be encouraged by making them more attractive and utilizing cross-registration consortia and cooperative efforts rather than strategies such as program transfer.

4. High school seniors should be counseled regarding strengths of other-race colleges.

5. We must remove barriers that discourage transfer from community colleges.

6. Educators must look to the family resources, types of high schools and their curricula, as well as academic and motivational skills on the one hand and characteristics of colleges on the other in helping students to choose colleges.

7. TBIs should recruit heavily at traditionally white high schools.

8. Colleges and universities, both TBIs and TWIs, should assist black students to improve their retention rates, progression rates, and college grade point averages.

9. TWIs must increase the proportion of black faculty they hire and tenure.

10. Both TWIs and TBIs must assure the availability of student financial aid.

11. Black students should become involved in campus life.

12. Black students should reside on campus.

13. To increase the production of blacks with graduate and professional degrees, universities, government, and the business community must engage in joint ventures.

14. Universities must encourage the creation of student networks that include black students.

15. Educators must promote efforts to increase the quality of elementary and secondary education.

16. High school students must be counseled to enroll in more than the minimum courses required for graduation, and to excel in their course work, especially mathematics.

17. We must raise the socioeconomic condition of black families, for it influences attendance of their children at integrated elementary and high schools, their ability to assist their children financially, their support of high academic achievement, and their children's options to attend a wide variety of colleges, both public and private.

18. Institutions must teach students how to cope with the new demands of succeeding in a college environment.

19. Programs to improve teacher effectiveness must alert faculty to the importance of their identifying early, and making overtures to, freshmen whom they suspect need to increase their ability to cope with college.

20. TBIs must intensify academic challenge.

21. TWIs must attend to the psychic needs of the black students enrolled at their institutions.

A Final Thought

The greatest benefit of *Adams* to higher education may be the light it shines on the process of equalizing educational opportunity. The pursuit continues, enlightened by the writing and research reported here. The education of black people in America has always presented challenges — from the illegality of teaching blacks to read to insensitivity about what it takes for blacks to succeed — and it has always been characterized by crises. To enable us to wrest control from crisis and challenges was the ultimate goal of this volume.

THE AUTHORS

Yvonne R. Abatso is chairperson of the Division of Continuing Studies at Bartlesville Wesleyan College. She has taught psychology and education at Langston University, Fisk University, and Chicago City College. Her area of specialization is coping and adaptive behavior. She holds the Ph.D. degree (University of Chicago) in educational psychology. She has lectured and organized counseling services in parts of the United States, North and West Africa, France, and Germany. She has published in the area of adaptive strategies for black urban families and the coping personality. As a research assistant, she conducted research under a grant from the National Institute of Education. She was assisted by *Kofi Semenya*. Semenya is a statistician and holds a Ph.D. from the University of North Carolina at Chapel Hill. He is at present Assistant Professor of Statistics at Tennessee State University.

Walter R. Allen is Associate Professor of Sociology and Director of the Center for Afro-american and African Studies at the University of Michigan–Ann Arbor. Since 1980, he has directed the National Study of Black College Students. A native of Kansas City, Missouri, he graduated from Beloit College (B.A., 1971) and the University of Chicago (M.A., 1973; Ph.D., 1975). He was Assistant Professor of Sociology at the University of North Carolina–Chapel Hill from 1974 to 1979; he has also held visiting appointments at Howard University, Duke University, and the University of Zimbabwe. He has been Associate Editor for *Social Forces* and the *Journal of Negro Education*. His publications focus on black students in higher education, black families and child socialization, and the demography of black America. Recently, he coedited *Beginnings: The Social and Affective Development of Black Children*. He is currently working on two other books, *Beyond Pathology: Black Family Research and Theory, 1965–1985* and *College in Black and White: Black Students in U.S. Higher Education*.

James E. Blackwell (Ph.D., Washington State University) is currently Professor of Sociology at the University of Massachusetts in Boston, where he served as department chairperson from 1970 to 1975. He has held full-time teaching positions at Case Western Reserve University, San Jose State University, and Grambling State University. He has lectured widely in the United States, East Africa, and Southeast Asia. He has also held administrative directorships in American foreign service programs in Tanzania, Malawi, and Nepal.

Blackwell served as President of the Eastern Sociological Society (1981–1982), President of the Society for the Study of Social Problems (1980–1981), and, from 1970 to 1972, he served as the founding President of the Caucus of Black Sociologists. In 1979, he received the Spivak Award of the American Sociological Association for his "systematic application of sociological knowledge to ongoing social problems." In 1984, he was elected to membership in the Sociological Research Association.

His major publications include *The Black Community: Diversity and Unity,* Second Edition (1984); *Mainstreaming Outsiders: The Production of Black Professionals* (1981); *Cities, Suburbs and Blacks* (1982) with Philip Hart; *Mentoring and Networking: Experiences of Black Professionals* (1983); *Black Sociologists: Historical and Contemporary Perspectives* (1974) with Morris Janowitz; and *Community Development Focus* (1971) with Boyd Faulkner *et al.* He has also published widely in journals and in anthologies.

Jomills H. Braddock II is a sociologist of education and a program director at the Johns Hopkins University's Center for Social Organization of Schools. His areas of specialization are race and sex differences in educational and occupational mobility processes and segregation in schools and adult life. He is currently using the National Longitudinal Survey of the High School Class of 1972 to examine the long-term occupational outcomes of different schooling experiences by blacks and whites, including the possible role of school desegregation experiences. His recent findings have been published in *Sociology of Education, Urban Education, Youth and Society,* and the *Urban Review.* He recently examined sources of racial discrimination or exclusion in professional sports and reported the results in his monograph, *Institutional Discrimination: A Study of Managerial Recruitment in the National Football League.* He earned his Ph.D. in sociology at Florida State University in 1973.

Marian E. Brazziel, Ph.D., is Chairman and Chief Operating Officer, Marian Brazziel Associates, Mansfield Center, Connecticut. She has served as a statistics professor at the University of Connecticut, a statistician at the National Aeronautics and Space Administration, and a U.S. Patent Officer. She is author of *CFAS: The College Freshman Adjustment Scales* and co-author of *Higher Education for All Americans, VGH Data for Twin-Engine Jet Airplanes During Airline Operations,*

Recent Enrollment Patterns of Students in States Affected by Adams–Califano Litigation and *Operational Experiences on General Aviation Aircraft.* She has completed research and policy studies under grants from the National Endowment for the Humanities, the Mott Foundation and the Ford Foundation

William F. Brazziel, Ph.D., is Professor of Higher Education and Coordinator of Higher Education Programs at the University of Connecticut. He is a charter member of the Connecticut Higher Education Master Plan Commission. He is the author of *Quality Education for All Americans* and co-author of *Recent Enrollment Patterns of Students in States Affected by Adams–Califano Litigation* and *Higher Education for All Americans* and has published numerous journal articles and technical papers. He has served as a visiting scholar at the University of New Mexico and the University of Wisconsin. He has completed research and policy studies under grants from the U.S. Office of Education, the National Institute of Education, the U.S. Labor Department, the National Endowment for the Humanities, the Southern Education Foundation, the Ford Foundation, and the Mott Foundation.

Jerry S. Davis is director of research and policy analysis for the Pennsylvania Higher Education Assistance Agency, where his duties include assessing the effects of financial aid policies at the state and federal levels on students and institutions in the Commonwealth. Since 1969, he has helped more than 25 states, associations, and consortia study their student financial aid and access needs and design programs to meet those needs. He holds a doctorate in higher education from the University of Georgia.

As a part of his professional activities and responsibilities at PHEAA, Davis guides production of the annual report of the state student grant program activities for the National Association of State Scholarship and Grant Programs. He is a member of that association's research committee and is also chairperson of the research committee for the National Council of Higher Education Loan Programs. He serves as a member of the National Association of Financial Aid Administrators' research committee, recently authored a NASFAA report on the characteristics of members of the financial aid profession, and is currently preparing a monograph for aid administrators on how to do financial aid research. He has published numerous books, articles, and reports on a wide variety of financial aid and related topics.

Edgar G. Epps has been the Marshall Field IV Professor of Urban Education at the University of Chicago since 1970. He previously held faculty positions at Tuskegee Institute, the University of Michigan, Florida A. and M. University, and Tennessee State University. He was educated at Talladega College, Atlanta University, and Washington State University, where he earned the Ph.D. degree in sociology (1959). His books include *Black Students in White Schools, Race Relations, Cultural Pluralism,* and, with Patricia Gurin, *Black Consciousness, Identity and Achievement.* He has authored or co-authored many articles on sociological and psychological factors that influence achievement and motivation. He is a member of the Southern Education Foundation's Research Task Force and of its Board of Trustees.

Cameron Fincher is Regents Professor of Higher Education and Psychology at the University of Georgia and director of its Institute of Higher Education. Educated at the University of Minnesota (M.A., 1951) and the Ohio State University (Ph.D., 1956), he has published widely in psychological and educational journals. He served for five years as a member of the Governor's Committee on Postsecondary Education (Georgia's 1202 Commission) and has been a participant on various planning committees and task forces for over 25 years. In 1982, he was the first recipient of the Ben W. Gibson Award, given by the Southern Regional Council of the College Board for outstanding contributions to higher education. In 1983, he was designated a distinguished member of the Association for Institutional Research. He has worked with the Southern Education Foundation on various projects for 20 years and at present serves as a member of SEF's Research Task Force.

Erica J. Gosman is a senior staff associate at the Western Interstate Commission for Higher Education, where she is conducting a series of manpower studies on public school teachers, pharmacists, and other professional practitioners. She is also actively engaged in research on college student retention, the participation of minorities in higher education, and racial differences in college student progression and performance. She serves as a member of the American Council on Education's Advisory Panel on Postsecondary Education to the National Center for Education Statistics. She has served as program evaluator and discrimination investigator for the state of Tennessee, and has many years of experience in testing and survey research in the fields of education, criminology, and mental health.

Charles M. Grigg is Professor of Sociology and former Director of the Institute for Social Research at Florida State University. He is the author of some 50 articles, 10 monographs and 4 books. He holds the Ph.D. degree (University of North Carolina, Chapel Hill) and has served as Visiting Professor at several institutions. Race relations has been one of his main areas of interest. During the past 10 years, he has been concerned primarily with the impact of the Civil Rights Act on public school desegregation in the South. At various times, he has been a consultant to the Department of Justice Community Relations Service and the Department of HEW, TRIO Project. He is a past president of the Southern Sociological Society and at present is on the Executive Committee of the Southern Regional Council.

Philip S. Hart currently is Associate Professor of Sociology, College of Public and Community Service, University of Massachusetts–Boston, and a Visiting Research Sociologist, Center for AfroAmerican Studies at UCLA. He holds an M.A. and Ph.D. in sociology from Michigan State University and a B.A. from the University of Colorado–Boulder.

Hart has authored numerous articles, reports, and research monographs and two books. He has a strong background in communications and has produced several films that have been distributed widely. He has served as a research consultant in studies of minorities in public broadcasting and of television audience measurement. He has served as project director in many urban development programs specializing in work that affects the lives of inner-city residents.

Kenneth W. Jackson is Assistant Professor of Sociology at the University of Houston–Downtown. He was Assistant Professor of Sociology at Texas Southern University during the 1982–1983 academic year and was Visiting Professor of Sociology at Rice University in 1982. His professional presentations include "Differences in Achievement Between Blacks and Whites" (National Black Studies Conference, 1982) and "Human Ecology: The Homeless Condition" (Southwest Sociological Association, 1983). He served as a consultant for the NAACP in the Houston Independent School District school desegregation case during 1984. He is currently working on a study of "Blacks in Higher Education" as a research collaborator on the University of Michigan's National Study of Black College Students. In addition, his current research interests focus on "Differences in Occupational Prestige among Blacks and Whites."

Kingston Johns, Jr., now a private consultant in Florida, received A.B. degrees from Franklin and Marshall College and from Guilford College and M.A. and Ph.D. degrees from Cornell University. He has served as Assistant Director of Counseling and Financial Aid Officer at North Carolina State University and as Assistant Director, Associate Director, and Director of the southern regional staff of The College Board.

He has published several instructional manuals for the Marine Corps and articles on high school teaching and administration and on student financial aid administration. He has served as director, consultant, advisor, and supervisor for many state financial aid studies.

Rhoda B. Johnson is Associate Professor of Sociology and Director of the Minority Access to Research Careers Training Program at Tuskegee Institute. She is a co-author of the report *Career Education in a University: An Evaluation.* She is currently involved in several other research efforts that examine the relationship between education and employment.

Gary D. Malaney, who earned the Ph.D. degree in higher education at the Ohio State University, is an emerging scholar. He holds a master's degree and a bachelor's degree in political science from Ohio State. Before returning to school to pursue his Ph.D., he spent six years as an administrator at Ohio State, serving first as a research administrator in the Department of Political Science and then as Assistant Director of the School of Public Administration. Malaney is currently a post-doctoral researcher in the Graduate School, where one of his primary responsibilities involves working with Ohio State's Graduate and Professional Study Fellowships Grant Program (formerly G*POP). His research interests include graduate student recruitment, organizational theory, and information systems in higher education. He has published in such higher education journals as *College and University, Journal of Student Financial Aid,* and the *Review of Higher Education.*

Michael T. Nettles is a research scientist in the Education Policy Research and Services Division of the Educational Testing Service. He was educated at the University of Tennessee at Knoxville (B.A.) and Iowa State University (M.S., M.A.,Ph.D.) and has received both universities' outstanding alumnus awards. He has published in education journals on the subject of student governance, state-level planning in higher education, and college students' performance. He is an active member in the Association for the Study of Higher Education, the

American Education Research Association, and the American Association for Higher Education. He presented two papers at the 1984 Southern Education Foundation conference on desegregation research on higher education. He developed an expertise on higher education desegregation after working on the Tennessee desegregation case for six years while serving as Assistant Director for Academic Affairs at the Tennessee Higher Education Commission.

Anne S. Pruitt is Director of the Center for Teaching Excellence and Professor of Education in the Department of Educational Policy and Leadership at the Ohio State University. She is a graduate in psychology of Howard University, with graduate degrees from Columbia University. Her experience includes serving as dean of students at Albany State College and at Fisk University and on the faculty of Case Western Reserve University. She has authored several publications dealing with desegregation in higher education, including the desegregation process in Nashville, Savannah, and Norfolk. She is a member of the Southern Education Foundation's Research Task Force. *Elisabeth C. Plax*, who served as associate investigator with Anne Pruitt on the research reported in Chapter 16, holds a doctorate in student personnel administration from Case Western Reserve University. She has worked as a consultant in career development for Project Choice, a Women's Education Equity Act funded two-year project, and has worked extensively with TRIO programs. Both her master's thesis and doctoral dissertation reflect specific research interest in the status of black professionals in higher education. *William R. Kennedy* served as statistical consultant on the Pruitt project. He holds a doctorate from Pennsylvania State University and has had broad experience in providing statistical consultation at Pennsylvania State, the University of Florida, the Cleveland Public Schools, Case Western Reserve University, and Cuyahoga Community College, where he served as Director of Instructional Development and Student Assessment. Currently he is Dean of Instruction at St. Louis Community College–Forest Park.

A. Robert Thoeny is the Associate Director for Academic Affairs at the Tennessee Higher Education Commission. He is a graduate of the United States Naval Academy and received the M.S. and Ph.D. degrees in political science from the University of Wisconsin (Madison). Prior to joining the Commission, Thoeny held faculty and administrative posts at the U.S. Air Force Academy and Memphis State University.

Gail E. Thomas is professor of Sociology at Texas A & M University. Her areas of specialization are race and sex differences in educational attainment, social and ethnic stratification, and research methodology. She has recently completed a primary data collection project on college students' major field choice and career aspirations. She has also worked extensively with secondary survey data. Thomas has published a number of articles in national and international journals and in books in sociology and higher education. She has also edited a volume published by Greenwood Press, *Black Students in Higher Education.*

Author Index

Abatso, Y.R., 123
Adams v. *Califano,* 21N
Adams v. *Richardson,* 21N
Admissions Testing Program of the College
    Board National College-Bound
    Seniors, 114N
Alexander, K.L., 39N, 115N
Allen, W.R., 38N, 132, 45N
American Association of University
    Professors, 103N
Astin, A.W., 38, 73N, 131N, 199N
Astin, H.S., 38N
Atelsek, F.J., 199N

Baird, L., 131N
Bayer, A.E., 38N
Bent, D.H., 161N
Blackwell, J.E., 21N, 38N, 48N, 73N, 76,
    146, 160N
Blau, P., 160N
Bobo, L., 145N
Bowen, H.R., 173N
Bowles, S., 48N
Boyd, W.M., 38N
Braddock, J.H., 32, 38N
Brazziel, M., 22N, 25, 74N, 103N
Brazziel, W., 22N, 25, 74N, 103N
Brown, F., 38N, 115N

Campbell, R., 104N
Caplow, T., 199N
Carlson, N., 174N
Carnegie Commission on Higher
    Education, 199N
Carnegie Council on Policy Studies
    in Higher Education, 173N
Cebula, R.J., 115N
Claffey, C.E., 74N
Clark, B.R., 48N
Cobb, H.E., 200N
Collins, E., 160N
Content, R., 200N
Creedon, C., 131N
Cross, P.H., 38N

Daedalus, 74N
Daughtry, D., 145N
Davis, J., 115N
Davis, J.S., 164, 173N, 174N
Duncan, O.D., 160N

Eckland, B.K., 39N, 115N
Egerton, J., 22N
Epps, E., 7, 96, 145N
Epstein, A., 160N
Epstein, C., 160N
Epstein, C.F., 161N
Eulau, E., 48N

Fairfax, J., 22N, 48N, 200N
Federal Register, 22N
Ferrin, R.I., 174N
Fincher, C., 5
Fleming, J., 145N
Fleming, J.E., 200N
Fleuranges, P., 145N
Fowler, D.L., 160N
Fox, L., 115N

Gill, G.R., 200N
Gillespie, D.A., 174N
Gintis, H., 48N
Gladieux, L.E., 174N
Glass, C.V., 74N
Goddard, J.M., 22N
Gomberg, I.L., 199N
Gosman, E.J., 49
Gottfredson, D.C., 39N
Granovetter, M., 160N
Gray, R.G., 161N
Green, M.F., 160N
Grigg, C.M., 38N, 40
Gurin, P., 145N, 200N

Haan, N., 131N
Haller, A.O., 39N, 104N
Hart, P.S., 64, 73N, 74N
Hasteltine, F.P., 161N
Hauser, R.M., 38N
Haynes, L.L., 200
Hedges, L.V., 74N

218

Hill, S.T., 24N, 200N
Homans, G., 161N
Hout, M., 104N
Hull, C.H., 161N
Hunter, J.E., 74N

Institute for Study of Educational
    Policy, 38N

Jackson, G.B., 74N
Jackson, K.W., 96
Janovich, J., 161N
Jenkins, J.G., 161N
Johns, K., 164, 174N
Johnson, R.B., 116
Kanter, R.M., 161N
Karabel, J., 48N
Kerckhoff, A., 104N
Kick, B.A., 131N
Klopf, G.J., 161N
Koch, J.V., 115N

Lederer, D.A., 115N
Levinson, D., 161N
Light, R.J., 74N
Lopes, J., 115N
Lynch, S.M., 161N

Malaney, G.D., 17
McCord, A.S., 39N
McGee, R.J., 199N
McLaughlin, M.B., 162N
McMillan, E.W., 4
McPartland, J.M., 39N
Miller, D.A., 74N
Mingle, J.R., 38N
Moore, K.M., 161N
Morgan, W.R., 104N
Morris, L.O., 161N
Moses, K., 161N

National Advisory Committee on
    Black Higher Education and Black
    Colleges and Universities, 200N
National Association of State Scholar-
    ship and Grant Programs, 174N
National Center for Education
    Statistics, 104N
National Commission on Student Financial
    Assistance, 174N
Nettles, M.T., 49

Nie, N.A., 161N
Nweke, W., 145N

Ohlendorf, G.W., 39N
Olkin, I., 74N

Pace, C.R., 131N
Pancrazio, S.B., 161N
Pantages, T., 131N
Parsons, T., 74N
Phillips-Jones, L., 161N
Pillemer, D.B., 74N
Portes, A., 39N, 104N
Poussaint, A., 30
Prestage, J.L., 22N
Pruitt, A.S., 7, 22N, 161N, 183, 200N, 203

Quinley, H., 48N

Reiss, A.J., 161N
Roche, G.R., 162N
Rossman, J.E., 131N
Rowe, M.P. 162N

Schmidt, F.L., 74N
Scott, J., 131N
Scott, P.B., 160N
Sells, L.W., 115
Sewell, W.H., 39N, 104N
Shah, V.P., 39N
Shapiro, E.C., 162N
Smelzer, N.J., 200N
Smith, D.H., 39N
Sower, C.A., 74N
Spady, W., 131N
Speizer, J.J., 162N
Steinbrenner, K., 161N
Stent, M.D., 38N, 115N
Swinton, D.H., 200N

Tanguay, S.L., 161N
Taylor, I., 162N
Thoeney, A.R., 49
Thomas, G.E., 32, 39N, 115N, 105, 162N
Tinto, V., 131N
Tuckman, H.P., 200N

U.S. Bureau of the Census, Current
    Population Reports, Series P-60,
    No. 139, 174N
U.S. Department of Education, Office for
    Civil Rights, 74N, 75N
U.S. News and World Report, 174N

Washington Office of the College Board, 174N
Webster, D., 131N
Wilson, K., 145N
Wilson, K.L., 39N, 104N

Willingham, W.W., 48N
Willie, C.V., 39N

Yates, F., 131N

Subject Index

Abatso, Yvonne, R., 11, 123, 210
Achievement
  educational, 93–103
  and ability, aspirations, track, grades,
    and influential others, 98–103
Acknowledgements, 6
Adams v. *Richardson,* 3, 7, 17–22
  and court order, 7
  and Kenneth Adams, et al., plaintiffs, 17
  and Elliott L. Richardson, 17
  and *Adams* v. *Califano,* 17
  and *Adams* v. *Bell,* 17
  and Guidelines, 23–24
Adams, Eula, 5
Admissions
  to graduate-professional schools, 83–84
  special admission programs to
    graduate-professional schools, 84–86
Alabama, 7, 21
  four year colleges, 116
Allen, Walter R., 11, 134, 210
Alexander, Elaine B., 5
Applications
  to graduate-professional schools, 82–83
Arizona State University, 133
Arkansas, 7, 19, 20, 21
  and employment of blacks, 191–192, 196
Aspiration, 95
  educational, 96–103
  and career choices, 205
Attainment
  educational, 96–103
  and ability, aspirations, track, grades,
    and influential others in males and
    females, 96–103
Attrition
  see retention
Austin, Sarah, 5

Bailey, Adrienne Y., 5
Bass, Jack, 5
Bell, Deborah H., 5
Bennett, William, 73
Black administrators in white colleges
  in 1975, 187
  in 1977, 189

Black colleges
  enhancement, 29
  racial balance, 29
  program transfer, 29
  and recruiting, 37
  and retention, 68–69
Black faculty
  attitudinal-behavioral characteristics,
    56–57
  employment of and student retention, 69,
    94
  mentoring, 94
  teaching black freshmen, 130
  in white colleges in 1975, 9–10 month, 187,
    11–12 month, 187, full time, by rank
    and tenure, 188
  in white colleges in 1977, 9–10 month, 187,
    11–12 month period, 190, full-time by
    rank and tenure, 190
  in community colleges, 195
Black students
  enrollment patterns, 25–31
  college destination, 32–39
  on white campuses, studies of, 33
  access, retention, and progression in
    Florida, 40–48
  achievement, racial differences, 33, 49–63
  institutional effectiveness, 64–73
  female, 69, 98
  male, 98
  educational attainment, 96–104
  major field choice, 105–115
  coping strategies, 123–133
  on black campuses, 139–143
  mentoring and networking, 148–164
  financial aid, 166–176
  and high school math, 112
  on white campuses, 134–139
Blackwell, James E., 5, 9, 10, 71, 76, 146,
  210–211
Bolden, Wiley, S., 5
Braddock, Jomills, H. II, 9, 32, 211
Brazziel, Marian E., 8, 25, 211–212
Brazziel, William F., 8, 25, 212
Brookover Self-Concept of Ability Scale, 125

California Achievement Test, Form 19, Vocabulary and Reading Comprehension, 126
Careers
  as consequence of progression and performance, 61
  of black graduates, 116–121, and characteristics of graduates 119–120
  and characteristics of colleges, 121
  choices, 95
  placement offices, 118–119
Carnegie Classification System, 186
Carter, Lisle C., 5
Central State University, 133
Charles Drew Medical Center, 88
Civil Rights Act of 1964, 17
College
  access, studies of, 32–33
  destination of black students, 32–39
  two-year, 40–48
  achievement, 49–63
  effectiveness, 64–94
  majors, 105–115
  coping strategies, 123–133
  black, 141–145
  white, 136–141, 185–202
  and Title III, 177–183
  selectivity, 35, 184
College access, students
  and personal characteristics, 35
  and academic and precollege program experience in high school, 35
  and characteristics of high schools, 35, 36
  and two-year colleges, 35
  and four-year colleges, 35, 36
  females, 35, 36
  males, 35, 36
Committee on Minorities in Engineering, 91
Community colleges, 40–48
  and black students in Florida, 44–48
  and employment of blacks, 194
Coping strategies, 123–133
  teaching of, 129–130, black students on white campuses, 137–138, black students on black campuses, 143–144, and grade point average, 129
  and locus of control, 125–128
  and self concept of ability, 125
  and expectation of success and failure, 125
  and coping-retention personality, 126–128
Congress, 170, 172

Counselors
  high school, 37
Court cases
  Adams v. *Bell, 17*
  Adams v. *Califano,* 17, 21
  Adams v. *Richardson,* 1, 17, 21
  Alan Bakke v. *The Board of Regents of the University of California/Davis,* 77, 84, 85, 87, 88
  DeFunis v. *Odegaard,* 84
Curlette, William L., 5

Davis, Jerry S., 11, 166, 212
Degrees conferred
  graduate and professional schools, 93
Delaware, 7, 21
Dental schools
  Howard University, 89
  Meharry, 89
  University of Georgia, 89
  University of Maryland, 89
  University of Pittsburgh, 89

Eastern Michigan University, 133
Effectiveness of colleges
  quotient (EQ), 65
  and institutional factors, 68
  and individual factors, 68
  and contextual factors, 68
  see also retention.
Employment
  in white colleges, 182–200
  faculty, 9 month, 187, 189
  faculty, 11–12 month, 187, 190
  tenured faculty, 188, 190–191
  temporary and part-time, 188–189, 191
  executive, administrative, managerial, professional non-faculty, 187, 189
  secretarial-clerical, technical–para-professional, skilled crafts, 188, 190
  service-maintenance, 188, 190
  nontenured, on-track faculty, 188, 190
  other faculty, 188, 191
  new hires, 191
  in Arkansas, 191–192
  in Florida, 192
  in Georgia, 192–193
  in Maryland, 193
  and Office for Civil Rights, 196
  policy implications, 196–198
  suggestions for further study, 188–189
  racial disparities in salary, 187–191

Enrollment patterns, 25–31
  correlates of state participation rates, 27
  in underrepresented fields, 26, 33
  zero-sum game, 26, 27
  graduate students-professional students,
    86–87
  professional students
    medicine, 87
    dentistry, 88
    optometry, 89
    pharmacy, 90
    veterinary medicine, 90–91
    engineering, 91–92
    law, 92
    social work, 92
Environment
  and graduate-professional education, 93, 94
  and retention, 123–130
  coping with, 128–129
  college, 206
Epps, Edgar G., 5, 7, 9, 96, 213
Equal Employment Opportunity Commission (EEOC), 196
  and EEO-6 information system, 183, 196
  and Office for Civil Rights, 196

Families
  and retention, 70
Fields, Richard B., 5
Financial aid, 206–207
  and retention, 69, 72–73, 128–129
  and graduate-professional education, 80–82
  for black students, 164–174
  and access to higher education, 166–167, 68
  past and recent trends in, 168–170
  future, 170–172
  to institutions, 175–181, 198
  for doctoral study, 198
Fincher, Cameron, 5, 12, 177, 213
Fisk University, 68
Florida, 7, 19, 20, 21, 88
  system of higher education, 42–43
  and employment of blacks, 192
Florida A. & M. University, 47, 90, 132
Ford Foundation, 4, 81
Foundations
  Ford Foundation, 4, 81
  Jeanes Fund, 1
  Peabody Fund, 1
  Southern Education Foundation, 1–4
  Robert Wood Johnson Foundation, 81

Alfred P. Sloan Foundation, 81
  Rockefeller Foundation, 81
  Slater Fund, 1
Friedman, Erwin A., 5

General Electric, 91
Georgetown University, 81
Georgia, 7, 19, 20, 21
  and employment of blacks, 192–193
Gosman, Erica J., 49, 213
Grade point average
  comparison by race and type of
    university, 54
  causal factors of, 58
Graduate and Professional Opportunities
  Program (G-POP), 81
Graduate-professional schools
  and black students, recruitment, enroll-
    ment, graduation, financial aid, 76–94
  medicine, 87
  law, 92
  dentistry, 88
  optometry, 89
  veterinary medicine, 90
  engineering, 91
  pharmacy, 90
  social work, 92
Graduate students
  need for compendium, 198
Grigg, Charles M., 5, 8, 40, 214

Hart, Philip S., 9, 64, 214
Harvard University, 81
Health Professions Scholarship and Health
  Professions Loan Program, 81
HEGIS
  enrollment tapes 1976 and 1978, 25
Herenton, Willie W., 5
High School and Beyond Study, 97–98, 99
Howard University, 88, 90, 91, 92

Indiana University, 90
Institutional differences in
  accessibility to students, 35–37
  access, retention, and progression of
    students, 44–47
  student attrition, 51
  student progression, 52–54
  grade point averages, 54
  student antecedent characteristics and
    college attitudinal characteristics, 54

family attitudinal characteristics, 56–57
predictors of students' college progression
  rates, 57–58
predictors of students' college grade point
  averages, 58–61
effectiveness of production of black
  graduates, 66–69
production of black graduate-
  professional schools graduates, 79–93
major field choices, 113–114
postbaccalaureate careers, 116–120
student experiences on black and white
  campuses, 134–144
mentoring and networking, 153–159
employment of blacks, 194
Integration
  of colleges, 29
  policies, 30
  remedial programs, 30
  transitional study programs, 30
  cross registration, 30
  consortia, 30
  racial steering, 30
  transfer, 30–31
Integration of students
  and qualitative changes, 49
  and attrition, 51
  and progression rate, 52
  and college grade point average, 54
  and antecedent characteristics and college
    attitudinal and behavioral charac-
    teristics, 54
  and effects of faculty attitudes, 56
  and causal factors of college progression
    rates, 57
  and causal factors of college grade point
    average, 58
  and employment, 61
Introduction, 7

Jackson, Kenneth W., 9, 96, 214
Jackson State University, 132
Jeanes Fund, 2
Johns, Kingston, Jr., 11, 166, 215
Johnson, Rhoda B., 10, 116, 215

Kelly, Eamon, M., 5
Kentucky, 7, 21

Landis and Scarpitti Awareness Scale of
  Limited Opportunities 1965, 125

Locus of control
  and Gurin's Adaptation of Rotter
    Internal/External Locus of Control
    Scale, 125
Loma Linda University, 81
Louisiana, 7, 19, 20, 21

Major field
  and high occupational expectations, 112
  male vs. female choices, 112
  impact of white vs. black colleges, 112
Malaney, Gary D., 17, 215
Maryland, 7, 19, 20, 21, 88
  and employment of blacks, 193–194
Mathematics
  and high school and college majors, 112
  and impact on college majors, by sex,
    112–113
Meharry Medical School, 87, 88
Mehrabian Achievement Motivation, 125
Memphis State University, 133
Men
  employees in white colleges, 187–191
Mentoring, 146–159, 198
  and networking, 147, 156–157
  characteristics, 146
  mentor-protegé relationship, 146, 148–149
  and role models, 153
  mentors, 154–156
Minorities in Engineering, 91
Minority Education Engineering Effort
  (ME³), 91
Minority Fellowship Program of the
  National Institute of Mental Health
  (NIMH), 81
Mississippi, 7, 19, 20, 21
Missouri, 7, 21
Mobility
  educational, 96–103
Morehouse College, 88
Morgan State University, 132

National Association for the Advancement
  of Colored People (NAACP), 76
NAACP Legal Defense and Educational
  Fund, 7, 76
National Center for Educational Statistics
  (NCES), 34
  and National Longitudinal Survey (NSL)
    of the High School Senior Class of
    1972, 34

National Longitudinal Survey
high school senior class of 1972, 34,
97–98
National Study of Black College Students,
134, 136, 146, 147
Nettles, Michael T., 9, 49, 215
Networking, 147
and mentoring, 147
see mentoring
North Carolina, 7, 17, 19, 20, 21, 88
North Carolina A. & T. University, 91, 132
North Carolina Central University, 91, 133

Office for Civil Rights, 17
Ohio, 7, 21
black college graduates, 29
Oklahoma, 7, 19, 20, 21

Peabody Fund, 1
Pennsylvania, 7, 19, 21, 88
Persistence
see retention
Personality
coping-retention, 126
Policy initiatives, 207–208
Prairie View A. & M. University, 91
Progression
and employment, 61–62
Pruitt, Anne S., 5, 6, 7, 12, 185, 205, 216

Quality of college experience
and academic performance, 52–54
and student personal and academic characteristics and attitudes, 54–56
and faculty attitudinal-behavioral characteristics, comparisons by race and
type of university, 56–57
and student employment, 61–62

Racial differences in
access, retention, and progression of-
students in Florida, 44–48
attrition, 51
progression, 52–54
grade point averages, 54
student antecedent characteristics and
attitudinal and behavioral characteristics, 54–56
faculty attitudinal-behavioral characteristics, 56–57
employment and salaries in white
institutions, 187–194

Reagan
administration, 72
Retention
comparison by race, 51
of black students, 65–73, 67
and black colleges, 68, 73
comparisons by race and predominant
race of university, 51
and white collegs, 68
Fisk University, 68
South Carolina State College, 68
Southern University, 68
institutional predictors, 68
individual predictors, 68, 69
contextual predictors, 68
private vs. public colleges, 69, 73
and institutional incentive system, 69–70
and community college articulation, 70
and consortia, 70
and financial aid, 70, 71
and campus involvement, 70, 72
and black faculty, 70, 72
and boards of trustees, 72
and state initiatives, 72
and federal initiatives, 72
and lobbying, 73
and coping strategies, 123–130
personality factors related to, 124
environment related to, 128–130
and college environment, 128–129
and personality, 126–128
Recruitment
of graduate-professional students, 79–80
Remedial programs, 30
Rotter Internal/External Locus of Control
Scale
Gurin's adaptation of, 125

Science
in high school and impact on college
major choice, 112–113
Sex differences in
influences upon educational attainment,
98–102
influences upon college choice, 35–37
influences upon major field choice,
107–114
employment in white colleges, 187–192,
194–196
ability, aspirations, track, grades and
influential others, 98–103

Simon, Senator Paul, 171–172
Slater Fund, 1
South Carolina, 7, 21
South Carolina State College, 68
Southern Education Foundation, 1
    mission, 1
    Board of Trustees, 5
    Research Task Force, 5, 8
Southern University, 68, 91, 92, 133
State system of higher education
    California, 40
    and community colleges, 40
    Florida, 40, 42–43
    access, distribution, retention,
        progression, 43–48
    two-tier system, 45
State University of New York,
    Stony Brook, 133
Status-attainment model, 96–97

Temple University, 81
Tennessee, 7
Tennessee State University, 91
Texas, 7, 21
Texas Southern University, 90, 92, 132
Thoeny, A. Robert, 49, 216
Thomas, Gail E., 9, 10, 32, 105, 217
Title III of the Higher Education Act of
    1965, 175
    and traditionally black institutions,
        175–181

and institutional management, 177
and program improvement, 178
and student services, 178–179
Title VI, Civil Rights Act of 1964, 17, 18,
    19, 20,
Tuskegee Institute
    School of Veterinary Medicine, 80, 90, 91

University of California, Los Angeles, 133
University of Georgia, 91
University of Maryland, 92
University of Michigan, 133
University of Mississippi, 91
University of Oklahoma, 92
University of North Carolina, 133
University of Southern California, 81
University of Tennessee, 91
University of Wisconsin, 133
U.S. Department of Education, 17
    (formerly Department of Health,
    Education, and Welfare)
    and policy initiatives, 28–29

Virginia, 7, 19, 20, 21
Virginia Commonwealth University, 92
West Virginia, 7, 21
Wisconsin model of status attainment, 96
Women
    employees in white colleges, 187–191

Xavier University of New Orleans, 90

3